Hot Rod Handbooks

Custom Auto Electrickery

How to Work with and Understand Auto Electrical Systems

Frank 'Choco' Munday

Published in 2006 by
Graffiti Publications Pty. Ltd.
69 Forest Street, Castlemaine, Victoria, Australia
Phone International 61 3 5472 3653
Fax International 61 3 5472 3805
Email: info@graffitipub.com.au
Website: www.graffitipub.com.au

Copyright 2006 by Frank "Choco" Munday
Publisher Larry O'Toole
Design Michael Wolfe

Printed in China by SC (Sang Choy) International Ltd.

Graffiti Publications books are also available at discounts in bulk quantity for industrial or sales promotional use.
For details contact **Graffiti Publications PH. 61 3 5472 3653.**

ISBN 0 949398 35 7

PUBLICATIONS PTY LTD

CONTENTS

Chapter 1

Electrickery

Today's automotive electronics have reached an unprecedented level of sophistication in all but the most basic of vehicles. There are no more carburetors, no more points and very few distributors. Engine Management by computer is "old hat", and there hasn't been a car built since the mid-80s that doesn't have at least one computer in it. It seems like only yesterday that the topic of "auto electronics" meant a magnetic distributor and a MSD box. Today, the topic covers most of the following:

- *Sensors and Actuators:* pressure sensors, linear and angle position sensors, flow sensors, temperature, heat and humidity sensors, exhaust gas sensors, speed and acceleration sensors, engine knock sensors, engine torque sensors.
- *Control Systems:* micro controllers, engine control, transmission control, cruise control, braking control, traction control, stability control, suspension control, steering control, lighting, wipers, air conditioning, heating.
- *Displays and Information Systems:* instrument panel displays, on/off board diagnostics. Safety Systems: electronic stability control, lane departure warning, pre-crash safety, automotive adaptive front lighting, heads-up display, tyre pressure monitoring.
- *Control-by-Wire:* in-vehicle networks, safe-by-wire, local interconnect network, time triggered automotive protocols, brake-by-wire, drive-by-wire, shift-by-wire.
- *Telematics and In-Vehicle Entertainment:* global positioning satellite, DSRC, DVD and entertainment products, PDA, hand set navigation, digital audio/video, multimedia node, bluetooth.
- *Security, Convenience, and Other Systems:* remote keyless entry, anti-theft, multiplex wiring systems, radio frequency identification, speech recognition.
- *Current and Emerging Technologies:* object detection, collision warning, collision avoidance, driver information systems, intelligent transportation systems, electric and hybrid vehicles, noise cancellation systems.

More and more of these sophisticated systems and components are being built into cars assembled by auto enthusiasts. Hot Rods, Customs, Classics and even restored cars are featuring engine management systems, security systems, entertainment systems, remote access, suspension control and instrumentation. Many of the auto electronic devices come from the donor vehicles, but how does the average back yard mechanic hook all of this together so that it will work in a '56 Chev or a fibreglass '33 Ford? What about an engine management system for a flathead?

Who Should Read This Book?

If you are an auto enthusiast or a Do-It-Yourself mechanic, and you want to take advantage of some of this automotive electronic technology to transplant it into your early car, this book is for you.

If you are sick of publications that just tell you to go buy an electronic distributor, an MSD 6 and a blaster coil, then follow the instructions to replace your old points system, this book is for you.

If you don't know what that tangle of wires and doo-dads are doing, this book is for you.

We tell you WHY, WHAT and HOW. In some cases, we include WHO and WHERE. We recognise that, as an enthusiast, you need to make your own choices, to customise the installation to suit your type of vehicle and to confidently hook everything together without the fear that it will all fall apart.

This book also takes into account the fact that technology takes leaps and bounds over a relatively short period in time.

Being aware of what works and what doesn't is half the battle.
The other half is putting it to use. This book will attempt to cover both these aspects as well. In addition to Electronic Ignition Systems, this book also covers the following technologies with the same approach:

- Electronic Fuel Injection systems
- Engine Management Systems and Components
- Wiring and Electrical Components
- Modern starting and charging systems
- Car Audio Systems
- Test equipment

Reference Material

This book makes references to after-market and factory manufacturers and suppliers of the components described in the various chapters. The Author (Choco Munday) and the Publisher (Graffiti Publications) are in no way tied to these companies, nor do they have any interest, financial or otherwise, in these companies. The Author has had some items of hardware made available for close scrutiny and to gain installation experience, but most of the companies listed below have been included because of their customer support, presence in the market place and long history of quality materials.

Contacts List

Painless Wiring
http://www.painlesswiring.com
Ultimate Wiring Harness
http://members.dcsi.net.au/ultimate/
Simon Muntz's Street Rods and Accessories
http://www.streetrod.com.au/
CAE - Castle Automotive Enterprises
http://www.castleauto.com.au
MSD
http://www.msdignition.com//
Kalmaker
http://www.kalmaker.com.au
Pertronix
http://www.pertronix.com/
Crane
http://www.cranecams.com/
http://www.cranecams.com.au/
Mallory
http://www.malloryperformance.com/
Accel
http://www.accel-ignition.com/
Holley
http://www.holley.com/

Chapter 2

Custom Auto Electrical - The Basics

A car's electrical system should be designed as an integral part of the car's structure. The steel body, frame and engine provide a ground, or the electrical return path, for the electrical supply (alternator/battery). Carrying the electrical supply throughout the car are wires. Interrupting the supply are switches (mechanical and electronic). Together, they form Electrical Circuits. In the electrical circuits are devices such as the windscreen wiper motor, radio, horn, lights, ignition coil, computer, cooling fan, relays etc. These devices are all Electrical Loads. So now, in our Electrical Circuit, we have loads controlled by switches.

Electrical Sources

Essentially, the source of your vehicle's electrical supply is the Alternator (or generator, for older cars). A Battery is used to store an electrical charge while the engine is not running, and the Alternator keeps the Battery charged when it is being driven by the engine, provided the drain on the alternator is not excessive. The correct installation of your electrical system should enable all electrical devices to operate simultaneously and still have sufficient power in reserve to charge the battery.

Short Circuit

If the electrical supply should meet with the return path (Ground) before it meets the load, we are shortening the length of the circuit - a Short Circuit. This will cause the current flowing in the conductor (wire) to take the quickest route to ground. In fact, it will travel so quickly it will heat the conductor to melting point, frazzle the insulation and cause short circuits with any other conductors bunched with it. Scratch one wiring harness! Fortunately, fuses and fusible links are built into our wiring harnesses to reduce this risk to a minimum.

Open Circuit

The opposite to a short circuit, and not as dangerous. An Open Circuit is a break anywhere in the path of the current flow. A switch is a device that creates an Open Circuit. If a fuse blows, the circuit it is protecting is open.

Series and Parallel Circuits

For a device to make use of electricity (a fan motor, headlight, horn, relay, etc) the electrical current must flow through the device from a negative (ground) to a positive.

> *Note: Electron Theory states that electrons (negative charges) move through a conductor in response to an electric field. The direction of electron movement is from a region of negative potential to a region of positive potential. This book uses the Electron Theory to describe electrical flow paths.*

Devices can be wired into the electrical circuit in one of two ways:

- In Series
- In Parallel

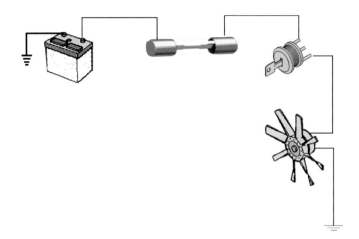

Figure 1 Simple Series Circuit

Series Circuit

In a simple series circuit (**Figure 1** Simple Series Circuit), electricity must flow from battery positive through the fuse, the ignition switch, then the fan on its way to battery negative. The circuit can be broken at any time by turning the switch off. In simple terms, the electricity must travel through a series of components (the fuse, the switch and the fan), one before the other. To operate two devices in the circuit, simply add another device in series. See **Figure 2** Devices in Series.

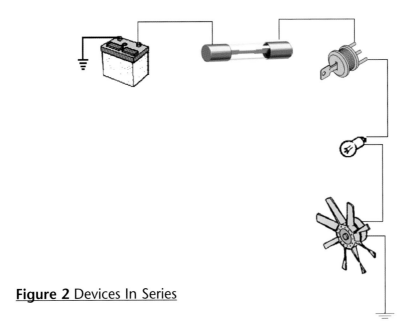

Figure 2 Devices In Series

Note that if the lamp burns out, the circuit is broken (or open), and no current will flow. The fan will not function. A problem also occurs when one component in series with another is of a much higher resistance. The current flowing through such a combined circuit may not be sufficient to drive the low resistance component. The component demanding the most current (the high resistance component) simply chokes the circuit.

Parallel Circuits

Another way to wire another device into the circuit is in parallel, as illustrated in **Figure 3** Parallel Circuits. Current now flows from the battery, through the fuse and switch, then through the two fans at the same time before returning to the battery. In this circuit, one fan will work if the other burns out.

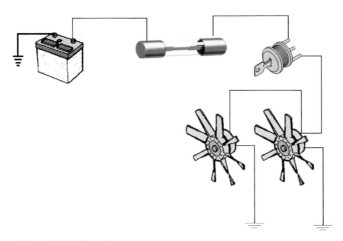

Figure 3 Parallel Circuits

Circuit Protection

Most automotive electrical circuits require protection from current draw that would exceed the capacity of the conductors or the load components. The excess current draw can be caused by an overload in the electrical components or by a circuit defect, such as a direct short to ground. To prevent damage to the components and conductors, these circuits must use some form of protection device. If an overload occurs, the protection device opens, preventing current from flowing in the circuit.

Fuse

A fuse is built into a circuit to be the weakest link. Under normal operating conditions, the fuse acts as a part of the circuit, and has no effect on current flow. If the circuit should draw more current than it is designed to, the fuse will melt, causing an open circuit (see **Figure 4** Fuses). The fuse is rated in Amps, at a rate representing the highest current drain allowable before the fuse will melt. A 10A (ten Amperes or Amps) fuse will melt if the current in the circuit exceeds ten Amps for a few seconds. This is the rate for which components in the circuit will function normally, such as a tail light circuit which, under normal operating conditions, draws six Amps.

Refer Table 2 - **Wiring Circuit Current Ratings** for a list of automotive circuit current ratings.

If one of the wires in the circuit should chafe or become damaged, the wire may touch a ground and draw the maximum current the battery will deliver. The fuse melts and the circuit is broken before the wires get so hot that they melt the insulation and cause a fire. It is therefore essential that the correctly rated fuses be replaced in the circuit for which they have been selected.

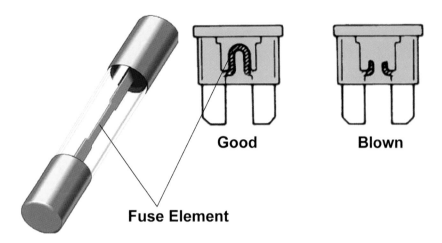

Good **Blown**

Fuse Element

Figure 4 Fuses

Fuse Types

There are two basic fuse types:

- Blade.
- Cartridge.

There are several variations of each, but the most common by far is the Blade type fuse.

Blade Fuses. There are four types of Blade fuse (**Figure 5** Blade Fuses):

- The standard Auto Fuse, also known as the ATO fuse
- Maxi Fuse
- Mini Fuse
- Fuse Element

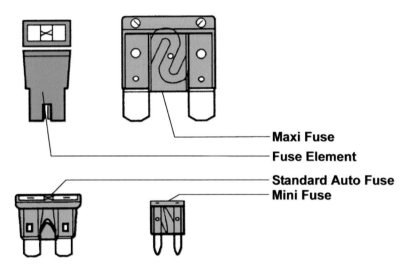

Maxi Fuse

Fuse Element

Standard Auto Fuse
Mini Fuse

<u>**Figure 5**</u> <u>Blade Fuses</u>

All blade fuses are a compact design with a transparent colour-coded insulated housing. The following table lists the current rating and the colour code:

Table 1 - Blade Fuse Colour Code

Auto Fuses and Mini Fuses		Maxi Fuses	
Current Rating	Colour	Current Rating	Colour
3	Violet	20	Yellow
5	Tan	30	Green
7.5	Brown	40	Amber
10	Red	50	Red
15	Blue	60	Blue
20	Yellow	70	Brown
25	Clear	80	Clear
30	Green		

The Fuse Element cartridge protects high current devices and the main supply line for the car's electrical system. Also known as a Pacific Fuse, the terminal and fusing portion form a single unit (see **Figure 6** Fuse Element or Pacific Fuse).

The housings are colour coded for each current rating and are available in two physical sizes as a plug-in or bolt-in design. The plug-in type is the most popular.

Fuse Element (Pacific Fuse) Current Rating and Colour Code

Current Rating	Colour
30	Pink
40	Green
50	Red
60	Yellow
80	Black
100	Blue

Figure 6 Fuse Element or Pacific Fuse

Cartridge fuses, made from glass or ceramic, were used in older vehicles and usually had the current ratings stamped into the end cap of the fuse.

Circuit Breakers

A more sophisticated device for circuit protection is the circuit breaker. Under normal operating conditions, the circuit breaker acts like a switch. A heat sensitive element inside the switch causes the circuit breaker to snap open if the current drain through the heat sensitive element exceeds its rated value. After a short, cooling down period, some circuit breakers reset themselves. Other types may require a manual reset after they have tripped.

There are many different types of circuit breaker (see **Figure 7** Circuit Breakers). Some can be flush mounted, like switches. Others need to be soldered into circuit boards. There are others which clip into fuse holders, and take the place of glass barrel type fuses and Auto mini fuses.

Note: Circuit Breakers that automatically reset after a brief cooling down period will cause the circuit to cycle through an on-off-on period, possibly damaging the circuit. These types are not recommended.

Figure 7 Circuit Breakers

Fusible Links

Like any other fuse, a fusible link protects a circuit from melt down if a component in the circuit fails, or short-circuits. A fusible link, however, is a fuse which protects the entire electrical system. It is usually installed between the Alternator and the Battery, and/or the Starter Solenoid and the Fuse Panel. A fusible link is simply a length of wire which is rated at less than the wire it is attached to so that it becomes the weakest link in the circuit.

The insulation is burn resistant to provide heat protection for the surrounding wires.

> **Note:** *Always determine the cause of a fusible link meltdown before replacing it.*

To see if a fusible link has blown, check for any discoloration of the insulation. Tug on one end of the fusible link, and it will come apart or at least stretch the insulation if it is blown.

Maxi Fuse

The Maxi Fuse (see **Figure 8** Painless Wiring Maxi Fuse) or the Pacific Fuse (see **Figure 6** Fuse Element or Pacific Fuse) are alternatives to the fusible link. You can purchase several variations of fuse holders to suit your custom electrical system.

This Maxi Fuse and holder is sold by Painless Wiring. There are several other variations that you can choose from to suit your application.

Figure 8 Painless Wiring Maxi-Fuse

> **You MUST include at least one fusible link, Maxi Fuse or Pacific Fuse in your main supply line. Do NOT omit this safety device from your custom wiring installation!**

Circuit Protection Installation

When designing and installing a custom wiring circuit, build sufficient circuit protection into the system to allow for future additional circuits.

> **Always install circuit protection in any custom wiring application! Never design a circuit without any protection.**

Also ensure that the design allows for as many fuses and/or circuit breakers as there are circuits. It is far better to give each minor circuit its own fuse than to feed a group of circuits together on the one fuse/circuit breaker. In addition, if a fuse continually blows, it is easier to chase down the offending
component or circuit if the fuse only feeds one or two devices.
Refer Table 2 - **Wiring Circuit Current Ratings**

Circuit Components

Most custom applications of auto electrical systems are made up of the same components. It doesn't matter whether you build your system from a wiring kit, a factory harness or build it from scratch, you will need to include some or all of the following circuit components:

Table 2 - Wiring Circuit Current Ratings

CIRCUIT CURRENT	(Amps)
Ignition	3.5
Starter Motor	up to 300
Starter Solenoid	12
Horn	20
Headlights	
High Beam	15
Low Beam	10
Dipswitch	3
Dash Lights	3
Parking Lights	1.5
Dome Light	1
Back–up Lights	5
Tail Lights	1
Stop Lights	5
License Light	1
Electric Wiper	7
Heater/Defogger	10
Air Conditioner	20
Power Antenna	10
Power Windows	20
Power Seat	50
Power Door Locks	5
Radio/CB	5
Electric Clock	5
Cigar Lighter	15

- Terminals and Connectors
- Wire
- Switches
- Relays
- Solenoids

Terminals and Connectors

A variety of terminal brands are available in the market place, however we shall deal with the common standard AMP terminals which come in three colours and sizes for a range of applications and current capacities. Table 3 - **Wire Terminal Colour Codes** lists the details.

Table 3 - Wire Terminal Colour Codes

Colour	Gauge (Imp)	Gauge (Met)
Red	18 to 20	2.0mm - 3.0 mm or 9 x 0.3mm - 14 x 0.3mm
Blue	14 to 16	3.0mm - 4.0mm or 14 x 0.3mm - 26 x 0.3mm
Yellow	10 to 12	5.0mm - 6.0mm or 40 x 0.3mm - 65 x 0.3mm

The common types of terminals and lugs are illustrated in **Figure 9** Terminals and Lugs.

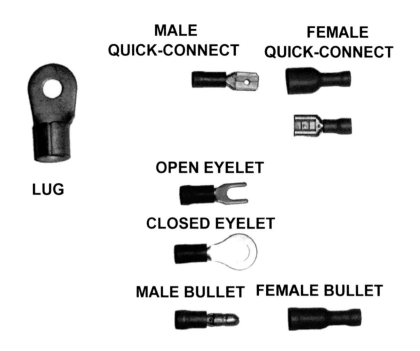

<u>**Figure 9** Terminals and Lugs</u>

See Chapter 11 **Crimping and Crimping Tools** for more information.

Weather Pack Terminals

GM Weather Pack Terminals, plugs and sockets are a soft metal termination with a waterproof cable seal for connecting ignition or accessories throughout your auto electrical project. The plugs and sockets are available with one to six male and female locking connectors. The terminals and seals are secured inside the weatherpack connector body with a hinge lock assembly.

See Chapter 11 **Crimping and Crimping Tools** for more information.

Wire

It is always important to use the correct gauge wiring for the circuit. Table 4 - **Wire Gauge** and Table 2 - **Wiring Circuit Current Ratings** can be used as a guide when wiring in various devices and circuits. More detailed wiring descriptions are given in Chapter 8 **Custom Wiring**.

Table 4 - Wire Gauge

GAUGE	METRIC	CURRENT
18	0.8mm	6A
16	1.0mm	8A
14	2.0mm	15A
12	3.0mm	20A
10	5.0mm	30A
8	8.0mm	40A

Switches

A switch is the most common means of providing control of electrical current flow to an accessory. A switch can control the on/off operation of a circuit or direct the flow of current through various circuits. The contacts inside the switch assembly carry the current when they are closed. When they are open, current flow is stopped.

A normally open switch will not allow current flow when it is in its rest position. The contacts are open until you flick the switch, which closes them to complete the circuit. A normally closed switch will allow current flow when it is in its rest position. The contacts are closed until you flick the switch, which opens them to stop current flow.

Single Pole, Single Throw Switch. The simplest type of switch is the single-pole, single-throw (SPST) switch. This switch controls the on/off operation of a single circuit. The most common type of SPST switch is the hinged pawl. The pawl acts as the contact and changes position as directed to open or close the circuit. Some SPST switches are designed to be a momentary contact switch. This switch usually has a spring that holds the contacts open until you push the switch, which closes them. The horn button on most vehicles is of this design.

Figure 10 Single Pole, Single Throw Switch

Single Pole, Double Throw Switch. Some electrical systems may require the use of a single-pole, double-throw switch (SPDT). The dimmer switch used in the headlight system is usually a SPDT switch. This switch has one input circuit with two output circuits. Depending on the position of the contacts, voltage is applied to the high beam circuit or to the low beam circuit.

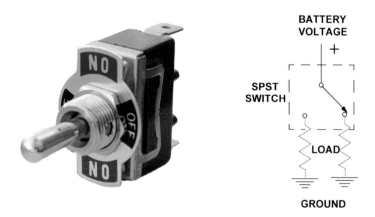

Figure 11 Single Pole, Double Throw Switch

Relays

Some circuits (refer **Figure 13** Relay Operation) utilise electromagnetic switches called relays. A typical late model car can have over twenty relays in the electrical system.

Relay Application. Relays are used as remote control switches that are controlled by another switch that the driver actuates, like the horn switch or the high beam switch. The relay controls a high current circuit with a low current switch, so it is OK to use as many as your system requires. The coil in the relay has a very high resistance, and draws very little current.

Relay Operation. All relays use the same principle of operation. In any relay, there are two circuits:

- Control Circuit. Pins 85 and 86 in **Figure 13** Relay Operation. The control circuit is a small electromagnet.

- Load Circuit. Pins 87 and 30 in **Figure 13** Relay Operation. The load circuit is a spring loaded switch. The size of the switch determines the amount of current it can handle, and is usually how we identify the type of relay, for example, 10 Amp Relay, 20 Amp Relay, 40 Amp Relay. Apart from the power ratings, mini relays have a standard configuration, as illustrated in **Figure 12** Mini Relay Pin Configuration.

> *Note: Make sure you select the correct rating relay for the circuit the relay is switching. See Table 2 - Wiring Circuit Current Ratings.*

When a voltage is applied to pins 85 and 86 (for example, press the horn button) a low current flows through the Control Circuit's coil, which is wrapped around an iron core. The ironcore intensifies the magnetic field.

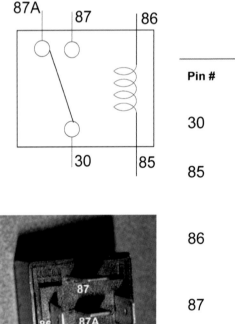

Pin #	Use
30	Always goes to the Main Power Feed
85	Always goes to a Ground source
86	Always goes to a Positive Feed from the Fuse Box
87	Always goes to the Electrical Device you are powering
87a	Always goes to a Secondary Electrical Device

Figure 12 Mini Relay Pin Configuration

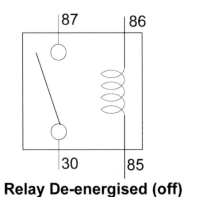
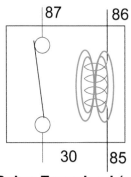

Relay De-energised (off)   **Relay Energised (on)**

Figure 13 Relay Operation

The magnetic field pulls the contacts closed and energises the relay. When the relay is energised, the contacts close and heavy battery current flows to the load component that is being controlled (for example, the horn).

Relay Design. There are two basic relay designs that are typical for automotive applications.

- Normally Open Relays. Normally Open relays have their contacts closed by the electromagnetic field.

- Normally Closed Relays. Normally Closed relays have their contacts opened by the magnetic field.

There are several variations in pin connections and relay design, but the ones that we shall focus on most of all are the ISO standard four and five pin Mini Relays used throughout the auto electrical industry (see **Figure 14** Standard 4 Pin Relay).

Figure 14 Standard 4 Pin Relay

Mini relays are a standard configuration, 1" x 1" (23mm x 23mm) cube, and you can plug them in to a standard relay socket (see **Figure 15** Mini Relay Socket). Note how easy it is to group the relay sockets together.

Figure 15 Mini Relay Socket

Solenoids

A solenoid is an electromechanical device comprising a coil surrounding a moveable metal core acting as a plunger. When a voltage is applied to the coil, it sets up an electromagnetic field, causing the plunger to move to the centre of the coil. A return spring pulls the core out of the coil when de-energised. The moveable core can be connected to various mechanical devices to carry out a variety of tasks, such as pulling the starter armature into the ring gear (starter solenoid) or pulling a cable connected to the door lock mechanism (door lock solenoids or central locking solenoids).

One of the most common uses of the solenoid is to control vacuum to other components. Many automatic climate control systems use vacuum motors to move the blend doors. The computer can control the operation of the doors by controlling the solenoid.

Chapter 3

Starting Systems

The Starting System (refer **Figure 16** Starting System) comprises the following components:

- Battery;
- Ignition Switch;
- Neutral Safety Start Switch;
- Starting Solenoid;
- Starter Motor.

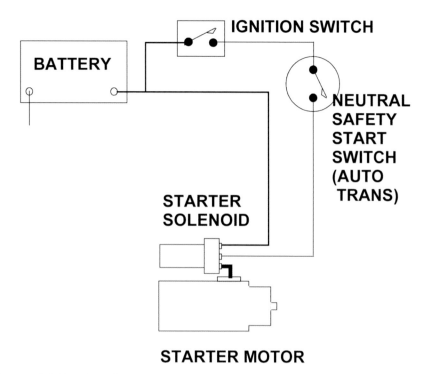

Figure 16 Starting System

Operation

As the ignition key is turned to the START position, the Starter Solenoid engages and pulls Battery Voltage over to the Starter Motor. The Solenoid can be remote or an integral part of the Starter Motor. If an automatic transmission is in use, a Neutral Safety Start Switch prevents the Starter Circuit from closing unless the transmission is in Park or Neutral.

With Battery Voltage available to the Starter Motor, the Starter Motor rotates, using the solenoid plunger to push the starter motor gear into the flywheel or ring gear of the flex plate (as is the case with most starter motors with an integral solenoid) or an Overrunning Clutch pushes the starter motor gear forward into the flex plate or flywheel ring gear (as is the case for earlier, remote solenoid type starter motors, sometimes called "Rat Trap" Starters). The high torque of the Starter Motor turns the flywheel or flex plate which cranks the engine over.

Starter Motor

A Starter Motor is an electric motor that is energised by the battery voltage of the car. The motor is geared to easily turn the engine over so that it will fire. The engine itself is turned by the starter gear at the flywheel (for manual transmissions) which has a toothed gear (called the Ring Gear) sweated on to the outer rim. In an Automatic Transmission, the Ring Gear is welded to the Flex Plate, which is bolted to the Torque Converter.

Starter Motor Components

The Starter Motor itself comprises the following components (refer **Figure 17** Starter Motor Exploded View):

- *Starter Motor Frame.* This houses the Pole Shoes. They are Electro Magnets, requiring Battery Voltage to establish a magnetic field around iron cores.
- *Pole Shoes.* Usually four pole shoes are built into the Starter Frame, each comprising an iron core around which many windings of copper wire are wrapped, forming a powerful Electro Magnet called Field Coils.
- *Drive Housing.* Facilitates the opening into the gearbox so that the Pinion Gear can engage the ring gear. Also houses the Overrunning Clutch.
- *Armature.* The metal framework around which several sets of windings are wrapped. At one end of the Armature is the Commutator and the Armature Windings connect to a segment of the Commutator.
- *Commutator.* Comprises many Segments, each of which is connected to a separate Armature Winding.
- *Solenoid.* Acts as a relay to apply power to the Commutator and thrusts the Pinion Gear into the ring gear of the engine via the Drive Yolk.

- *Brush Holder and Brushes.* Applies electrical power to the Commutator, segment by segment.
- *Drive Yolk.* A fork that acts on the Overrunning Clutch and Pinion Gear via the action of the Solenoid.

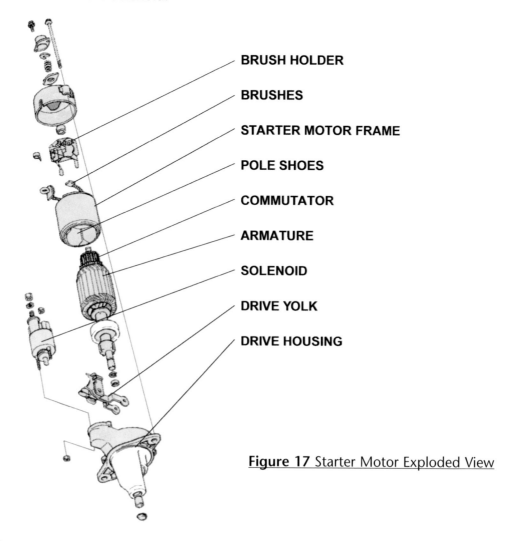

BRUSH HOLDER

BRUSHES

STARTER MOTOR FRAME

POLE SHOES

COMMUTATOR

ARMATURE

SOLENOID

DRIVE YOLK

DRIVE HOUSING

Figure 17 Starter Motor Exploded View

Operation

The Starter Motor operates as follows (refer **Figure 17** Starter Motor Exploded View):

1. The Ignition Key is switched ON and primary ignition voltage established.
2. The Ignition Switch is forced over to the START position. Secondary ignition voltage (eg supplies for electric fan, wipers, etc) and accessory supplies (eg radio, heater fan, A/C fan, etc) are temporarily disconnected to ensure full supply is available for starting.
3. Battery Voltage is applied to the Solenoid terminals.
4. The Solenoid pulls the Drive Yolk in, forcing the Overrunning Clutch and the Pinion Gear to mesh with the ring gear.

5. Contacts in the Solenoid close, applying Battery Voltage to the Brushes and Field Coils.

6. Power flows through a segment of the commutator via the Brushes.

7. The Magnetic Field around the Field Coils force the Armature to spin inside the Pole Shoes.

8. Contact is made with the next segment of the Commutator, repeating step 7 again.

9. Steps 7 and 8 continue until the engine fires.

10. The Overrunning Clutch freewheels as the engine speed exceeds starter motor speed.

11. Overrunning Clutch slides back with spring pressure, pulling the Drive Yolk with it.

12. The Drive Yolk disconnects and forces the electrical contacts in the Solenoid apart, removing power from the Starter Motor and Solenoid.

Permanent Field Magnets. Later model starter motors come with permanent magnets constructed from iron, boron and neodymium, which replace the Pole Shoes. This means that no electrical power is required to establish the strong magnetic field needed by the Pole Shoes to set the Armature spinning. Instead, these new permanent magnets are sufficiently powerful to do the job themselves.

Starter Motor Types

There are two basic types of Starter Motors in use today;

- Remote Solenoid. Sometimes called Positive Engagement or Rat-Trap Starters (refer **Fig 18** Rat Trap Starter Motor); In the Remote Solenoid type, a moveable Pole Shoe is attached to the Drive Yolk. When the Field Coils are energised (via a remotely located solenoid, which acts as a relay only), the moveable Pole Shoe acts upon the Yolk forcing the Overrunning Clutch to thrust the Pinion Gear into the Ring Gear. At the same time, electrical contacts held open by the Moveable Pole Shoe are closed and the starter is turned by normal starter action. When the engine speed reaches starter speed, the Overrunning Clutch freewheels and is forced back, breaking the electrical contact and removing power from the starter.

- Solenoid Actuated. This is the more common type of starter, with an integral solenoid, and has already been described. The solenoid mounted on the starter completes the circuit from the battery to the starter motor and also engages the pinion gear.

The difference between the two is only in the method used to move the Pinion Gear into meshing with the Ring Gear.

Figure 18 Rat Trap Starter

Gear Reduction Starter

In engines which develop high compressions, a Gear Reduction Starter (refer **Figure 19** Gear Reduction Starter Motor) or Hi Torque starter may be necessary. Extra gears are built into the starter to increase the amount of torque available at the Pinion Gear. There are a number of after market Gear Reduction starters available from many suppliers, although there are some factory Gear Reduction starters (eg Chrysler) fitted to various engines as standard equipment.

Figure 19 Gear Reduction Starter

One advantage of the Gear Reduction starter is the size of the electric starter motor. It is much smaller than a non-geared starter motor and therefore draws less current, relying on its gearing to turn the most stubborn of high compression engines. In addition, it is less affected by heat, so in cases where an older style starter motor refuses to turn over because the headers are too close to it, a high torque starter motor will cure the problem.

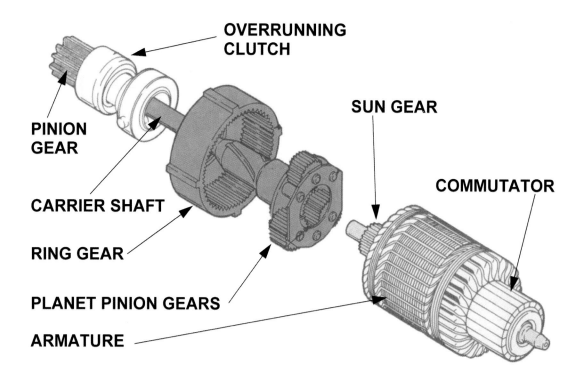

OVERRUNNING CLUTCH

PINION GEAR

SUN GEAR

COMMUTATOR

CARRIER SHAFT

RING GEAR

PLANET PINION GEARS

ARMATURE

Figure 20 Planetary Gear Reduction Starter

Another variation of the Gear Reduction Starter is the GM type Planetary Gear. In this configuration (refer **Figure 20** Planetary Gear Reduction Starter) a planetary gearset is used to produce the reduction. A planetary gear is very compact and strong, eliminating the sometimes bulky engineering required for conventional gearsets.

Chapter 4

The Charging System

The automotive storage battery is not capable of supplying the demands of the electrical system for an extended period of time. Every vehicle must be equipped with a means of replacing the current being drawn from the battery. A charging system is used to restore the electrical power to the battery that was used during engine starting. In addition, the charging system must be able to react quickly to high load demands required of the electrical system. It is the vehicle's charging system that generates the current to operate all of the electrical accessories while the engine is running.

The purpose of the charging system is to provide the electrical energy needed to charge the battery and to power all the electrical components and systems on the car. When the engine is not running, the battery provides this electrical energy. When the engine is running, the charging system takes over. The basic parts of a charging system are shown in **FIGURE 21** Basic Charging Circuit. The alternator is the heart of the charging system. It is an alternating-current generator mounted on the engine, which is driven by a belt from the crankshaft. The alternator develops alternating current, which is changed to direct current. Alternating current changes from positive (+) to negative (-) at a regular cycle. Direct current does not change from positive (+) to negative (-). Only direct current can be used to charge a battery.

A voltage regulator, either inside or outside the alternator, senses the electrical needs of the vehicle and adjusts the output of the alternator accordingly. An indicator light, ammeter or voltmeter on the instrument panel allows the driver to observe whether the system is operating properly.

Two basic types of charging systems have been used. The first was a DC generator, which was discontinued in the 1960s. Since that time the AC alternator has been the predominant charging device. The DC generator and the AC alternator both use similar operating principles.

As engine speed increases, the charging system produces sufficient electrical energy to keep the battery charged and supply the car's electrical loads. If there is an increase in the electrical demand, the battery and charging system work together to supply the required current.

The entire charging system consists of the following components:

- Battery

- Alternator, with integral or remote regulator

- Drive belt

- Charge indicator (lamp or gauge)

- Ignition switch

- Cables and wiring harness

- Starter relay (some systems)

- Fusible link (some systems)

The charging system is illustrated in **Figure 21** Basic Charging Circuit.

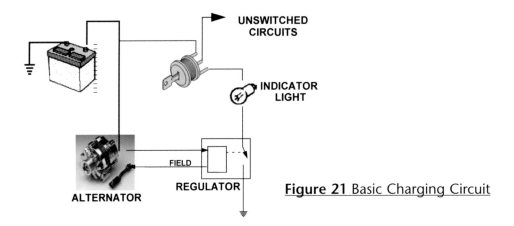

Figure 21 Basic Charging Circuit

Battery

The battery, put simply, stores electricity. A chemical reaction takes place inside the battery which produces electricity, however, it is easier to describe it as an electrical storage device. Inside the battery, two dissimilar metals (conventionally, lead and lead peroxide) are immersed in an electrolyte of sulphuric acid and water. When a load is connected across the two dissimilar metals, a chemical reaction causes current to flow, discharging the battery. Eventually, both metals will become lead sulphate and the electrolyte will change to pure water, and no more electricity will be produced. The charging process, however, ensures this will not happen. Connecting an electrical supply across the dissimilar metals causes the reverse action to take place, i.e.the sulphuric acid and water solution is made stronger, and the lead sulphate turns to lead.

> **Electrolyte is very corrosive. It will cause severe injury if it comes in contact with skin and/or eyes. If you come into contact with battery acid, wash immediately with water. If you get the acid in your eyes, flush them immediately with cool water or a commercial eye wash then seek medical treatment immediately. If you swallow any electrolyte, do not induce vomiting. Seek medical treatment immediately.**

When discharging the battery (current flowing from the battery), it changes chemical energy into electrical energy. It is through this change that the battery releases stored energy. During charging (current flowing through the battery from the charging system), electrical energy is converted into chemical energy. As a result, the battery can store energy until it is needed.

The automotive battery has several important functions, including:
- It operates the starting motor, ignition system, electronic fuel injection, and other electrical devices for the engine during cranking and starting.

- It supplies all the electrical power for the vehicle accessories whenever the engine is not running or at low idle.

- It furnishes current for a limited time whenever electrical demands exceed charging system output.

- It acts as a stabilizer of voltage for the entire automotive electrical system.

- It stores energy for extended periods of time.

The largest demand placed on the battery occurs when it must supply current to operate the starter motor. The electrical current requirements of a starter motor may be over several hundred Amps. This requirement is also affected by temperatures, engine size, engine compression and engine condition.

After the engine is started, the vehicle's charging system works to recharge the battery and to provide the current to run the electrical systems. Most alternators have a maximum output of 60 to 90 Amps. This is usually enough to operate all of the vehicle's electrical systems and meet the demands of the accessories. Under some conditions (such as engine running at idle) alternator output can be below its maximum rating. If there are enough electrical accessories turned on during this time (heater, wipers, headlights, and stereo) the demand may exceed the alternator output. The total demand may be 20 to 30 Amps. During this time the battery must supply the additional current.

Even with the ignition switch turned off, there are electrical demands placed on the battery. Clocks, alarm systems, engine computer memory, body computer memory and electronic sound system memory are all examples of key-off loads. The total current draw of key-off loads is usually less than 30 milliAmps, hardly significant but could cause problems over extended periods of non-use.

In the event that the vehicle's charging system fails, the battery must supply all of the current necessary to run the vehicle. Most batteries will supply 25 Amps for a couple of hours before discharging low enough to cause the engine to stop running.

The amount of electrical energy that a battery is capable of producing depends on the size, weight, active area of the plates, and the amount of sulphuric acid in the electrolyte solution.

The battery in a car loses its charge when under pressure, such as when starting the engine, but regains its charge once the engine is running and driving the Generator or Alternator. This continuous charge/discharge cycle enables the battery to remain in service for up to five years.

The process of charging and discharging a battery produces hydrogen gas, which is highly flammable. When exposed to a naked flame, An explosion may take place, which will cause personal injury and damage to the car.

State of Charge. A Battery is at its optimum charge when the Specific Gravity of the Electrolyte is at approximately 1.270. The Specific Gravity measurement is a measurement of the combined specific gravity of the water and sulphuric acid. Table 5 - **Specific Gravity** shows how a Battery should read in its various states of charge.

Table 5 - Specific Gravity

VOLTAGE	STATE OF CHARGE	SPECIFIC GRAVITY
12.6	100%	1.270
12.4	75%	1.225
12.2	50%	1.190
12.00	25%	1.155
11.8	0%	1.120

BATTERY VOLTAGE WHILE THE ENGINE IS RUNNING SHOULD READ CLOSE TO 14.40 VOLTS IF THE CHARGE RATE IS CORRECT.

Specific Gravity is measured by sucking up some electrolyte into a Hydrometer.

When designing a custom wiring system, it is highly desirable to include a Battery Isolation Switch. Such a switch is included in all circuits in this book. It is also important to determine the location of the battery and to consider the distance between the battery positive terminal and the first main junction point, which is normally the starter motor solenoid. It is highly recommended to locate the battery as close as possible to the starter motor for a number of reasons.

- The length of cable required to connect the battery + to the solenoid may be excessive enough to drop a considerable voltage across the length of the cable, impairing the cranking voltage.

- A danger exists through chafing of the main feed cable against the chassis or body panels. If this chafing can be reduced or eliminated, there is less danger of a battery fire due to short circuiting the main feeder cable.

Wherever you may locate the battery, the type of battery selected must also be decided. A high compression, high performance engine will need a battery of sufficient cranking power to turn the engine over, and keep turning it over until it fires. A high torque starter motor may need to be considered in these cases. A factory stock engine, however, will only require the type of battery recommended by the manufacturer of the car the engine originally came from.

Trunk Mounted Battery

A Hot Rod or Custom project rarely utilises the original battery location or factory replacement cables. A battery box and thick welding cable or 0 gauge battery cable is often used. Special consideration must be given, however, when installing the battery in the trunk (boot). Welding cable is a very good conductor, but there are some drawbacks which you must be aware of if you are going this route.

Welding cable conducts well because of "skin effect", which is the action of alternating current passing through a conductor on the outside cross-section of the wire, or the "skin". Welding cable is composed of hundreds of fine conductors, taking full advantage of skin effect and making it very flexible at the same time. Even in Direct Current applications, electron flow is on the outer cross sectional area of the conductor.

Positive Cable. At the starter motor end of the custom built battery cable, the lug will be hotter than the rest of the cable, and any moisture present will soak into the cable in much the same fashion as a wick. Welding cable is not designed to operate in a wet environment such as what you would find on a rainy road under a car. If there is a gap between the connector and the insulation, it will suck up water like a wick very quickly. Also consider that the insulation is made of rubber and deteriorates much faster than high temperature plastic or teflon. If welding cable is used in your project, make sure you seal the connection end at the engine with heat shrink and glue to prevent the wicking affect. Cover the cable with convoluted tubing to prevent chafing of the insulation and always use insulated clamps to secure the cable.

Negative (Ground) Cable. Many trunk mounted battery installations route the negative (ground) cable to the nearest piece of bare metal on the chassis and/or body.

This is the weakest link in your charging system!

If the positive cable runs from the trunk to the starter motor, so too should the ground cable. Way too much voltage is dropped across these long cables, so everything you can do to prevent this will help improve your wiring system.

Battery Case. The battery case is made of polypropylene, hard rubber, and plastic based materials. The battery case must be capable of withstanding temperature extremes, vibration, and acid absorption. The cell elements sit on raised supports in the bottom of the case. By raising the cells, chambers are formed at the bottom of the case, trapping the sediment that flakes off the plates. If the sediment was not contained in these chambers, it could cause a conductive connection across the plates and short the cell. The case is fitted with a one-piece cover. The entire battery must be secured properly. In custom applications or where the battery is to be mounted away from its factory position, a good quality battery box is the way to go. An example of an after market battery box is illustrated in **Figure 22** Battery Box.

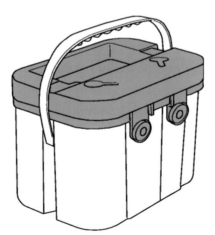

Figure 22 Battery Box

Maintenance-Free Batteries

The maintenance-free battery contains cell plates made of a slightly different compound to reduce gassing and selfdischarge. The use of calcium, cadmium, or strontium reduces the amount of vaporization that takes place during normal operation. The grid may be constructed with additional supports to increase its strength and to provide a shorter path, with less resistance, for the current to flow to the terminal posts.

Each plate is wrapped and sealed on three sides by a plastic envelope or separator. By enclosing the plate in an envelope, the plate is insulated and reduces the shedding of the active material from the plate. The battery is completely sealed so the electrolyte and vapours cannot escape. An expansion chamber allows internal expansion and contraction to occur. Because the vapours cannot escape from the battery, it is not necessary to add water. Containing the vapours also reduces the possibility of corrosion and discharge caused by electrolyte on the surface of the battery.

Some maintenance-free batteries have a built-in hydrometer that shows the state of charge. If the dot at the bottom of the hydrometer is green, then the battery is fully charged (more than 65% charged). If the dot is black, the battery charge is low. If the battery has a built-in hydrometer it cannot be tested with a hydrometer because the battery is sealed.

If the dot is yellow, do not attempt to recharge the battery. If the 'eye' is clear, the electrolyte is low. In either case the battery must be replaced.

Many manufacturers have revised the maintenance-free battery to a "low maintenance battery", in that the caps are removable for testing and electrolyte level checks. The advantages of maintenance-free batteries over conventional batteries include:

- A larger reserve of electrolyte above the plates.

- Increased resistance to overcharging.

- Longer shelf life (approximately 18 months).

- Ability to be shipped with electrolyte installed, reducing the possibility of accidents and injury to the technician.

- Higher cold cranking current rating.

The major disadvantages of the maintenance-free battery include:

- Grid growth when the battery is exposed to high temperatures.

- Inability to withstand deep cycling.

- Low reserve capacity.

- Faster discharge by parasitic loads.

- Shorter life expectancy.

Hybrid Batteries

The hybrid battery can withstand up to six full discharge/ recharge cycles and still retain 100% of its original reserve capacity by the selection of compounds used in the plate construction. This improves its reserve capacity for better cranking performance. There is also a reduction in grid growth and corrosion as the lead calcium has less gassing than conventional batteries.

The hybrid battery is capable of providing more current at a faster rate. This is accomplished by designing separators which are constructed of glass with a resin coating. The glass separators offer low electrical resistance with high resistance to chemical contamination.

Recombination Batteries

One of the most recent variations of the automobile battery is the recombination battery. The recombination battery does not use a liquid electrolyte. Instead, it uses separators that hold a gel-type material. The separators are placed between the grids and have very low electrical resistance. Because of this design, output voltage and current are higher than in conventional batteries. The extra amount of available voltage (approximately 0.6Vdc) assists in cold weather starting. Also, gassing is virtually eliminated.

The following are some other safety features and advantages of the recombination battery:

- Contains no acid. If the case is cracked, no acid will spill.

- Can be installed in any position, including upside down.

- Is corrosion free.

- Has very low maintenance because there is no electrolyte loss.

- Can last as much as four times longer than conventional batteries.

- Can withstand deep cycling without damage.

- Can be rated over 800 cold cranking Amps.

Note: Refer to the manufacturer's manual before attempting to test the battery.

If your car has an unusual number of electrically powered accessories, you will have to consider the size of the battery required to sustain the electrical supply should the alternator fail to charge sufficiently. Electric water pumps, fuel pumps, cooling fans, dry sump motors, air conditioning, etc. will determine battery size, alternator size and wiring complexity.

Battery Selection

Batteries come in many different sizes and configurations. When choosing a battery, consider the following three things:

- the size (height, width, length and post configuration),

- whether your battery has top or side posts, and

- how many amps will be needed for reliable cold starting and vehicle operation.

Sizes. Because there are many different sizes, many after market replacement battery suppliers consolidate similar sizes to simplify inventory requirements, so some replacement batteries may not fit exactly the same as the original. The battery may be slightly shorter, taller, narrower or wider than the original, but as long as it fits the battery tray and there are no interference problems, it will do the job.

Too tall a battery may cause the cables to make contact with the hood causing a dangerous and damaging electrical short!

Some replacement batteries come with both side and top posts to accommodate custom applications. Some also have folding handles to make handling and installation easier.

Battery Ratings. Though many replacement batteries are marketed by the number of "months" of warranty coverage provided (36, 48, 60, etc.), what's more important in terms of performance is the battery's power rating which is usually specified as the "Cold Cranking Amps" (CCA) rating. The CCA rating tells you how many amps the battery can deliver at 0 degrees F for 30 seconds and still maintain a minimum voltage of 1.2Vdc per cell. In the past, the rule of thumb was to always buy a battery with a rating of at least one CCA per cubic inch of engine displacement, but twice that is probably a better recommendation for reliable cold weather starting.

At the very least, you should buy a replacement battery with the same or better CCA rating as your old battery or one that meets the vehicle manufacturer's requirements. For most small four-cylinder engines, this would be a 450 CCA or larger battery, for a six cylinder application, a 550 CCA or larger battery, and for a V8 a 650 CCA or larger battery. Bigger is usually better. Extra battery capacity is recommended if your vehicle has a lot of electrical accessories such as air conditioning, power windows, seats, electric rear defogger, etc.

Battery Installation. Most batteries are "dry charged" at the factory, which means they're activated as soon as acid is poured into the cells. Even so, the battery may require some charging to bring it all the way up to full charge. It is recommended that the battery be charged before it is installed regardless of whether it is dry charged or not. This will ensure the battery is at full charge and lessen the strain on your charging system.

When the battery is installed, it must be locked down and held securely by a clamp, strap or bracket. This will not only keep the battery from sliding around on its tray (which might allow the positive cable to touch against something and short out the battery or start a fire!), but will also help to minimize vibration that can damage the battery. Refer **Figure 22** Battery Box.

The battery cables should also be inspected to make sure they're in good condition, too. If the cables are badly corroded, the cables should be replaced. At the very least, you should clean the cable clamps and battery posts with a post cleaner, sandpaper or a wire brush to ensure good electrical contact. A light coating of grease, petroleum jelly and/or installing chemically treated felt washers under the cable clamps will help prevent corrosion.

Alternator

Restorers and nostalgia purists may keep their generators, but modern vehicles use an alternator for their charging system. The remote regulator type are almost extinct, so we will proceed with an explanation of the common, internally regulated alternator seen on 99% of engines today. Refer **Figure 23** Alternator.

Alternator Housing and Cooling Fan. Most alternator housings are of two-piece construction cast from aluminium. The two ends provide support for the rotor and the stator. The end furthest from the pulley contains the diodes, regulator, heat sinks, terminals and other components of the alternator. The two end pieces are referred to as:

FIGURE 23 Alternator

- The drive end housing: This housing contains a bearing to support the front of the rotor shaft. The rotor shaft extends through the drive end housing and holds the drive pulley and cooling fan.
- The slip ring end housing: This housing also holds a rotor. The cooling fan draws air into the alternator through the openings at the rear of the alternator housing. The air leaves through openings behind the cooling fan.

Do not pry open the alternator housing - any excess force can damage the cast aluminium.

Alternator Operation Overview
The Alternator operates as follows:
1. When the engine is running, the drive belt spins the rotor inside the stator windings.
2. A magnetic field is set up inside the rotor via the field current flowing through the slip rings to the rotor creating alternating north and south poles.
3. Current flows in the windings of the stator.
4. The induced current in the stator is an alternating current because the magnetic fields are alternating.
5. As the magnetic field begins to induce current in the stator's windings, the induced current starts to increase. The current peaks when the magnetic field is the strongest.
6. As the magnetic field begins to move away from the stator windings, the amount of current starts to decrease.
7. Each of the three windings of the stator generates current, so the three combine to form a three-phase voltage output.
8. The current induced in the stator passes through the bridge rectifier.

Figure 24 External Regulators

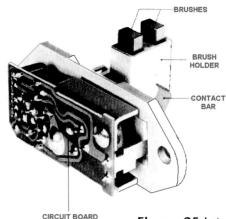

Figure 25 Internal Regulator

Regulation

To maintain the output voltage at a constant battery voltage, a regulator is fitted either externally or as an integral part of the alternator. In automotive applications, Solid State, or Transistorised, regulators are now built in to the Alternator. **Figure 24** External Regulators illustrates the external regulator, both mechanical and solid state types. They are a separate device mounted on the firewall.

Internal regulators are all solid state and are the most common in operation. **Figure 25** Internal Regulator illustrates the typical Internal Regulator (Ford/Bosch type shown). There are two basic types of regulators:

- electromechanical; and

- electronic.

Electro Mechanical Regulators. The electromechanical regulator is obsolete, and is not discussed in detail in this book. Suffice to say that the external electromechanical regulator is a vibrating contact point design. The regulator uses two electromagnets to control Charging Output. The first, a Voltage Limiter Relay, regulates output from the Alternator. When the output from the Alternator gets too high, the high current flow through the Voltage Regulator coil pulls the contacts together (to the grounded contact). This action stops current flow to the Alternator field windings, decreasing Alternator output. When Alternator output gets too low, less current flows through the regulator coil. This action weakens the electromagnetic pull and the force of the contact spring opens the contacts. This connects the alternator field to the battery voltage, and alternator output increases. Cycling at approximately 100 times per second, smooth regulation is achieved.

The other coil is the Field Relay Coil, and simply disconnects power from the charging system when the ignition is in the OFF position.

Electronic Regulators. Electronic regulators can be mounted either externally or inside the alternator. There are no moving parts, so it can cycle between 10 and 7,000 times per second. This quick cycling provides more accurate control of the field current through the rotor. The Electronic Regulator is a sealed unit and not repairable. Sealing the unit prevents damage by moisture, heat and vibration. The most common type of Electronic Regulator today is the Integral Voltage Regulator mounted on the alternator. Most use an IC to provide regulation.

When Alternator output is low, the regulator allows more current to flow through the rotor windings. This strengthens the magnetic field around the rotor. More current is then induced into the stator windings and, as a result, charging output rises.

As the output reaches its upper limits, the regulator introduces higher resistance between the battery and the rotor windings, causing field strength to drop. Less current is induced in the stator windings and charge output reduces.

This increase and decrease in charge output is a direct result of Alternator rpm and the electrical load on the car. If the load is high or the rotor speed is low (for example, idling) the regulator reacts to a drop in system voltage. Charge output increases accordingly. If load drops or rotor speed increases, the opposite occurs.

Note: if not operating correctly, the electronic regulator must be replaced.

Computer-Controlled Regulation. On many vehicles after the mid-1980s, the regulator function has been incorporated into the vehicle's engine management system. The operation is the same as the internal electronic regulator. The on board computer makes decisions concerning voltage regulation based on output voltages and battery temperature. When the
desired alternator output voltage is obtained (based on battery temperature) the computer activates a switching transistor. This transistor grounds the alternator's field to control output voltage.

General Motors introduced an alternator called the CS (charging system) series. This alternator is smaller than previous designs and features two cooling fans (one external and one internal) and terminals designed to permit connections to an onboard computer through terminals L and F. The voltage regulator switches the field current on and off at a fixed frequency of about 400 Hz. Varying the on and off time of the field current controls voltage output.

Voltage/Battery Sensing
Remote Voltage-sensing, or Battery Sensing, has been a standard auto electrical voltage control method for most makes since the late 80s. Because the alternator is the power source for the ignition system, engine management system, lighting,

cooling and all other electrical system parts, it stands to reason that your electrical system will perform at its best when operating at a constant, optimum level - about 14 volts. This is what the voltage regulator is for. In a custom auto electrical system, it is more than likely that the wire harness will feed power to these parts from a main junction, like the fuse panel or a maxi-fuse, which might be some distance from the alternator. In earlier, internally regulated alternators, voltage sensing takes place inside the alternator. The battery charge will be dependant on this voltage. No adjustment is made for the voltage drop that will inevitably occur along the wires that connect the alternator output to the main electrical junction.

For example, if we have a 2.5V drop across the long length of wire between the alternator and the main junction, 14V at the alternator means we only have 11.7V at the main junction! This is what commonly causes dim lights, slow cooling fans and inadequate battery charging in single wire charging systems.

> **Note:** *The voltage regulator will maintain 14V at the junction if its Voltage Sensing circuit reads the voltage from here.*

A Voltage Sensing alternator has three wires - Battery (the big, red wire), Ind (idiot light, or Alternator Warning light) and Sense (see **Table 12** - Alternator Terminals). The Sense connection is the voltage-sensing terminal for the voltage regulator. The Sense terminal of the voltage regulator monitors electrical system voltage. Changes to this voltage due to switching electrical components on and off (cooling fan, stereo system, lights, etc) causes the regulator to adjust alternator output to maintain the 14 volts at the spot where the sensingwire is connected.

> **Note:** *The sensing-wire can be routed to a place remote from the alternator.*

Wiring an Alternator

The Remote Voltage Sensing feature is a big advantage when running a non-factory, custom built wiring system.

The alternator output adjusts accordingly, even though the main electrical system's junction is far removed from the alternator. As lighting or any accessories are switched ON, more power is drawn from the main junction, which lowers voltage at the junction. The voltage regulator, however, will increase alternator output as needed to maintain the 14V level at the junction. With the same 2.5V voltage drop across the wire between the alternator and the junction, the voltage regulator makes the alternator produce 16.5V to compensate.

This system only works properly when a properly rated wire connects the battery to the junction (see **Figure 26** Correctly Wired Alternator). You should never connect the alternator directly to the battery.

In the example illustrated in **Figure 27** Incorrectly Wired Alternator, the installation of the alternator includes a heavy gauge charging wire from the alternator directly to the battery. The voltage sensing wire is routed to the junction, and the voltage regulator will maintain the junction at the correct 14V level. However, as the voltage regulator compensates for the voltage drop, the alternator output could be over 16 volts, overcharging the battery via the extra charging cable.

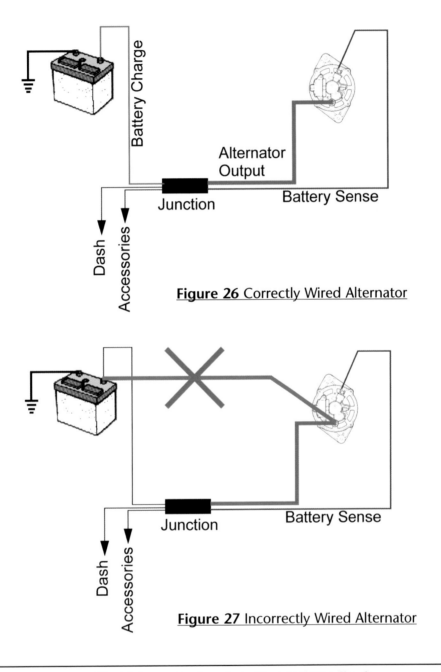

Figure 26 Correctly Wired Alternator

Figure 27 Incorrectly Wired Alternator

Chapter 5

Ignition Systems

The purpose of the ignition system is to supply a spark across the spark plug electrodes in the combustion chamber at the correct time under all engine operating conditions. This precisely timed spark is responsible for igniting the air-fuel mixture in the combustion chamber so the burning, expanding gases in the cylinder always create maximum downward force on the piston. All ignition systems include some form of ignition advance control.

There are many different types of ignition systems. Most of these systems can be placed into one of three distinct groups:

*   The conventional breaker point type ignition systems, in use since the early 1900s (see FIGURE 28 **Points Distributor Ignition System**).

*   Electronic Ignition (EI) systems. Electronic Ignition systems were introduced in the 1970s to take over from points type systems of the previous 50 years. These systems still had distributor advances.

*   Distributorless ignition system.The introduction of semiconductor controlled spark advance during the late 70s and early 80s was the fore-runner of the modern electronic ignition system, with no distributors and computer-controlled spark advance.

Note: *Since the 1980s, most engines came equipped with some form of electronic ignition.*

The following major components make up most of the various configurations of ignition systems popular with custom auto electrical systems:

- Distributors. Magnetic and Hall Effect distributors, crank triggered distributors and distributor advance techniques.

- Distributorless. Coil packs, crankshaft position and camshaft position systems used in Engine Management Systems.

- Control Units. Electronic Control Units (ECU), Capacitive Discharge Ignitions (CDI), Ignition Modules and microprocessors (computers).

- Ignition Coils. Single coils, Coil packs and coil on plug (COP) systems.

- Spark Plugs.

Distributor Ignition System

Both the distributor-type and distributorless systems can have computer-controlled spark advance. The ignition system must supply the spark to each spark plug in the firing order of the engine regardless of the number and configuration of engine cylinders.

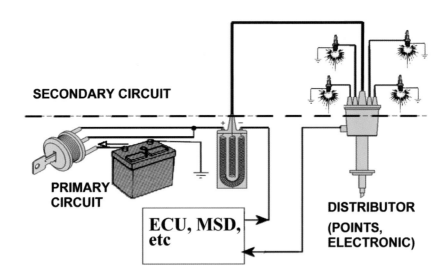

Figure 28 Points Distributor Ignition System

The ignition system provides a spark at just the right time when each cylinder is ready for a power stroke. The spark ignites the air-fuel mixture in the cylinder to push the piston down. The ignition system consists of the following basic parts:

- Primary Circuit, consisting of:
  - Ignition Switch
  - Battery

- Coil Primary Winding
- Distributor
- Secondary Circuit, consisting of:
    - Rotor
    - Distributor Cap
    - Plug Leads, and
    - Spark Plugs.

If a V8 engine is rotating at 3,000 rpm, and the ignition system must fire four spark plugs per revolution, the ignition system must supply 12,000 sparks per minute. These plug firings must also occur at the proper instant, without misfiring. If the ignition system misfires, or does not fire the spark plugs at the proper time, fuel economy, engine performance, and emission levels are adversely affected.

A source of electrical energy is required for ignition. This source is the battery and alternator. When the engine is being started, the battery supplies the needed current. After the engine is running, current is supplied by the alternator or by the alternator and battery working together.

The ignition switch allows the driver to start and stop ignition by opening and closing the circuit between the electrical energy source and the other ignition components. The key switch usually has four positions:

- OFF
- ACCESSORY
- ON
- START

The voltage developed by the battery or alternator is not high enough to ignite the air-fuel mixture in the engine's cylinders. The function of the ignition coil is to step up, or transform, the low voltage available from the battery or alternator to the 35,000 or more volts required for ignition on earlier points and transistor assisted ignitions and upwards of 70,000 volts for modern CDI and distributorless ignitions.

Electronic Control
The need for higher mileage, reduced emissions and greater reliability has led to the development of the electronic ignition systems. These systems generate a much stronger spark which is needed to ignite leaner fuel mixtures. Breaker point systems needed a Ballast Resistor to reduce the operating voltage of the primary circuit in order to prolong the life of the

points. The primary circuit of the electronic ignition systems operate on full battery voltage which helps to develop a stronger spark. Spark plug gaps have widened due to the ability of the increased voltage to jump the larger gap. Cleaner combustion and less deposits have led to longer spark plug life.

> *Note: On some systems, the ignition coil has been moved inside the distributor cap. This system is said to have an internal coil as opposed to the conventional external one.*

Like conventional distributor ignition systems, electronic systems have a primary circuit and a secondary circuit. The entire secondary circuit is the same as in a conventional ignition system. In addition, the section of the primary circuit from the battery to the battery terminal at the coil is the same as in a points ignition system. Electronic ignition systems differ from points ignition systems in the distributor. Instead of a distributor cam, breaker plate, points and condenser, an electronic ignition system has a reluctor (or trigger wheel), a pick-up coil (or stator, or sensor), and an electronic control module (ECM). See **Figure 29** Reluctor and Pick-up Coil.

Distributor Operation
The distributor in an electronic ignition system can have three jobs:

- Emits a controlling signal at a precise point in the engine's cycle. This controlling signal, or "pulse", is used by the ignition module or control unit to output a low voltage to the primary circuit of the ignition coil.

- The distributor times the pulses to engine speed. This is accomplished with centrifugal and vacuum advance mechanisms or electronic timing control in the ignition module or engine management system.

- The distributor directs the high voltage developed by the cables to the spark plugs.

There are two types of electronic distributors that are detailed in this section:

- Magnetic Pulse
- Hall Effect

Magnetic Pulse. In a Magnetic Pulse system, the distributor pick-up coils contain an inductive winding on a permanent magnet, all of which are bolted to a pick-up plate (see **Figure 29** Reluctor and Pick-up Coil). The pick-up windings are connected to the ignition Electronic Control Unit (ECU) and is the means by which the ECU knows when to fire the spark.

A trigger wheel, or reluctor, is pressed onto the distributor shaft and has a high point for each engine cylinder. When the reluctor high points rotate past the pick-up coil, the gap is narrowed considerably. Since the pick-up coil is bolted to the pick-up plate, the gap between the reluctor high points and the pick-up is adjustable.

RELUCTOR

PICK-UP COIL ASSEMBLY

Figure 29 Reluctor and Pickup Coil

Note: Should the reluctor high points become misaligned with the pick-up coil, a larger gap appears and the magnetic field weakens. Realignment by way of the adjustment will be necessary.

With the ignition switch turned on, primary (battery) current flows from the battery through the ignition switch to the coil primary windings. Primary current is turned on and off by the action of the reluctor as it revolves past the pick-up coil or sensor. As each tooth of the reluctor nears the pick-up coil, it creates a voltage that signals the Electronic Control Unit (ECU) to turn off the coil primary current. A timing circuit in the module will turn the current on again after the coil's magnetic field has collapsed. When the current is off, however, the magnetic field built up in the coil is allowed to collapse, which causes a high voltage in the secondary windings of the coil. It is now operating on the secondary ignition circuit, which is the same as in a conventional points system.

The Distributor directs the spark voltage to the appropriate spark plug via the Rotor, which completes the circuit between the centre tower of the distributor cap and the lobe corresponding to the spark plug.

Figure 30 Distributor Cap

Distributor Cap. The distributor cap should be checked to see that the sparks have not been arcing from point to point within the cap. The inside of the cap must be clean. The firing points should not be eroded, and the inside of the towers must be clean and free from corrosion.

Distributor Rotor. A distributor rotor (refer **Figure 31** Distributor Rotor) or "Rotor Button" is designed to rotate and distribute the high voltage to the towers of the distributor cap. The firing end of the rotor, from which the high voltage spark jumps to each of the cap terminals, will wear out eventually which will result in resistance to the high voltage spark. The rotor with a worn firing end will have to be replaced.

The rotor is mounted on the upper end of the distributor shaft and must have a snug fit on the end of the shaft. On some models, two screws are used to attach the rotor to a plate on the top of the distributor shaft. In most cases, built-in locators on the rotor ensure correct location.

The rotor is driven directly by the camshaft, but is "advanced" (turned) by the centrifugal advance mechanism. Advancing the spark timing allows the engine to run efficiently. A vacuum advance is also fitted on some cars for the same reason.

Figure 31 Distributor Rotor

Hall Effect Distributor

Hall Effect is the phenomenon where an electric current flowing through a semi-conductor material is deflected when a magnetic field passes through at right angles to the direction of current flow in the semi-conductor. The deflection is the Hall Voltage, and its strength is dependent on the strength of the magnetic field. If the magnetic field is varied in time with the ignition sequence, pulses of Hall Voltage can then be utilised to trigger the ignition spark.

Hall Generator. The Hall Generator, located in the distributor (refer **Figure 33** Hall Generator and **Figure 32** Hall Effect Distributor) produces the Hall Voltage. It comprises the following components:

- Trigger Wheel and rotor button.
- Permanent Magnet Conductive Element.
- Hall IC, encapsulated in plastic with one of the conductive elements.

TRIGGER VANE

HALL IC

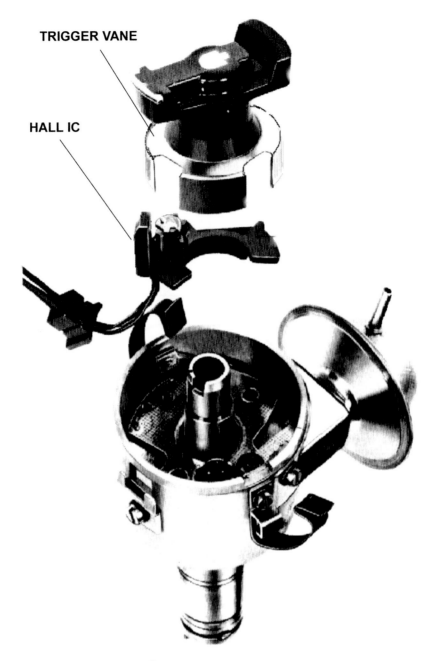

Figure 32 Hall Effect Distributor

Operation of the Hall Generator. The magnetic Trigger Wheel rotates with the distributor shaft. The vanes of the trigger wheel correspond to the number of cylinders in the engine, and every time a vane passes between the Hall IC and the Permanent Magnet (refer **Figure 33** Hall Generator), a Hall Voltage is generated at the output wires. The Vane Width determines the Dwell Angle, therefore the Dwell Angle remains constant for the life of the distributor.

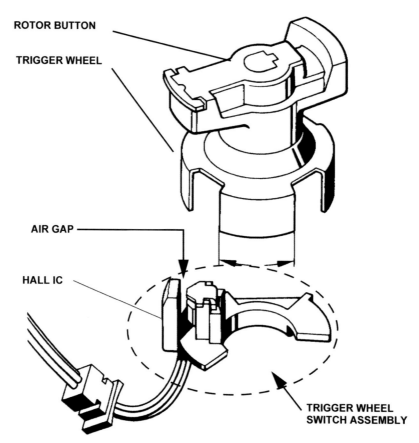

ROTOR BUTTON

TRIGGER WHEEL

AIR GAP

HALL IC

TRIGGER WHEEL
SWITCH ASSEMBLY

Figure 33 Hall Generator

Hall Electronic Control Unit. The ECU is similar in operation to the Pulse Generator type ECU except that there is an extra wire to supply power for the Hall IC (refer **Figure 32** Hall Effect Distributor, **Figure 33** Hall Generator).

Optical Pulse Distributor

This type of distributor uses a Light Emitting Diode (LED) to trigger a power module. To time the trigger pulses of light, the light is directed through a control rotor which fits on to the distributor shaft and rotates with the shaft. Openings in this control rotor permit the light to shine through at strategic points in its rotation and the light beams are picked up on the other side of the rotor by a photo-electric transistor. From this point, the operation is identical to that of the other two systems.

Distributor Crankshaft Triggered Ignition

To take this system one step further, the Crankshaft Triggered Ignition System transfers the Reluctor and Pick-up Coil locations to the engine crankshaft. The distributor is simply used as a rotary switch to transfer high voltage to each spark plug. The rotor and distributor cap are standard components. This eliminates the inaccuracies inherent in a cam driven distributor system, like the camshaft drive system, camshaft torsional twist and lash between the cam and distributor gears. In high performance and custom applications, these tolerances can create spark scatter that can vary ignition timing by several degrees.

Operation of the Crankshaft Triggered system is the same, except that the Crankshaft Position Sensor is mounted next to the Crankshaft Pulse Ring and take the place of the Pick-up Coil and Reluctor (respectively). A Crankshaft Triggered system maintains more precise timing than with a distributor as there is no backlash or play in the distributor gears, no timing chain slack to contend with and piston height is read straight from the crankshaft.

A variation on this application is the MSD Flying Magnet system, which utilises a non-magnetic pick-up. The magnets are located on the trigger wheel, and induce a pulse whenever the "Flying Magnet" passes the non-magnetic pick-up. See **FIGURE 34** Crankshaft Triggered Ignition (MSD Flying Magnet)

Figure 34 Crankshaft Triggered Ignition (MSD Flying Magnet)

Magneto Ignition

A Magneto is a self-contained device which generates and distributes the High Tension electrical impulses for igniting the air-fuel mixture. The Magneto generates the high voltage from the battery ignition supply voltage and distributes it to the various cylinders at the correct time, in a similar manner to a distributor. A magneto does not require a battery or other source of electrical supply, instead it relies on engine speed to generate its own excitation voltage. Once the Magneto is firing, the spark voltage does not decrease with engine speed but actually increases.

The Magneto today is primarily a racing car ignition system, even though they were the earliest forms of ignition in automobiles. Battery ignition took over early in automotive history in most automotive applications because Magnetos require higher cranking speeds than battery ignition. In addition, a battery or some other power source is still needed for lights and accessories.

Timing

Ignition timing is the point at which the spark plugs fire in each of the cylinders. It is measured in degrees of crankshaft rotation before or after Top Dead Centre (TDC) of the compression stroke. Ideally, the ignition of the air/fuel mixture should take place exactly at the piston's TDC, because that's where most power will be made (when the mixture is fully compressed). In reality, the spark plug fires a little bit before the piston reaches TDC because of the time it takes for the spark to ignite the mixture. For example, if the ignition timing is set to 5 degrees before TDC (BTDC) the spark plug fires when the crankshaft is 5 degrees away from TDC (where TDC is 0 degrees).

This setting is fine at idle, but as engine speed increases (that is, the pistons travel faster and faster), the ignition of the mixture has to happen sooner so that it still fires at TDC. To do this, we advance the spark timing as the engine speed increases. On older vehicles, this was accomplished using centrifugal force - weights inside the distributor alter the position of the mechanism controlling the spark. Springs attached to the weights, and the density of the weights themselves, determine how much, and when, the ignition timing advances. Engine vacuum is also used by acting on a vacuum diaphragm mounted on the side of the distributor to control ignition advance at low engine speeds. Later vehicles are equipped with an electronic spark timing system in which no vacuum or mechanical advance is used.

If the ignition is set too far advanced (that is, the spark occurs too far before TDC), the ignition of the fuel in the cylinder happens before the mixture is completely compressed, forcing the piston down while it is still travelling up. This causes engine detonation, or pinging. If ignition is retarded (that is, the spark occurs to far after TDC), the piston will have already passed TDC and is on its way down when the fuel is ignited. The piston is forced down for only a portion of its travel, resulting in poor engine performance and lack of power.

Distributor Mechanical Advance

The distributor can have three advance mechanisms:

- Centrifugal Advance, (**Figure 35** Distributor Centrifugal Advance) which is usually mounted under the pick-up plate, and

- Vacuum Advance, (**Figure 36** Distributor Vacuum Advance) which is positioned on the side of the distributor.

- Electronic Advance. Controlled by the ECU or the Engine Management System.

Centrifugal Advance. The centrifugal advance mechanism comprises pivoted weights mounted on a plate attached to the distributor shaft (refer **Figure 35** Distributor Centrifugal Advance). As the engine and distributor shaft speed increase, the centrifugal force moves the weights outward. The amount of movement is controlled by a precise spring tension on each weight. Pins on the upper weight surface are mounted in slots in the reluctor plate. The reluctor and plate rotate on top of the distributor shaft and a snap ring retains the reluctor and plate assembly to the shaft. Outward weight movement causes the reluctor to rotate in the direction of distributor shaft rotation.

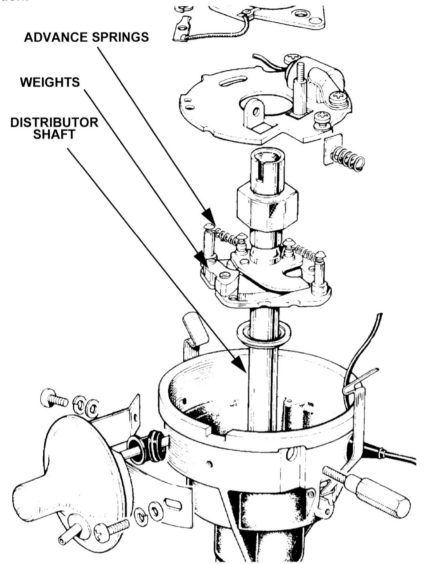

ADVANCE SPRINGS

WEIGHTS

DISTRIBUTOR
SHAFT

Figure 35 Distributor Centrifugal Advance

This reluctor movement means that the high points will line up sooner with the pick-up coil, which in turn causes the spark to occur sooner. Since the pistons move up and down faster as engine speed increases, and the burning time of the air-fuel mixture is about the same, the spark must occur sooner at the spark plug electrodes to be sure that the air-fuel mixture has just started to burn when the piston is at TDC (maximum compression). If the spark is not advanced in relation to piston speed, the piston will be partially down in the power stroke before the air-fuel mixture has had sufficient time to completely burn, which reduces combustion force on the piston and, as a consequence, engine power.

Vacuum Advance. The vacuum advance unit (refer **Figure 36** Distributor Vacuum Advance) is bolted to the side of the distributor housing. A diaphragm contained in a sealed housing is pushed inward toward the distributor by a spring located between the diaphragm and the opposite end of the sealed housing. A vacuum hose is connected to an outlet on the housing. The vacuum hose can be connected to supply manifold vacuum directly from the intake manifold, or port vacuum from the carburettor just above the throttle plate. The diaphragm is pushed inward toward the distributor housing by the spring and an arm is attached to the side of the diaphragm next to the distributor housing. The inner end of the arm is mounted over a pin on the pick-up plate.

When high intake manifold vacuum is applied to the vacuum advance diaphragm, such as at moderate cruising speed, the diaphragm is moved

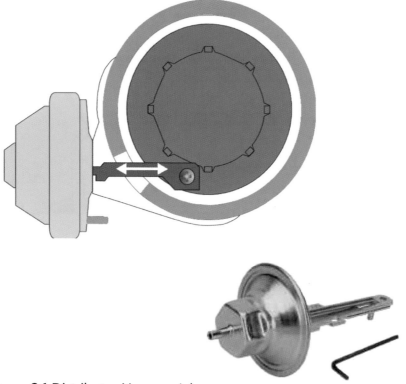

Figure 36 Distributor Vacuum Advance

away from the distributor housing against the spring tension. This diaphragm movement rotates the pivoted pick-up plate in the opposite direction to distributor shaft rotation, which means that the pick-up coil will sign up with the reluctor high points sooner - the spark will then occur sooner. All this must happen under high vacuum because compression pressure and compression temperature are lower, therefore the air-fuel mixture does not burn as fast.

Additional spark advance provided by the vacuum advance increases fuel economy and engine performance.

At or near wide-open throttle, the amount of air intake, compression pressure and compression temperature are increased, which causes faster burning of the air-fuel mixture. The spark advance, then, must be retarded to prevent engine detonation. The intake manifold vacuum is very low at wide open throttle, therefore the spring moves the vacuum advance diaphragm inward toward the distributor housing. This causes the pick-up coil to move back to a retarded position and spark advance is reduced. Put simply, when the engine is operating at light load, moderate cruising speed conditions, the vacuum advance is fully advanced. Under heavy load, wide-open throttle, the vacuum advance is almost inoperable, allowing the centrifugal advance to set total advance.

Those systems using port vacuum work in the opposite manner, except that the vacuum advance does not provide any spark advance when the engine is idling. Port vacuum is developed above the throttle plates, and the vacuum is the action of air rushing through the venturi.

Figure 37 Adjustable Vacuum Advance Unit

Vacuum Advance Adjustment. On some Vacuum Advance units (refer **Fig 37** Adjustable Vacuum Advance Unit), an Allen Key can be inserted through the vacuum outlet to turn an adjusting nut. Clockwise rotation decreases spring tension on the diaphragm which increases the amount of spark advance supplied by the vacuum advance. When this adjusting nut is rotated counter clockwise, the spring tension is increased and vacuum advance is reduced.

Electronic Advance

Ignition timing on most of today's vehicles is controlled by the engine management system's computer and is not adjustable. Timing is determined by the position of the crankshaft (using a Crankshaft Position Sensor or a distributor reference). The computer uses the following inputs to determine ignition timing across the engine's speed range:

- Engine Speed. Crankshaft Position Sensor or distributor reference.

- Crankshaft Position. Crankshaft Position Sensor or distributor reference.

- Engine Load. Manifold vacuum read by the MAP Sensor.

- Engine Temperature. Read by the Coolant Temperature Sensor.

- Throttle position. Read by the Throttle Position Sensor.

- Park/Neutral Safety Switch. In an auto, there won't be any ignition unless the P/N Safety switch detects the transmission is in park or neutral.

- Detonation. The Knock Sensor tells the computer to retard timing if the engine starts to ping.

- Vehicle Speed. The Vehicle Speed Sensor tells the computer how fast the car is travelling.

Ignition Coil

The Ignition Coil is a compact, electrical transformer which boosts the 12V supply from the battery to as high as 20,000 volts. The Ignition Coil comprises two windings (refer **Figure 38** Ignition Coil and **Figure 39** Ignition Coil Magnetic Field):

- The Primary Winding; and

- The Secondary Winding.

Connecting battery voltage across the Primary Winding produces an Electro Magnet. Disconnecting the voltage causes the electro magnetic field surrounding the winding to suddenly collapse (refer **Figure 39** Ignition Coil Magnetic Field).

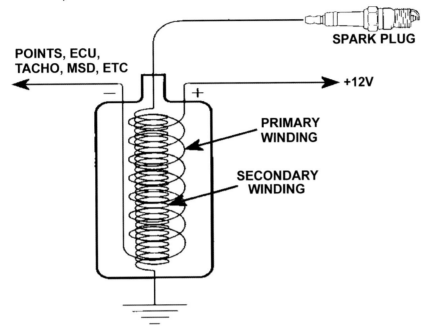

Figure 38 Ignition Coil

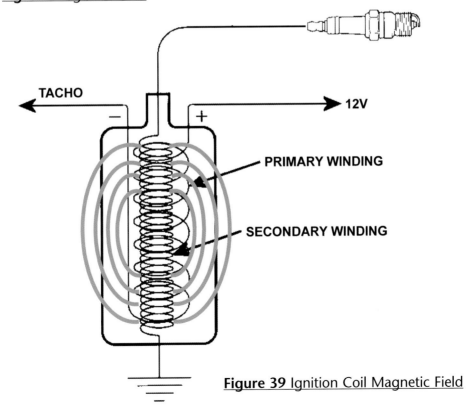

Figure 39 Ignition Coil Magnetic Field

When this happens, a voltage is induced in the secondary winding, which is tightly wrapped around the primary winding. Because the secondary winding has many more turns in it than the primary winding, the induced voltage in the secondary winding is much higher than that in the primary winding. This process is called Magnetic Induction, and is the principle behind Transformers. In effect, the induced voltage in the secondary of the coil is around 25,000 Volts. This charge is routed through the Distributor to the spark plug, and the arc ignites the air/fuel mixture.

Operation

In earlier points and the first electronic ignition systems, power from the battery was fed through a resistor or resistance wire to the primary circuit of the coil. The ignition points provide a ground when they close, energizing the coil primary circuit as current flows through the primary windings. This induces a very large, intense magnetic field while the points remain closed.

As the distributor cam rotates, the points are pushed apart, breaking the primary circuit and stopping the flow of current. Interrupting the flow of primary current. The magnetic field collapses. In the same manner that current flowing through a wire produces a magnetic field, moving a magnetic field across a wire produces current. As the magnetic field collapses, current is induced in the secondary windings. Since there are many more turns of wire in the secondary windings, the voltage from the primary windings is magnified considerably - up to 40,000V (40Kv, or Kilovolts).

The voltage from the coil secondary windings flows through the coil high-tension lead to the centre of the distributor cap, where it is distributed by the rotor to one of the outer terminals in the cap. From there, it flows through the spark plug lead to the spark plug. This process occurs in a split second and is repeated every time the points open and close, which is up to 1500 times a minute in a four cylinder engine at idle.

Condenser. In a points ignition system, a Condenser is fitted in the ground circuit of the points (see **Figure 40** Condenser).

One of the main properties of a Condenser (or Capacitor) is that it opposes the rate of change of voltage. To prevent the high voltage from burning the points, a condenser is installed in the circuit. It absorbs some of the force of the surge of electrical current that occurs during the collapse of the magnetic field. A condenser which is defective or improperly grounded will not absorb the shock from the fast-moving stream of electricity when the points open and the current can force its way across the point gap, causing pitting and burning.

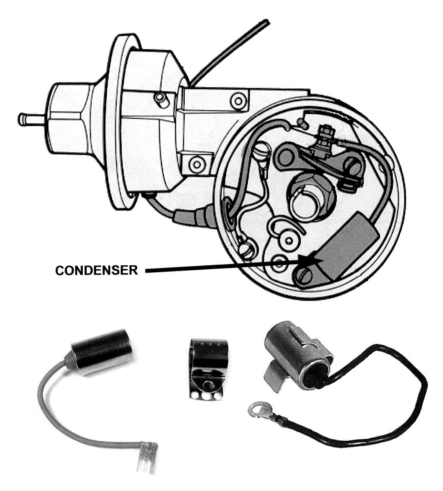

CONDENSER

Figure 40 Condenser

High Energy Ignition Systems

The General Motors High Energy Ignition System (HEI) was introduced in 1975 in the GM passenger cars and light trucks. A reliable and efficient electronic ignition system, the HEI was not designed for use in race cars and high horsepower Hot Rods and Street Machines, however with some modifications, they can be made to produce the timing accuracy and reliability to launch any high compression, high revving (>6500 rpm) Small Block Chev.

There are after market companies that manufacture HEI distributors for non-GM engines (see **Figure 41** HEI Distributors for GM and non-GM engines). Pertronix make one for Ford 221, 260, 289, and 302 engines. Proform and Mallory also make an HEI distributor for Chrysler small and big block V8 and DUI make one for the AMC engine.

Pick-up Coil, Pole Piece, and Timer Core. In a HEI system, the pick-up coil surrounds the distributor shaft, and a flat magnetic plate is bolted between the pick-up coil and the pole piece.

A timer core that has one high point for each engine cylinder is attached to the distributor shaft. The number of timer core high points matches the number of teeth on the pole piece. This design allows the timer core high points to be aligned with the pole piece teeth at the same time.

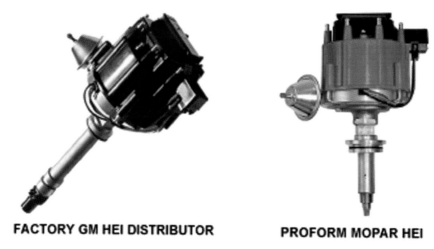

FACTORY GM HEI DISTRIBUTOR   **PROFORM MOPAR HEI**

Figure 41 HEI Distributors for GM and non-GM engines

Module. The dual pick-up lead wires are connected to the HEI module, which is bolted to the distributor housing. Reversal of the pick-up wires on the module is impossible because the wire terminals are different sizes. Heat dissipating grease must be placed on the module mounting surface to prevent excessive module heat. A capacitor is connected from the module voltage supply terminal to ground on the distributor housing.

Ignition Coil. In some HEI systems, the coil is mounted in the top of the distributor cap, whereas other HEI systems have an externally mounted coil. The coil battery terminal is connected directly to the ignition switch, and the coil tachometer (tach) terminal is connected to the module.

Figure 42 HEI Distributor Components

A wire also extends from the coil battery terminal to the module. In many HEI systems with an integral coil, a ground wire is connected between the coil frame and the distributor housing to dissipate induced voltages in the coil frame. HEI coils are similar to Ford TFI ignition E core coils, because they both have windings set in epoxy and a laminated iron frame surrounding the windings. The HEI centrifugal advance mechanism is mounted under the rotor, and the rotor is bolted to the centrifugal advance plate. The vacuum advance is not equipped with an adjusting nut.

High Energy Ignition System Operation. When the ignition switch is on and the distributor shaft is not turning, the module opens the primary ignition circuit. As the engine is cranked and the timer core high points approach alignment with the pole piece teeth, a positive voltage is induced in the pick-up coil. This voltage signal causes the module to close the primary circuit, and current begins to flow through the primary circuit. Under this condition, the magnetic field expands around the coil windings.

At the instant of alignment between the timer core high points and pole piece teeth, the pick-up coil voltage drops to zero. As these high points move out of alignment, a negative voltage is induced in the pick-up coil. This voltage signal to the module causes the module to open the primary circuit. When this action occurs, the magnetic field collapses across the ignition coil windings, and the high induced secondary voltage forces current through the secondary circuit and across the spark plug gap.

HEI modules have a variable dwell feature, which closes the primary circuit sooner as engine speed increases. In an eightcylinder distributor, there are 45 degrees of distributor shaft rotation between the timer core high points. At idle speed, the module closes the primary circuit for 15 degrees and opens the circuit for 30 degrees. If the engine is operating at high speed, the module may close the primary circuit for 32 degrees and open the circuit for 13 degrees. This dwell increase in relation to engine speed provides a stronger magnetic field in the coil and improved secondary voltage at high speed. Since dwell is a function of the module, there is no dwell adjustment.

Electronic Ignition Control Unit

Older ignition systems used points and cam lobes to control spark distribution and dwell. Electronic ignition systems use an Electronic Control Unit (ECU). Early factory systems were nothing more than transistorised switching systems, providing more durability than points, but that was about the only advantage. Later, the ECU became more sophisticated and controlled dwell angle (spark duration), amplitude (spark voltage) and operated at full battery voltage, negating the need for a ballast resistor.

These systems, however, were relatively short lived. Before too long, engine management systems resumed full ignition control and the distributor

B - Battery
C - Battery - (Ground)
W - Magnetic Pickup
G - Magnetic Pickup

The GM HEI Ignition Module was used to control magnetic pickup type ignition systems for many points conversions. Today's after-market CDI systems are far more efficient and reliable.

<u>**Figure 43** GM HEI Ignition Module</u>

disappeared, going the same way as the carburettor, points, condenser and ballast resistor. We can, however, use the more modern electronic ignition components available today to improve reliability, performance and emissions of older, carburetter engines.

How It Works

The ignition control unit switches the primary current in the ignition coil in accordance with the pulses sent to it from the magnetic or Hall Effect pulse generator in the distributor. It serves three main functions:

- Pulse shaping. The pulse shaper converts the alternating voltages from the pulse generator into rectified pulses.

- Dwell angle control. The dwell angle controller changes the duration of these pulses as a function of engine speed.

- Voltage stabilisation. The voltage stabilisation system ensures the supply voltage remains constant.

Capacitor Discharge Ignition

Originally developed as an ignition system for specific applications such as all out racing, the Capacitive Discharge Ignition System (CDI) is the basis for the popular Multiple Spark Discharge (MSD, see **Figure 44** Multiple Spark Discharge ECU) systems available for the enthusiast.

Figure 44 Multiple Spark Discharge ECU

With the CDI, the trigger box contains a capacitor as the ignition energy storage device, a thyristor as a power switch and related electronics for dwell angle control and wave shaping. The principle advantages of a CDI system, apart from breakerless control, are:

- Very short spark duration;

- Very fast voltage rise - makes the system impervious to voltage shunts (high resistances) which would appear as open circuits to lesser systems.

- Highest efficiency of any distributor type ignition system.

NEVER USE A CDI IGNITION TRANSFORMER WITH ANY OTHER ELECTRONIC IGNITION SYSTEM. THE ECU WILL BE DESTROYED!

The after market industry has developed CDI systems for use on street driven high performance vehicles. It will increase the overall performance of everything from the loaded work truck to the bracket street cars. The basic technology involves hot multiple sparks to ensure complete combustion of the air/fuel mixture even under the worst conditions possible. The MSD system illustrated outputs 50,000 volts using a 450Vdc Primary Voltage. The multiple sparks fire during 20 degrees of crankshaft rotation, ensuring the mixture is completely burned and never snuffed out by rich or lean conditions.

Ignition Controllers

Often called Ignition Modules, Ignition Controllers are used in conjunction with the Engine Management System to set and control ignition advance at start, cruise and, in some cases, diagnostic mode. There are many different Ignition Controllers in use today, but they can be broken down into two basic types:

- Smart Module. Handles ignition advance without the aid of the ECM.

- Dumb Module. Has limited control of ignition and relies on the ECM to determine timing.

To describe an example, the Delco ECM uses a standard four wire interface to communicate with the "dumb" ignition controller. Ignition controllers can be any of the following:

- TBI ignition module as used on many US engines, and Australian 1.8 and 2.0 Camira. The TBI module uses a reluctor input.

Figure 45 TBI Ignition Module, Factory and After Market

- Bosch Module (all 8 cylinder), uses a Hall-Effect input.

- Coil Pack (all 6 cylinder), uses a Hall Effect input.

Note: The ECM does not know which device it is connected to. All devices use the four wire interface.

The four wire interface is as follows:

- Reference high

- Reference low (ground)

- EST output (ECM to ignition controller)

- Bypass control.

All GM ignition controllers operate in three modes:

- Backup Mode (also called Module Mode). This is the mode that is used to start the engine. When the engine is cranking, spark advance is fixed at 10 degrees. The computer has no control over this. In theory, you could unhook the computer and the engine would continue to run at 10 degrees (if it had fuel).

- EST Mode. When the engine reaches 450 rpm, it is considered to be running and switches to EST Mode. In EST Mode, the computer controls the amount of advance.

- Diagnostic Mode. This mode is mainly for setting timing, and is also controlled by the computer. It should not be confused with Module Mode, as it is just coincidental that it also fixes timing at 10 degrees.

Diagnostic mode is activated by bridging the diagnostic link in the ALDL connector. This switches the computer to a fixed timing output (10 degrees by default).

Ignition Module Operation The ECM determines engine rpm from the period between reference pulse inputs, and outputs spark accordingly. It effectively estimates engine speed from the last reference pulse. At engine speeds below 400 rpm this scheme becomes inaccurate because of cycle to cycle fluctuations. The ECM therefore starts with a fixed spark (Backup Mode, or Module Mode) and switches control to the ECM (EST Mode) at engine speeds greater than 400 rpm.

Figure 46 Ignition Module illustrates the magnetic reluctor type ignition module as used in the four cylinder Holden Camira JE, and the Chev V8 TPI and TBI distributors. These ignition modules can be connected to any magnetic reluctor type distributor through pins P and N, for example, Ford, Chrysler, Nissan, MSD, Mallory, etc. Used in conjunction with the matching GM coil, the ignition module connects to the Delco ECM via the standard four wire ignition interface. This includes all the Australian Delcos and many USA models including the '86 to '89 Chev TPI 1227165 and the '90 TPI 1227730.

The pinouts vary between Delco computer models, but provided you match the four wire interface (EST, Reference, Bypass, and Ref Low) in accordance with the factory wiring diagram for the computer model you are using, it will work fine.

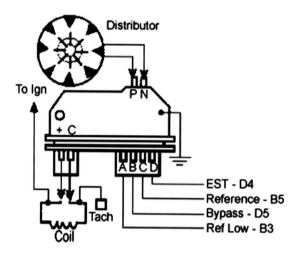

Figure 46 Ignition Module

The four wire interface for the 808 Delco ECM, for example, is as follows:

• EST = D4   • Ref = B5   • Byp = D5   • Ref Low = B3

Similarly, if using a Hall Effect distributor from any brand of 4, 6, or V8, use a Hall Effect EFI ignition module. Connect the three wires from the Hall Effect pick-up inside the distributor to the matching Hall Effect ignition module. Connect the ignition module to the ECM in accordance with the factory connections of the model computer you are using. If using a 808 or 165, it will still be the same four wires as above.

If using a GM 4, 6, or V8 DFI coilpack system with either Magnetic or Hall Effect Crank Trigger, the same principle applies.

These are the three types of ignition interface that GM use with these model computers. Unfortunately, engines that use optical or sequential ignition systems often will not interface with the Delco easily, for example, the Lexus V8.

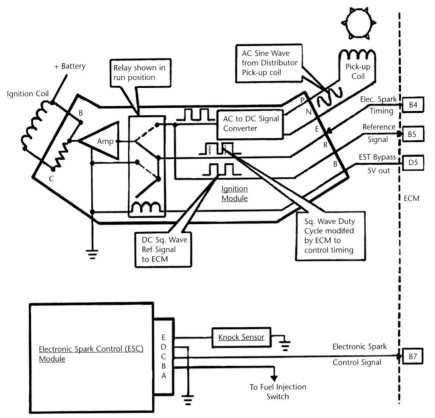

Figure 47 Schematic of GM Ignition Module

Many older points type distributor engines can use an electronic distributor from a newer engine, or an aftermarket items such as MSD or ProComp, which are are easily adapted to the GM ignition module.

Newer engines can either have a Hall Effect trigger added to the crank (such as Lexus) and then use existing distributors, or add DFI Coilpaks which require quite a basic easy to fabricate crank trigger.

The magnetic reluctor pickup type coilpaks are the type GM use on the following vehicles:

- 4 cyl - Chev S10, Cavalier, Lotus, Lada Niva TBI etc

- 6 cyl - Chev V6

- 8 cyl - Corvette ZR 1 (LT-5 engine only)

The Buick / Commodore V6 use a twin Hall Effect 3 x 18 type pickup, and is a very nice system, but it is more difficult to fabricate the trigger to suit other applications.

Distributorless Electronic Ignition

This section deals with electronic ignition systems, where the spark is controlled electronically, generated electronically and distributed electronically. These systems are often called Direct Ignition Systems or Direct Fire Ignition Systems, and are usually incorporated into the Engine Management System. The Direct Ignition System (DIS) uses either a magnetic crankshaft sensor, camshaft position sensor, or both, to determine crankshaft position and engine speed. This signal is sent to the ignition control module or engine control module which then energizes the appropriate coil.

Figure 48 Coil Packs (Eight Cylinder Shown)

Multiple ignition coils, in conjunction with the ECM, fire the spark plugs. A crankshaft timing sensor is mounted over the crankshaft and sends a signal to the computer regarding engine speed and crankshaft position. Some systems also use a camshaft sensor to determine camshaft position relative to crankshaft position. This information, along with that from other sensors, allows the computer to control ignition timing.

> **Note:** *There is no need for the centrifugal and vacuum timing systems used on conventional ignition systems.*

Unlike a distributor system, distributorless types are not prone to worn drive gears, broken shafts and worn bushings, all of which cause erratic ignition timing and spark advance. In addition:

- There are no timing adjustments

- There is no distributor cap and rotor

- There are no moving parts to wear out

- There is no distributor to accumulate moisture and cause starting problems

Another important advantage is the amount of time required for the coil to charge. In a single coil, there is little time between firing, but with one coil divided between two spark plugs, the coil can charge to its full capacity before the next compression stroke comes along.

Obviously, the installation of a distributorless system would result in better economy and performance with less exhaust emissions. Without a distributor, the ignition timing remains more stable over the life of the engine.

Note: Distributorless ignition systems produce much more energy than conventional electronic ignition systems.

DIS Spark Plugs

Distributor points ignition and breakerless electronic ignition systems both fire the spark plugs with approximately the same gaps, therefore the voltage required to fire the spark plugs in both systems is similar. Widening the gap on breakerless systems, unlike points type systems, maintains the same voltage level but puts more strain on the secondary circuit to provide the same energy. The additional energy in the distributorless systems is not produced in the form of voltage, but as current flow, allowing longer duration arcs across the spark plug electrodes. The average length of time which current flows across the spark plug electrodes in a distributorless electronic ignition system is 1.5 milliseconds compared to approximately 1 millisecond in a distributor system. This extra current flow duration of 0.5 milliseconds may seem insignificant, but it makes a big difference. The additional spark duration on distributorless electronic ignition systems helps to prevent cylinder misfiring with leaner air-fuel ratios.

Most DIS applications are factory built and supplied, however there are several after market manufacturers such as Electromotive Inc that can convert any points or electronic ignition to a DIS.

Spark Plugs

Spark plugs use ignition coil voltage to ignite the air-fuel mixture in the cylinder heads (see **Figure 49** Spark Plugs). They are screwed into the combustion chamber of an engine (the thread length is referred to as spark plug reach) and are constructed with a side electrode and an insulated centre electrode spaced far enough apart to form an air gap (refer **Figure 50** Spark Plug Components). Ignition voltage arcs across the air gap to provide the flame to ignite the compressed air-fuel mixtures.

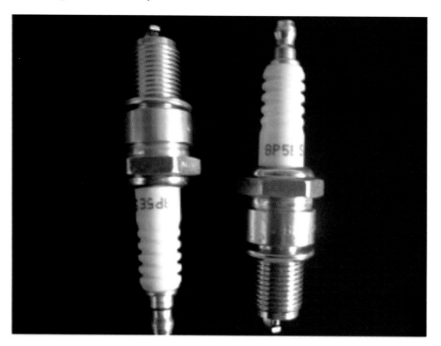

Figure 49 Spark Plugs

The high-voltage burst from the coil via the distributor is received at the spark plug's terminal and conducted down a centre electrode protected by a porcelain insulator. Ribs on the insulator increase the physical distance between the terminal and the shell to help prevent electric arcing on the outside of the insulator.

Many spark plugs have a centre electrode made from a copper alloy. The centre electrode on most spark plugs contains a resistor which drops 15,000Vdc to 7,500 Vdc. This voltage drop reduces radio frequency interference (RFI), which prevents noise on stereo equipment. Voltage peaks from RFI could also interfere with, or damage, on-board computers.

> **When resistor-type spark plugs are used as original equipment, replacement spark plugs must also be resistor-type.**

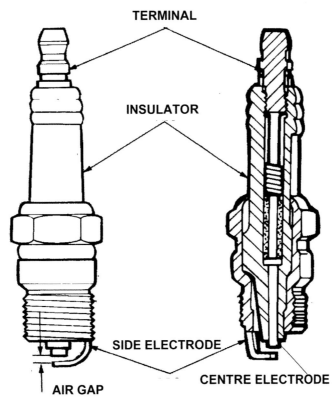

TERMINAL

INSULATOR

SIDE ELECTRODE

CENTRE ELECTRODE

AIR GAP

Figure 50 Spark Plug Components

Various thread lengths are designed to match the cylinder head and combustion chamber design. Some spark plugs have a metal gasket positioned between the seat on the steel shell and the cylinder head, whereas other spark plug shells have a tapered seat with a matching seat in the cylinder head. Some spark plugs have platinum-tipped electrodes, which greatly extend plug life. The average replacement interval for conventional spark plugs is often 30,000 miles or 48,000 kilometers. Platinum-tipped spark plugs have a replacement interval of 60,000 mi (96,000 km) or more.

Spark Plug Heat Range

Every spark plug has a thermal load indicated by an IMEP rating. IMEP (Indicated Mean Effective Pressure in pounds per square inch) is determined by a SAE (Society of Automotive Engineers) standard. This, in simple terms, is the heat range of the spark plug.

Spark plugs are designed to operate within certain heat ranges to compensate for various operating conditions. When the engine is running, most of the heat is concentrated in the centre electrode. Heat from the ground electrode is dissipated quickly because it is threaded into the cylinder head and the engine coolant circulating through the cylinder head passage surrounding the spark plug assists the dissipation process.

The heat path for the centre electrode is through the insulator into the shell and cylinder head, therefore the spark plug heat range is determined by the thickness of the insulator. For cold spark plugs, the depth of the insulator is short before it contacts the shell. This short heat path means cooler electrode operation. In a hot spark plug, the insulator depth is increased before it makes contact with the shell. This extended heat path means increased electrode temperature.

The engine manufacturer will recommend the spark plug type for that particular engine and engine application. There may be more than one spark plug recommended for different applications. For example, if an engine is to be driven continually at low speeds, the spark plugs may become carbon fouled. A hotter range spark plug may be required for this engine's application. Severe high-speed driving over an extended time period may require a colder range spark plug to prevent electrode burning from excessive combustion chamber heat.

The spark plug structural factors that determine heat range are:

- Volume, determined by the space formed between the metal shell and the insulator nose at the firing end.

- Surface area and/or length of insulator nose at the firing end.

- Thermal conductivity of the materials for the insulator, centre electrode and, more importantly, the overall design.

- The total structure of the centre electrode.

- The relative position of the insulator tip to the shell end.

- The number of ground electrodes.

The spark plug operational factors affecting temperature are:

- The internal combustion engine's air-fuel ratio.

- The overall compression ratio of the engine.

- The internal combustion engine ignition timing.

- The octane rating of the fuel.

- The engine speed and load.

The voltage required to create the optimum spark across the spark gap is affected by the following conditions:

- Less voltage is required as the of the air/fuel ratio decreases (that is, gets richer).

- Higher voltage is required as cylinder pressure increases.

- Ignition timing. As the compression pressure at top dead centre reaches its maximum, the spark strength needs to be greater to maintain optimum firing temperature. The required strength of the spark decreases in relationship ignition advance, since the compression pressure lowers and the spark plug temperature rises.

- Fuel types and mixtures.

- The spark plug gap (and resulting temperature) affects the spark voltage.

Spark Plug Identification

Numbering and lettering arrangements indicate various spark plug features. Spark plug heat range is usually indicated by the number on the insulator, and a higher number indicates a hotter spark plug. Many spark plug manufacturers use an 'R' prefixing the number to indicate a resistor spark plug. A 'T' after the number often indicates a tapered seat spark plug, while a 'C' indicates a copper alloy centre electrode. Other letters may be used to identify spark plug reach. The following table describes the numbering code for NGK spark plugs. The designation is broken down into six fields:

Note: Some fields are optional and some have multiple characters.

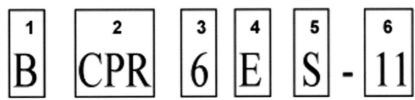

Figure 51 Spark Plug Number Fields

Field one: Thread diameter. A = 18mm, B = 14mm, C = 10mm, D = 12mm.

Field two: Construction. C = hex size 5/8", K = hex size 5/8 with projected tip (ISO), M = compact type, P = projected insulator type, R = resistor, SD = surface discharge for rotary engines, U = semi-surface discharge, Z = inductive suppressor.

Field three: Heat Range. 2 = hot, up to 10 = cold.

Field four: Thread reach. E = 19mm, F = tapered seat, H = 12.7mm (1.5"), L = 11.2mm (7/16").

> *Note: If this field is blank, an 18mm diameter plug has 12mm reach, and a 14mm plug has a 9.5mm (3/8") reach.*

Field Five: Firing end construction. A, B = special design (no details given), C = special ground electrode, G = racing use, GV = racing use V type, H = half thread, K = 2 ground electrodes for certain Toyotas, L = half heat range, LM = compact lawn mower type, M = 2 ground electrodes for Mazda rotary engine, N = special ground electrode, P = platinum tip (premium), Q = 4 ground electrodes, R = delta ground electrode for BMW, S = standard 2.6mm centre electrode, T = 3 ground electrodes, V = fine-wire centre electrode, gold palladium, VX = platinum tip (high performance), W = tungsten electrode, X = booster gap, Y = v-groove centre electrode.

Field Six: (after the dash) Wide gap. 8 = 0.032", 9 = .036" 10 = .040", 11 = .044", there is no 12, 13 = .050", 14 = .055", 15 = .060", 20 = .080".

Spark Plug Cables

Spark plug cables are high tension or secondary ignition cables. One cable transfers the electrical energy from the coil tower to the centre of the distributor cap, and the others from the cap terminals to the spark plugs. Most spark plug cables are carbon-cored resistance cables which suppress RFI, and can be identified by the words Electronic Suppression stamped on the outside of the cable. A graphite-impregnated woven fibre core at the centre of the cable is surrounded by insulation and covered by a glass and cotton braid Some have a hypalon jacket over the braid, and high-temperature wires have a silicon jacket.

Spark plug cables are terminated at either end by metal caps. Boots on the end of each plug wire slide down over the spark plug insulators and prevent high-voltage arcing from the end of the wire. Most plug cables have a maximum voltage drop of 8,000V to 12,000V per foot. Some spark plug cables have a locking connection at the distributor cap. The distributor cap must first be removed and the terminals squeezed together before the spark plug cable can be removed from the distributor cap.

To work effectively in modern ignition systems, it is important to choose a spark plug cable which is rated at a specifically designed resistance. The cable must also have enough insulation so that it can withstand heat, cold, moisture, oil, grease, and chafing. High voltage in a cable builds up a surrounding electrical field. The electrical field frees oxygen in the surrounding air to form ozone, which will attach to the rubber insulation if it is not properly protected. Ozone causes the rubber to deteriorate and lose its insulating qualities. Electrical losses will seriously weaken the spark at the plug gap.

Spark Plug Wear. The ability of the spark to ignite the fuel is badly affected if the plugs are damaged or the spark gaps are abnormal. It is therefore important to examine used spark plugs closely and to clean them periodically. The gaps of old and new plugs should also be checked before installing them. There are three basic types of spark plug fouling:

- carbon fouling,

- high speed or lead fouling, and

- oil/carbon fouling.

Carbon fouling is caused from low-speed operation or a fuel mixture that is too rich. It causes missing or roughness and creates soft black soot that is easily removed. Lead fouling is caused by tetra ethyl lead used in some fuels and by extended high speed operation. Lead compounds which are added to the fuel have a bad effect on some spark plug insulators. At high temperatures, it is a good conductor and may give good results under light loads, but often fails under full loads and high combustion temperatures. In some cases, it is possible to run the engine at a speed just below the point where missfiring will occur; then, increase the speed (always keeping below the missing speed) to burn off the lead fouling. Lead fouling appears as a heavy, crusty formation, or as tiny globules.

Oil/Carbon fouling is found on engines that are so badly worn that excess oil reaches the combustion chamber past the piston ring, or the valve guides. In all cases of fouling or wear, it is advisable to replace the plugs. To avoid having to replace plugs one at a time as they wear out, always replace the entire set, even though only one plug may be bad.

Chapter 6

Electronic Ignition Conversions

This Chapter describes the various methods and procedures to follow in order to convert a points type ignition system or an early transistor assisted electronic ignition system to a magnetic pulse or hall effect electronic ignition system. We will deal with the most popular electronic ignition system conversions which are available for earlier, pre-EFI engines. For the auto enthusiast who wishes to retain these older engines, the conversions will increase performance, reduce pollutants and run more efficiently without losing their aesthetic appeal. An early, or "traditional" Hot Rod just wouldn't look right with a SVO port injected Ford, but with the proper application of these products, your Windsor, Cleveland, 390 Cadillac, early Hemi or flathead engine can be fired by the most modern, high tech means available.

Breakerless Ignition
There are three primary components required for a conversion to Magnetic Pulse or Hall Effect ignition:

- The Distributor

- The Electronic Control Unit

- The Ignition Coil

Distributors
The billet distributors available from manufacturers such as MSD, Mallory, Accel, Holley, far exceed the quality and reliability of the older factory systems in several ways.

- Bearings. The distributor shafts run on bearings, not bushes. Shaft wobble is eliminated.

- Voltage. Billet replacement distributors use the full 12 volts, and do not require a ballast resistor.

- Accurate Advance. The advance mechanism is far more accurate and easier to dial in than the old counter-weight systems. No vacuum advance is required.

- Lockout. Most billet distributors can be locked out (the advance mechanism locked in place) for racing or for Engine Management System control.

Electronic Control Unit

The ECU switches the primary current in the ignition coil in accordance with the pulses sent to it from the pulse generator in the distributor. It serves three main functions, as follows:

- Pulse shaping;

- Dwell angle control; and

- Voltage stabilisation.

The pulse shaper converts the alternating voltages from the pulse generator into rectified pulses. The dwell angle controller changes the duration of these pulses as a function of engine speed. The voltage stabilisation system ensures the supply voltage remains constant.

Ignition Coil

The ignition coil is specially designed to suit the ECU, and cannot be replaced by a coil designed for a points system. The coil incorporates safety devices. Because this type of ignition system is designed to handle larger currents than conventional systems, the coil is protected at the primary terminals to prevent contact, as voltages in the range of 350V are possible. In the event of a failure of the switch transistor, the coil primary current can reach values which may overheat the ignition coil and cause oil seepage past the coil cap. A cut out in the coil cap crimping ring discharges the hot oil.

Conversion Kits

There are many third party brands of electronic ignition kits (MSD, Accel, Mallory, Jacobs, Crane, Pertronix, to name a few) designed to simplify the conversion to electronic ignition on many different engines. Because of the large range of kits available for this conversion, the procedures to install the kits vary from manufacturer to manufacturer. It would not be wise to include installation instructions here, as they may differ from the manufacturer's. Instead, we shall describe one manufacturer's system to give you an idea as to what is involved in the installation process.

MSD Ignition

Employing CDI Technology, the Multiple Spark Discharge (MSD) system takes advantage of the short spark duration of CDI systems and fires the plug several times for each ignition cycle. **Figure 52** MSD Ignition depicts the control box for the MSD 6AL ignition system.

Figure 52 MSD Ignition

One of the easiest Electronic Ignition System to install is the MSD System. The distributor can be a points distributor or a pulse (magnetic or hall effect) type. The procedure is simple. The MSD control unit is installed between the ignition coil and the distributor.

A ballast resistor is not required, as the MSD accepts the full ignition voltage. The triggering system can be either points or pulse, magnetic or hall effect. If a points system is used, the wire from the distributor to the MSD box is the White wire. In a Pulse Triggered system, the Magnetic Pick-up cable to the MSD box is used, but NEVER BOTH!

For points systems, the dwell angle is controlled by the MSD Control Box. Where a dual point distributor is used, the trailing points should be removed to take full advantage of the electronic dwell angle control.

The Installation Instructions for all MSD products cover most makes and models of factory and after market systems and include recommendations for other components that will enhance the capabilities of the MSD system.

It is highly recommended that a points distributor be replaced with either a replacement magnetic/hall effect distributor or converted to magnetic using a Pertronix or similar points conversion. Discarding the points:

- Improves power, quickens throttle response.

- Smooths out idle and starting.

- Reduces spark plug fouling.

- Improves mileage and reduces emissions.

The following information has been provided by Autotronic, and details the MSD 6 Series Ignition Technical Data:

- All sparks, including each multiple spark, is 110 milliJoules of spark energy.

- Steps up the primary voltage to 470 volts.

- Spark duration lasts for 20 degrees of crankshaft rotation.

- Operates at full power with a supply of 10-18 volts and will run down to 5 volts.

- Cast aluminum housing and Humi-Seal coated circuits protect the electronics.

- Can be triggered using points, electronic ignitions or magnetic pick-ups.

Crankshaft Triggered Ignition. To obtain the most accurate ignition timing possible, the ignition control is handed over to a triggering device on the crankshaft, usually in the form of a Trigger Wheel and a sensor. The sensor is typically magnetic in design, and each time a tooth on the trigger wheel passes the sensor, it "triggers" an ignition pulse.

MSD manufacture an innovative system called the Flying Magnet system. This one is different because the sensor is not magnetic. The magnetic pulse is obtained from a magnet on the trigger wheel, thus the term "Flying Magnet"

The trigger wheel is machined from 6061-T6 aluminium andanodized MSD Red. Each "rare earth" magnet is pressed and then riveted into the wheel to handle high rpm situations and the resultant vibration. By installing the magnets in the trigger wheel, MSD has done away with the chance of false triggering. As the crankshaft rotates, the magnet passes the nonmagnetic sensor, triggering the ignition.

All MSD Flying Magnet Crank Trigger Kits must be used with an MSD Ignition Control.

Figure 53 MSD Flying Magnet Kit

Note: A locked-out distributor must be used with a crank trigger system.

Distributorless Ignition System

There are few after market manufacturers of Distributorless Ignition Systems (or Direct Ignition Systems as they are also called), but Electromotive Inc is the best known and most reputable.

The Electromotive DIS claims a 0.1 degree timing accuracy. An integral rev-limiter can be set anywhere between 4,000 and 15,000 rpm. A MAP sensor can be integrated to accommodate timing changes for both light load cruise conditions and/or high load forced induction.

To obtain engine speed and position, a 60 tooth trigger wheel, with 2 of the teeth missing, is attached to the crankshaft, and a magnetic sensor is aimed at the wheel. The two missing teeth are sensed by the ECM to provide information on the crankshaft position for each revolution. The ECM is housed in a billet aluminum casing and provides a solid mount for the coils. The system can be mounted under the hood for quick and easy maintenance and adjustment.

The crankshaft trigger wheel is mounted between the harmonic balancer and the first pulley. In situations where this kind of mounting would be inappropriate, a Camshaft trigger wheel can be installed and even a distributor wheel is available for installing in a factory distributor. The Magnetic Sensor is mounted in an aluminium bracket. Kits are provided for most common installations, but custom installations are well catered for.

Wiring a DIS. When wiring up DIS such as the Elecromotive kit, special attention must be paid to grounds. There are at least five grounding points on the vehicle:

- Battery to engine block

- Battery to chassis

- Engine block to chassis

- ECM to engine block

- Ground wire from ECM to battery (preferred) or engine

> *Note:* *When wiring the magnetic sensor, avoid passing the wires close to high current/high voltage sources, such as spark plug wires, as this could cause interference in the ECM.*

Spark Plugs in DIS. Because a DIS creates significantly higher energy levels than other ignition systems, a colder heat range spark plug is required. Plug gaps, typically, are from 0.025" to 0.032". For high boost or high compression applications, set gaps at the narrow end of the range. For street use, a wider gap is appropriate. Thick, tight fitting plug boots are also highly recommended. Plug wires must be high quality, 8mm or larger RFI/EMI suppressed carbon core.

Chapter 7

Electronic Fuel and Ignition Control

It is impractical to expect home handypersons to have a working knowledge of computers in order to install and repair engine management systems. When it comes time to fixing "the Black Box", it is a case of repair by replacement. A very EXPENSIVE replacement, so you want to be sure that the Black Box is definitely busted before you go ripping it out. When building a Hot Rod, Custom, Street Machine or any other project involving a drivetrain managed by a Black Box, a working knowledge is essential in order to hook all the technology up to the engine. Anything less is a waste of time. You may as well go and bolt in a carburetted, points ignition drivetrain for all the good it will do.

The term "computer" is used loosely throughout the automotive industry, and there are several references used by different manufacturers to represent their particular "computer". The following terms are commonly used:

- Electronic Control Module (ECM);

- Electronic Control Assembly (ECA);

- Programmable Control Module (PCM);

- Processor;

- Microprocessor;

- Electronic Control Unit (ECU).

Note: This book will generally use the term ecm when referring to the engine management system computer

The reason for using computerised modern engines is simple. They burn cleaner, they are more efficient (and therefore cheaper to run), they are more reliable (less moving parts) and they are plentiful. Although more complex in their operation, it is now only necessary to pull out a laptop and a Digital Multimeter to fix the modern engine. Firstly, however, a basic understanding of the concepts and functions of Engine Management Systems (EMS) will be necessary. A brief description of Analog and Digital technology follows.

Digital vs. Analog

There are two basic types of electronic signals or impulses:

- Analog; and

- Digital.

Analog signals are the most familiar type to all of us. Analog information is in the form of an AC or DC voltage or current which varies smoothly or continuously. It does not change abruptly, or in steps.

Digital signals are a series of pulses or rapidly changing voltage levels that vary in discrete steps. Digital signals are pulses of voltages which switch between two fixed levels.

Digital information is presented as a series of particular points, not ranges or curves. A switch is digital. It only has two values, on or off, represented as a 1 or 0. A digital voltmeter displays the voltage as exact numbers. A digital speedometer displays the speed at any given time as an exact value. The value is determined by the speedometer's interpretation of the rate and frequency of on-off signals it receives through it's circuitry. Computers are digital devices.

Digital and, consequently, computer technology is made possible by the binary concept - on or off, 1 or 0, voltage present or not present. Each 1 or 0 is called a "bit," and there are eight bits in a "byte," also known as a "word." The pattern of bits in a byte represents a particular number or character, called a Binary Coded Decimal (BCD). The most common coding standard is ASCII (American Standard Code for Information Interchange), in which alphanumeric characters (az, 0-9 and other printable characters) are represented by an eight bit code.

Analog to Digital Conversion

In most instances, sensor input is analog (although there are some ON/OFF inputs from switches that qualify as sensor input). For example, the oxygen sensor signal ranges from 0.1Vdc to 1.0Vdc. The TPS is really a variable resistor, and as such doesn't produce voltage. Instead, it receives a 5.0Vdc reference signal from the ECM (GM calls this "VRef"), and its position determines the degree of resistance that signal encounters, determining the amount of voltage returned to the computer (the ECM). Inside the ECM, all is digital. The incoming analog signal is converted via an Analog/Digital converter (A/D) which assigns the analog signals their numeric values which the computer can deal with.

Memory

Memory in a computer is simply a storage area for millions of digital levels. There are several types of memory components, although we will confine ourselves to the more common ones which are used in automotive applications. Read Only Memory (ROM) and Programmable Read Only Memory (PROM) hold the computer program, which is a set of instructions on how information from sensors and to actuators are to be handled. Also contained here is vehicle-specific data such as axle ratio, engine type, options, and a host of information preset at the factory. This information is permanently etched into the ROM, PROM or EPROM (the 'E' in front of PROM means Erasable) and is usually called the Look Up Table(s) (Para). The data can be cleared by exposure to UV light or, in the case of EEPROMS (Electrically Erasable Programmable Read Only Memory) a 'kill' pulse. It can then be reprogrammed with a different set of instructions.

Random Access Memory (RAM) is active and volatile, that is, once power is removed, information held in RAM disappears. Data from the engine's sensors is loaded into RAM and then read from RAM at random rates and intervals. When the information from the sensors is required to be retained when the engine is not in use, another type of RAM is used. In the case of GM products, NVRAM (Non-Volatile RAM) or (for Ford products) KAM (Keep Alive Memory) retain their data as long as the computer is connected to the vehicle's battery. Adaptive learning, or Block Learning, uses this technology (found in GM's integrator and block learn). The GM adaptive learning strategy makes minor closed-loop adjustments in fuel delivery on the basis of what the oxygen sensor has been reporting recently. This can compensate for such things as a minor vacuum leak.

Operation

Automotive computers receive a combination of inputs, then cross-check stored information in memory called "look-up tables" to find the best values for pulse width, timing, dwell, etc. This data, sometimes referred to as a "map," is established at the factory for each particular engine through testing on dynamometers and actual driving. In this way, the optimum settings for performance, fuel efficiency, low emissions and driveability can be burned into the ROM/PROM chip of the ECM. The program uses the look up tables and input from sensors to issue commands which will control fuel injectors, ignition, solenoids, and many other devices.

There can be more than one computer on board a vehicle. The most common computers are as follows:

- *Main Computer (ECM).* Usually the more powerful computer in any EMS controlled car. Other computers provide the ECM with data.

- *Instrument Computer.* Receives inputs from sensors to operate dash gauges and indicators.

- *Engine Controller.* The computer which accepts inputs and issues commands for engine operation only.

- *Ignition Computer.* Controls ignition timing, dwell, spark duration, etc.

- *Anti-Lock Brakes Computer.* Utilises wheel sensor inputs to prevent wheels from locking up under hard braking.

- *Climate Controller.* Heating, ventilation, Air Conditioning, etc. are all controlled by this computer.

- *Suspension System.* A computer controlled module controls ride stability and torsion via inputs from shock absorber sensors, steering wheel position sensor, speed sensor, etc.

Note: *Only the main ecm will be dealt with in this book*

Inputs

The ECM accepts inputs to check against the look-up tables. As a result, the ECM will control the actuators (such as fuel injectors, idle air control valves) until the value in the look up tables are obtained. The inputs can come from other computers, the driver, the technician or through a variety of sensors and switches. Switches can be used as an input for any operation that only requires an on-off condition, and can be mechanical or electronic. Sensor inputs may be in the form of analog voltages (such as that being returned from a powered O2 Sensor), analog resistances (e.g. the resistance from the Throttle Position Sensor) or ON/OFF (grounded/not grounded) status.

Feedback signals are independent inputs which report the operation of an actuator as having been successful or unsuccessful. For the ECM to monitor critical points of the Engine Management System, it must receive some confirmation that various conditions have been met, such as the operation of a relay, switch or other device. The failure to receive a correct feedback signal usually results in a trouble code being set.

Sensors

There are many different types and designs of sensors. Some are simply switches which complete an electrical circuit while others are complex devices which generate their own voltage under different conditions. The most common types of sensors are:

- *Potentiometers.* A constant voltage value (usually 5 volts) is applied to one end of the resistance. The wiper is connected to the shaft or the moveable mechanism of the monitored unit, such as the Throttle Position Sensor (refer *Throttle Position Sensor* on page 122). As the wiper is moved toward the opposite terminal, the sensor signal voltage to the source terminal decreases. The ECM measures the voltage at different shaft positions which translates to linear or rotary movement of the shaft. As the wiper is moved across the resistor, the position of the unit can be tracked by the computer.

- *Thermistors.* A thermistor is a resistor which changes its resistance as the temperature changes. By monitoring the thermistor's resistance value, the ECM can determine the operating temperature of such things as the engine coolant (refer *Temperature Sensors* on page 117).

- *Magnetic Pulse Generators.* Magnetic pulse generators send speed information (e.g. individual wheel speed, vehicle speed) to the ECM. The ECM uses the data for such things as instrumentation, cruise control, antilock braking, speed sensitive steering, and automatic ride control systems. One of the original functions of the Magnetic Pulse Generator was for distributor controlled electronic ignition (discussed elsewhere in this book) and, in later distributorless systems, to inform the ECM of the degree of revolution of the crankshaft or camshaft for ignition timing.

Table 6 - Common Sensors lists the sensors used in most of the common applications across many makes and models of engines.

Table 6 - Common Sensors

Sensor	Abbreviation	Remarks
Manifold Air Temperature	MAT	Measures air temperature in the inlet manifold
Coolant Temperature Sensor	CTS	Measures temperature of the engine coolant
Oxygen Sensor	O2 Sens,EGO	Measures the amount of oxygen in the exhaust
Heated Exhaust Oxygen Sensor	HEGO	Same as the EGO except that a heating element is added to the sensor
Manifold Absolute Pressure	MAP	Measures the vacuum in the inlet manifold
Barometric Pressure Sensor	BAR, BAP	Measures atmospheric pressure in the engine bay
Throttle Position Sensor	TPS	Measures the angle at which the throttle is open
Vehicle Speed Sensor	VSS	Measures vehicle speed
Engine Speed Sensor	ESS	Measures engine rpm
Crankshaft Position Sensor	CPS	Measures angle of rotation of crankshaft at any given time
Mass Airflow Sensor	MAF	Measures the air as it flows into the engine
Knock Sensor	Knock Sens	Detects detonation in the cylinders
Brake Sensor		Detects application of the brakes
Camshaft Position Sensor	CPS	Checks camshaft position in degrees of rotation
Exhaust Gas Recirculation	EGRVP	Measures position of EGR valveposition Sensor valve
Air Charge Temperature Sensor	ACT	Measures the temperature of the air charge entering the motor

Temperature Sensors

Temperature sensors are thermistors that change resistance with temperature. As the temperature goes up, the resistance goes down.

Coolant Temperature Sensor (CTS). The CTS tells the ECM, obviously, how hot the motor is. The Engine Management System needs to know what the coolant temperature is so that it can initiate a cold start, go into closed loop operation when the engine warms up, and help determine proper timing and fuel mix. The CTS is not to be confused with the Temperature Sender unit, which is sometimes combined with the CTS. The sender operates an idiot light and/or temperature gauge. See **Figure 54** Coolant Temperature Sensors.

The CTS should not be confused with Temperature Sender. In this application, the CTS is installed in a heater outlet, right next to the sender.

Figure 54 Coolant Temperature Sensors

Manifold Air Temperature. There are more molecules of oxygen per cubic foot of cold air than of warm air, therefore the cooler the intake stream, the leaner the mixture (given the same amount of fuel).

The computer has to know about the temperature of the air entering the manifold in order to keep the blend right, and that's the job of the MAT (Manifold Air Temperature) or Air Charge Temperature Sensor (ACT). Although its business end is exposed to a gas instead of a liquid, it works in the same way as a CTS. With a cold engine, a scan tool should give you a MAT reading equal to ambient. See **Figure 55** Manifold Air Temperature Sensor.

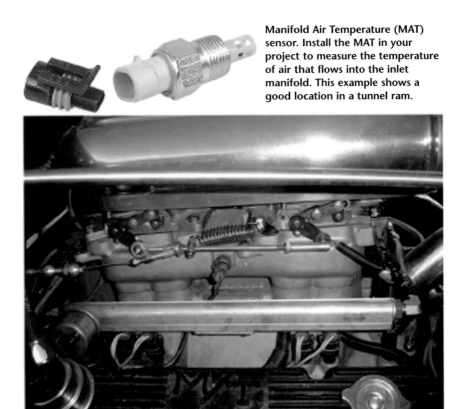

Manifold Air Temperature (MAT) sensor. Install the MAT in your project to measure the temperature of air that flows into the inlet manifold. This example shows a good location in a tunnel ram.

Figure 55 Manifold Air temperature Sensor

Thermal Time Sensor. Sometimes called the Start Injector Time Switch, this temperature sensitive sensor activates the cold start injector when cranking a cold engine.

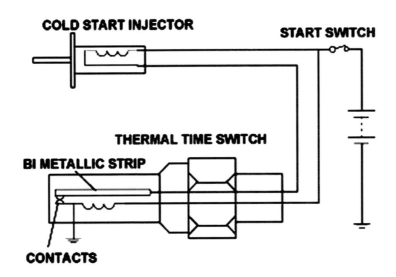

Figure 56 Cold Start Injector and Thermal Time Switch

The cold start injector provides excess fuel to the cylinder(s) in much the same way that a carburettor choke supplies a rich mixture to start a cold engine. When engine temperature is low, the bi-metallic strip in the TTS (refer **Figure 56** Cold Start Injector and Thermal Time Switch) causes the electrical contacts to be closed, energising the cold start injector during engine cranking and cold start. As temperature rises, the bimetallic strip flexes, causing the electrical contact to break and de-energising the cold start injector. Because the TTS is screwed into the engine block or intake manifold, it will not engage the cold start injector as long as the engine is warm.

This system is becoming outdated. The cold start feature of most Engine Management Systems is based on fuel enrichment when the CTS detects a cold engine.

Oxygen Sensor

The Oxygen Sensor (O2 Sensor, Lambda or EGO) is the primary measurement device for the Engine Management System (EMS) fuel control in your car. It tells the computer if the engine is running too rich or too lean. The O2 sensor is active any time it is hot enough, but the computer only uses this information in the closed loop mode. Closed loop is the operating mode where all engine control sensors including the O2 sensor are used to get best fuel economy, lowest emissions and good power.

Operation of O2 Sensor. An Oxygen sensor is a chemical generator. It consists of a hollow element (usually made of zirconium dioxide (ZrO2), a ceramic material) and coated with a thin layer of platinum. The outer layer is exposed to the exhaust stream, while the inner layer is vented to the atmosphere and attached to a wire from the ECM.

This is a lot like a battery cell. The zirconium dioxide acts as an electrolyte, and the platinum layers serve as electrodes. Once the ZrO2 reaches about 600° F, it becomes electrically conductive and attracts negatively-charged ions of oxygen. These ions collect on the inner and outer platinum surfaces. Because there is more oxygen in plain air than in exhaust gas, the inner electrode will always have a larger number of ions than the outer electrode, and this difference results in a voltage potential.

The O2 sensor constantly compares the Oxygen inside the exhaust manifold and air outside the engine. As a result, the voltage generated swings between 0Vdc and 1.1Vdc, in accordance with the air:fuel ratio. All spark combustion engines need the proper air fuel ratio to operate correctly. For gasoline this is 14.7 parts of air to one part of fuel. When the engine has more fuel than it can handle, all available Oxygen is consumed in the cylinder

Use a heated nO2 sensor in your custom exhaust system. You can buy weld-in bungs (they are all the same size and thread) and locate them just about anywhere in the exhaust flow. Single wire systems need exhaust heat from near the exhaust port to operate.

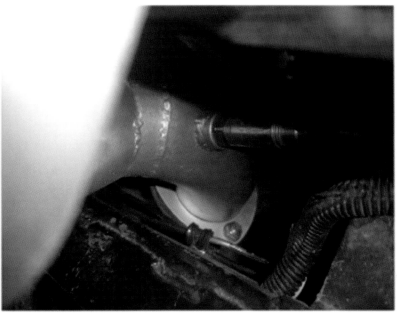

Figure 57 Oxygen Sensors

and gasses leaving through the exhaust contain almost no Oxygen. This causes the O2 sensor to generate a voltage greater than 0.45Vdc. If the engine is running lean, all fuel is burned and the extra Oxygen leaves the cylinder and flows into the exhaust. In this case, the sensor voltage goes lower than 0.45Vdc. Usually the output range is between 0.2Vdc to 0.7Vdc.

The O2 sensor does not begin to generate its full output until it reaches about 600° F. Up until this time, the sensor is not conductive, as if the circuit between the sensor and computer is not complete. The mid point is about 0.45Vdv. This is neither rich nor lean. A fully warm O2 sensor will not spend any time at 0.45Vdc. In many cars, the computer sends out a bias voltage of 0.45Vdc through the O2 sensor wire. If the sensor is not warm, or if the circuit is not complete, the computer picks up a steady 0.45Vdc. Since the computer knows this is an "illegal" value, it judges the sensor to not be ready. It remains in open loop operation, and uses all sensors except the O2 Sensor to determine fuel delivery.

Any time an engine is operated in open loop, it runs somewhat rich and makes more exhaust emissions. This translates into lost power, poor fuel economy and air pollution

The O2 sensor is constantly in a state of transition between high and low voltage. Manufacturers call this crossing of the 0.45Vdc mark "O2 cross counts". The higher the number of O2 cross counts, the better the sensor and other parts of the computer control system are working. It is important to remember that the O2 sensor is comparing the amount of Oxygen inside and outside the engine. If the outside of the sensor should become blocked or coated with contaminants such as oil, paint, undercoating or antifreeze etc., this comparison will not take place efficiently, if at all.

Throttle Position Sensor
The Throttle Position Sensor (TPS, see **Figure 58** Throttle Position Sensor) allows the ECM to sense the position of the throttle and to use that information to control fuel delivery. The TPS is simply a variable potentiometer whose output signal is dependent upon the position of its rotating wiper arm. At idle, the throttle plate in the throttle body is closed, and the air that's breathed by the engine is supplied by the Idle Air Control (IAC) Valve. When the accelerator is depressed, the throttle spindle rotates and the plate "opens" to admit more air.

The Throttle position sensor is connected to the throttle spindle and as the spindle rotates, the position of the TPS wiper changes, changing the

Figure 58 Throttle Position Sensor

output voltage, which should vary from about 0.3Vdc at idle to about 4.7Vdc at full throttle.

Vehicle Speed Sensor

The VSS produces an AC signal at a frequency proportional to the transmission's speedometer gear. When converted by the car's computer, the result is a DC signal proportional to the vehicle's speed. The VSS is used to store the vehicle speed in the computer's memory to operate the cruise control, transmission converter lockup and engine cooling fan (after a certain speed, the fan is turned OFF).

Crankshaft Position Sensor

The CPS is usually mounted in front of the engine block and is aligned with a Crankshaft Pulse Ring or Interuptor Ring. The CPS detects the actual position of the crankshaft and sends a corresponding signal to the computer. This signal is used to trigger the breakerless distributor pick-up and adjust spark advance or is used in conjunction with the Camshaft Position Sensor to pulse the injectors is a distributorless system.

Stable ignition timing is a necessity in performance engines. In most cases, a distributor will do just fine, but when you start making big-time

Figure 59 After Market Crankshaft Triggered Ignition System

horsepower with extreme cylinder pressures, the timing is critical to both the performance and the life of the engine. The ignition must be triggered at a precise time in relation to the position of the piston on the compression stroke. However, think of all the mechanical stretching and flexing that takes place through the timing chain, gears and cam before the distributor pick-up triggers the ignition. The crankshaft on the other hand, knows exactly where each piston is, plus it is the most stable component of the engine in relation to piston position. That's why a crank trigger is so important in high horsepower engine applications.

Most crank triggers use steel studs that stick out of the wheel to trigger a magnetic pick-up. However, the stationary magnet can be triggered by track debris, vibration or even bolts. MSD uses a non-magnetic pick-up which gets triggered by powerful magnets that are embedded in the trigger wheel. This "flying magnet" design cannot be false triggered. The only way to trigger the ignition is when a magnet passes the pick-up.

This non-magnet pick-up is securely held in position by CNC machined aluminium brackets made for a specific application. These brackets feature a long adjustment slot providing a large range of accurate timing adjustments. Plus, many of the brackets can be used on either side of the balancer for easy installation. Most kits are supplied with several spacers for different accessories and pulley systems.

Knock Sensor

Detonation due to low octane fuels is a problem which has haunted the average Hot Rodder for years, particularly since refining fuel for environmental purposes has eroded the octane rating. From state to state, you never know which fuels are going to cause detonation. With this ingenious system, however, there's no danger of the internal engine damage heavy detonation can cause.

The concept is based on piezoelectricity (from the Greek "piezein," to squeeze or press), which is the generation of current in dielectric crystals subjected to mechanical stress. In automotive applications, the crystal is commonly quartz (sandwiched between two electrodes inside the sensor), and the pressure involved is in the form of the high-frequency vibrations caused by detonation. The pressure on the quartz crystal is caused by engine knock, resulting in a voltage at the electrodes.

The knock sensor is screwed into the block or intake manifold where it 'listens' for detonation. See **Figure 60** Knock Sensor. When it 'hears' the knocking (detonation), it sends a warning signal to the computer, which responds by retarding the spark. As soon as this abnormal combustion condition subsides, the sensor stops generating the signal, and timing is once again advanced to the optimum setting.

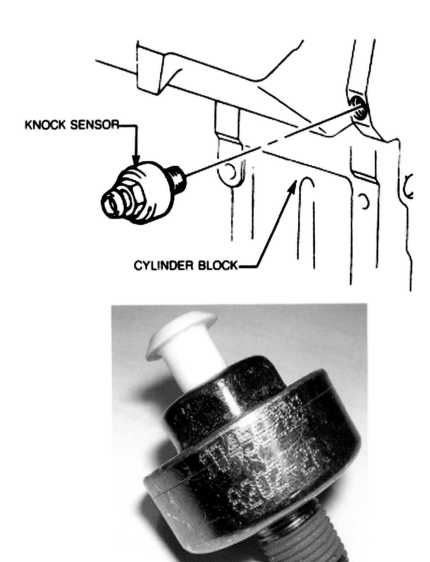

Figure 60 Knock Sensor

Exhaust Gas Recirculation Valve Position Sensor
The EGRVP Sensor tells the computer the exact position of the EGR valve. It is simply a linear potentiometer which is mechanically moved by a rod connected to the EGR valve. As the EGR Valve opens and closes, the air/fuel ratio is adjusted and the EGR valve responds accordingly.

Mass Air Flow Sensor
The Mass Air Flow Sensor (MAF) measures the weight of the air entering the engine. This information is used by the computer to supply the correct amount of fuel. The MAF Sensor heralded the refinement of electronic fuel injection.

This Mass Air Flow Sensor is an integral part of the throttle body on the rear of this V6 supercharger. Also note the IAC Valve and the TPS.

This view of a GM LT1 type Mass Air Flow sensor shows he hot wire elements in the air flow path.

Figure 61 Mass Air Flow Sensor

A typical MAF has a wire or film element that's kept heated to a specified temperature above ambient (180° F in Bosch units) and is exposed to intake air. The amount of current required to maintain that temperature becomes the signal to the computer. High air flow obviously has a greater cooling effect than low, but so does the denser air of cold days and low altitudes, so the PCM/ECM gets the true data on mass it needs to provide the longer injector pulse width that extra oxygen needs to fire dependably. Bosch versions and GM 5.0/5.7L V8 units produce an analog voltage output, but Hitachi and most AC Delco MAF's send out a square-wave signal. There are some ingenious versions of the Karman-Vortex air mass measurement principle, such as those that can be found on the Lexus LS 400 and '87 and up Toyota Supras. The speed of vibration of a thin metal mirror in the intake vortex is monitored optically to generate a frequency signal that varies according to the mass of air entering the engine. Various Mitsubishi units use sound waves to exploit the vortex idea.

Manifold Absolute Pressure Sensor

The Manifold Absolute Pressure Sensor (MAP) measures vacuum inside the intake manifold. The ECM receives information on engine load via this sensor. High pressure (low vacuum) indicates a heavy load and high power output. The ECM issues commands to enrichen the fuel mixture and decrease the spark advance. The opposite occurs for high vacuum conditions, where there is little load. A leaner mixture is sufficient and more spark advance is required.

Figure 62 MAP Sensor

Inside any pressure sensor is a silicon diaphragm which flexes when vacuum or pressure acts upon it. This movement alters its electrical resistance - the more it flexes, the higher the resistance. In an absolute pressure sensor, the variable value acts against a reference pressure, whereas a differential pressure sensor has one side open to manifold vacuum and the other open to the atmosphere.

Barometric Pressure Sensor. The barometric (BARO) sensor reads atmospheric pressure as it changes with altitude and weather conditions. Some are combined in one differential-type "MAP-BARO" sensor, but more commonly, the Engine Management System reads the MAP sensor's output between ignition ON and START to get the BARO reading.

Mass Air vs Speed Density

Mass Air Flow systems measure airflow rate directly. These systems have an air flow meter in the inlet air ducting. Speed Density systems calculate the amount of air the engine is ingesting by measuring engine speed (that's the speed part) and vacuum/boost (that's the density part). Throttle position and intake air temperature are also used in the calculation. Speed density ECUs compare these measured criteria against known air flow characteristics of the engine.

There is one other type of system that should be mentioned. The Alpha-N system of EFI (sometimes referred to as TPS Mode or Speed Alpha), uses the Throttle Position Sensor and engine speed (tacho) to determine engine load. Similar to Speed Density, Alpha-N systems may utilise a MAP sensor for fuel control at cruise speeds or whenever a reliable vacuum signal is present. These systems are useful for engines with very large cams and/or throttle bodies which are exposed to a lot of air, such as stack injection conversions, twin four barrel conversions that are unstaged or multiple throttle body conversions. The ECU simply responds to the angle of the GO-Pedal.

Mass air flow systems:

- Are ultimately more accurate, since deterioration in engine condition and changes in combustion components (cams, blowers, bigger throttle bodies) are automatically accommodated.

- They respond better to changes in atmosphere (elevation, temperature).

Speed density systems adjust for loss of compression (for example leaks past rings or valves) or other departures from new engine specifications only if the EMS has Self Learning, a feature normally found on later model, factory cars. However, the ease with which after market ECUs are reprogrammed for changes to a speed density engine compensates for this lack of flexibility.

Speed density systems are at least as satisfactory in practice and have a couple of advantages:

- The flow meter in a mass air flow system imposes a pressure drop which degrades performance somewhat.

- The air inlet ducting must conform to certain requirements for accurate metering.

- There is some built in lag time with Mass Air systems due to the distance between the throttle body and the air meter.

• Throttle response is faster, as the ECU does not have to process data. With speed density, the information is already processed and stored in tables.

It is the simplicity of speed density systems which makes them good candidates for EFI/EMS conversions and the best choice for high performance and race engines.

Actuators

Actuators are electromechanical devices such as solenoids, relays and electrical motors, which receive commands from the ECM to carry out a mechanical action. This process requires the translation of the electronic signals into mechanical motion, and is accomplished via an output driver in the ECM. The output driver supplies the electrical impulse which controls the actions of switches, vacuum flow controllers, door locks, valves and other actuators. The output driver usually operates by applying or completing the ground circuit of the actuator. The ground is applied to the actuator for varying periods depending on the circuit. For example, if the automatic door locks are to be activated, the actuator is energized (its ground is applied) until the locks are latched. A feedback signal tells the ECM that the job has been done, so the ground is removed.

Other actuators are required to be turned on and off very rapidly or for a set number of cycles per second (called the "Duty Cycle"). One cycle is OFF-ON-OFF, and most duty cycled actuators cycle ten times per second. If the cycle rate is ten times per second, one actuator cycle is completed in one tenth of a second. If the actuator is turned on for 30% of each tenth of a second and off for 70%, it is referred to as a 30% duty cycle. The most common actuator encountered in EFI systems is the fuel injector itself.

Fuel Injectors

There are so many different types of fuel injectors around that it would be impossible to document them in the space available. Described here are the basics, which should be used as a guide for injector choice.

Pulse Width and Duty Cycle. The length of time an injector is open and squirting fuel is called the pulse width, and is measured in milliseconds (ms). That's thousandths of a second. As engine speed increases, an injector can only be held open for so long before it needs to be held open again for the next engine revolution. This is what is known as the injector's duty cycle and is measured as a percentage of open to closed.

Injector Size. Injectors are measured in accordance with their Flow Rate in lbs/hr (pounds per hour) or cc/min (cubic centimetres per minute). A fuel injector's flow rate is measured at its maximum duty cycle (100%), but in real life they should never be operated at more than 80%. The following formula is used to "guestimate" injector size for a particular application: BSFC = Brake Specific Fuel Consumption, generally accepted to be around 0.5 for calculating injector sizes.

Injector Flow Rate (lb/hr) – <u>Engine HPx BSFC</u>
　　　　　　　　　　　Number of Injectors x 0.8

For example, to calculate the individual injector size for a 650 HP V8 using 8 injectors and assuming a BSFC of 0.5:

Injector Flow Rate (lb/hr) – <u>650 x 0.5</u> = 50.78 lb/hr
　　　　　　　　　　　　　8x0.8

To convert lb/hr to cc/min, multiply by 10.5.

Injector Types. For simplicity, these articles describe injectors as being one of two different types according to their internal electrical resistance:

- *Saturated.* High resistance. Saturated injectors are used in almost all standard production, engines, mainly because of the cost and simplicity. Saturated Injectors are more suited to Batch Injection.

- *Peak and Hold.* Low resistance. Peak and hold injectors respond faster than Saturated injectors. They require more electrical power to open (4-6 Amps vs. 0.75 -1 Amp). Peak and Hold injectors squirt fuel more accurately, and sustain the accurate squirt for longer, than the saturated type. This is important in high-pressure systems. Using Peak and Hold injectors costs more because they require one computer injector driver per injector in most applications. This is a design requirement in Sequential Electronic Fuel Injection (SEFI) systems where each injector is fired at a very precise time in the intake cycle.

Most mass produced cars use Saturated 12 to 16 Ohm Injectors. Peak and Hold injectors are generally reserved for high performance applications or in Turbo/Blower applications.

Fuel Injectors come in many sizes and types, but are generally divided into two groups - Low Impedance (Peak and Hold type) and high Impedance (Saturation). Injector drivers are rated differently for the two types, so care must be taken to fit only those injectors that are compatible with your ECM. Fitting the wrong injectors may damage the ECM or, at best, will perform poorly.

Figure 63 Fuel Injectors

Injector Choice. Choosing an injector means selecting the correct flow rate and the type supported by your ECM. See Table 7 - **Injector Flow Rates** for details on injector flow and horsepower to assist with injector selection.

Injector Flow Rate. The following table lists the maximum horsepower obtainable from injectors based on the injector flow rate operating on a 100% duty cycle. The horsepower figures assume a Base Specific Fuel Consumption (BSFC) of 0.55 lbs of fuel per hour at maximum HP (this is an average figure).

Table 7 - Injector Flow Rates
Horsepower @ 100% Duty Cycle

Injector Size Lb/Hr (cc/Min)	4Cyl	6Cyl	8Cyl
20 (210)	145	218	291
22 (231)	160	240	320
24 (252)	175	262	349
26 (273)	189	284	378
28 (294)	204	305	407
30 (314)	218	327	436
32 (335)	233	349	465
34 (356)	247	371	495
36 (377)	262	393	524
38 (398)	276	415	553
40 (419)	291	436	582
42 (440)	305	458	611
44 (461)	320	480	640
46 (482)	335	502	669
48 (503)	349	524	698
50 (524)	364	545	727

Injector Size

Lb/Hr (cc/Min)	4Cyl	6Cyl	8Cyl
52 (545)	378	567	756
54 (566)	393	589	785
56 (587)	407	611	815
58 (608)	422	633	844
60 (629)	436	655	873
62 (650)	451	676	902
64 (671)	465	698	931
66 (692)	480	720	960
68 (713)	495	742	989
70 (734)	509	764	1018

Note: You should choose injectors based on a duty cycle of no more than 85%.

Stepper Motors

There are parts of the EMS which require the use of a stepper motor to move the controlled device to whatever location is desired. By applying voltage pulses to selected coils of the motor, the armature will turn a specific number of degrees. When the same voltage pulses are applied to the opposite coils, the armature will rotate the same number of degrees in the opposite direction.

Different engine makes have different Actuators and call the same actuators by different names. The following actuators represent only the most common designations:

- Idle Air Control (IAC);

- Electric Drive Fan (EDF);

- A/C Controller;

- Wide Open Throttle A/C Shut-off;

- Vehicle Speed Control (VSC).

Idle Air Control

The Idle Air Control (IAC) device uses a small stepper motor which operates an adjustable tapered valve. The valve maintains engine idle speed at closed throttle by controlling the amount of air allowed to bypass the closed throttle valves in the twin bores of the throttle body.

Figure 64 Idle Air Control Valve

The engine's idle speed is determined by the calibration in the ECM, and is not mechanically adjustable beyond setting what is referred to as "base idle", which in most stock applications is approximately 500 rpm. This base idle is set by removing the connector from the IAC unit (which eliminates ECM control), and adjusting the throttle plate stop screw.

Factory Engine Management Systems

When transplanting a factory EFI engine, no computer modifications are necessary if you retain the factory computer and connect it the same way as it was connected in the donor vehicle. Modifications to the engine, however, are not recommended for speed/density Engine Management Systems unless you have a programmable engine management system or software to calibrate a factory engine management system like Kalmaker.

Large cams that change the engine's manifold vacuum will confuse a Speed Density EFI system and will improperly calculate engine load. Higher compressions, larger throttle bodies, injector changes, will all cause a factory speed/density engine to fail. A Mass Air system, however, can handle quite radical modifications without accompanying calibration changes to the factory computer. Large cams that cause a surging or pulsing of air at idle may cause poor idle on a Mass Air Flow EFI system.

In this section, two popular factory engine management systems are discussed. The Ford and GM systems are popular because they are readily available and can be easily transplanted into other cars. The GM system can also be installed on non-GM engines, using software from the public domain to alter the calibrations or by using Kalmaker real time software. The Mass Air versions can be used on modified engines.

Ford Electronic Engine Control

Engine Management of Ford vehicles from 1985 is called the Electronic Engine Control (EEC) system. The first of these systems was the EEC 3, which used a Crankshaft Position Sensor (CPS) as its ignition strategy. They also used a 9.0Vdc Reference Voltage in the Electronic Control Assembly (ECA, a variation of the ECM). The next generation EEC 4 used a distributor with a Hall Effect ignition and a Thick Film Integrated (TFI) Module to determine crankshaft position. In both the EEC 3 and 4 systems, the ignition control pulses are processed by the ECA before opening and closing the primary ignition circuit to fire the spark plugs. The ECA makes the following adjustments to the engine:

- Ignition timing;

- Air/Fuel ratio;

- Exhaust Gas Recirculation (EGR) flow rate;

- Thermactor Air Control;

- Engine idle speed.

The Ford EEC system also uses two sets of tables to make computations and apply optimum performance characteristics to the engine management system. These tables are actually figures stored in memory which have been predetermined as the optimum sensor values which should be read by the engine management system. The two types of tables are:

- Look Up Table. Incorporated in the ECA, these tables are used for all vehicles. The various sensor inputs are compared to the values in the Look Up Table and the ECA provides the necessary output to optimise engine performance.

- Calibration Table. On EEC 3 systems, Calibration Tables are mounted externally to the ECA as a Calibration Assembly. EEC 4 systems house the Calibration Assembly inside the ECA. The Calibration Tables contain Look Up Tables applicable to that specific vehicle. Computations are made by the ECA to provide optimum performance when the values stored by the Calibration Tables are compared with actual values from the sensors.

Adaptive Strategy. As a feature of the EEC 4, continual adjustment of the Calibration Tables was made possible to allow for wear and aging of applicable components. The adjustments are retained in the Keep Alive Memory so that when power is removed (engine turned off) the values are retained.

This strategy will incur a brief "learning" period of approximately 5 Km of driving when either of the following occur:

- On new vehicles;

- When battery has been disconnected during normal service;

- When an EEC component is disconnected or replaced. In this case, the memory must be cleared to prevent the system from running with the new component as if it were an old and worn component.

Note: During the learning process, there may be some symptoms of surge, hesitation, high idle speed, etc. as the EEC system compensates

Failure Mode Effects Management. Failure Mode Effects Management (FMEM) was introduced (in the US) in 1986 EEC 4 systems. Basically, most sensors now have an input operating range, and the EEC can monitor each sensor and determine whether it is operating within its limits. If the sensor is not functioning correctly, the ECA performs the following actions:

- Stores the signal in memory;

- Substitutes a signal which is within the correct limits. This alternate signal then allows the engine to continue running until the problem can be investigated and fixed. Without this strategy, the engine may have stalled or perhaps never even started. For example, if the MAP sensor should fail, the last valid signal is used by the ECA and the following actions would be carried out by the ECA as a consequence of assuming the FMEM mode:

  - The BAR (Barometric) pressure signal is inferred;

  - The adaptive (learning) strategy for fuel delivery stops;

  - Idle speed is fixed;

  - EGR is made inoperative.

Ignition Control

EEC 3. The Crankshaft Position Sensor (CPS) on EEC 3 systems sends ignition pulses to the ECA for processing. These pulses are counted by the ECA and used in conjunction with engine RPM to control fuel and timing. The ignition advance is also adjusted by the ECA at this point, taking into consideration such things as engine load and other operating conditions. The resultant output signal is sent to the ignition module. Refer **Figure 65** EEC 3 Ignition Control.

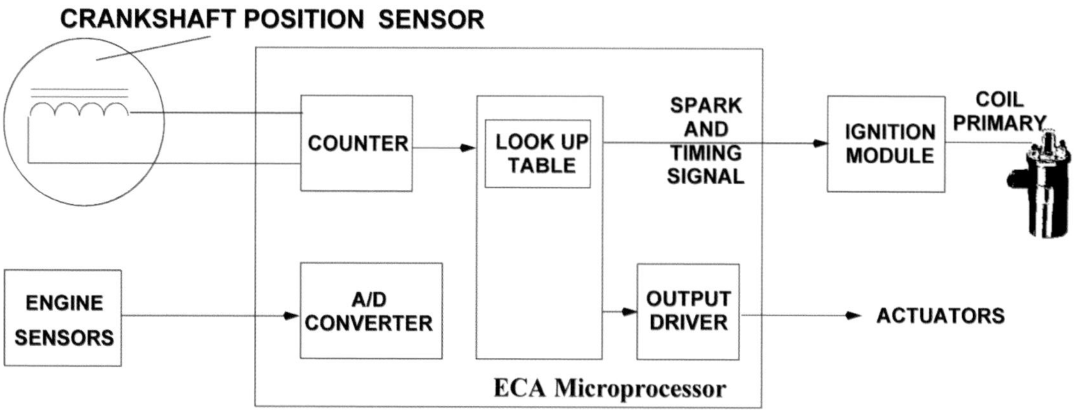

Figure 65 EEC 3 Ignition Control

The Ignition Module amplifies the input signal from the ECA and uses this signal to open and close the coil primary as with any other ignition control.

EEC 4. The EEC 4 system uses the Hall Effect technology for ignition. The Hall Effect voltage is generated in the distributor and sent to the Thick Film Integrated (TFI) module, mounted on the side of the distributor. The resultant control pulses are then transferred to the ECA for processing. These pulses are known as the Profile Ignition Pick-up (PIP) signal. The ECA calculates Dwell and timing from the PIP, then sends a resultant square wave back to the TFI module to fire the ignition. Ford calls this signal the Spark Out (SPOUT) signal.
The three wires connecting the TFI module to the ECA are as follows:

• Circuit 349 pin 56 - PIP Signal from TFI module to ECA.

• Circuit 324 pin 36 - SPOUT from ECA to TFI Module.

• Circuit 60 pin 16 - Common Ground.

> *Note: The TFI module is grounded on the distributor. The ECA is grounded to the engine block.*

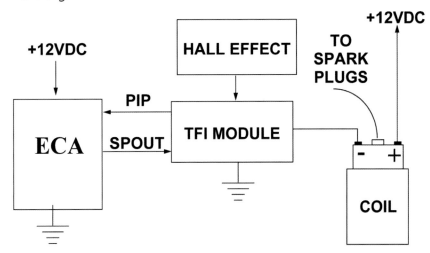

Figure 66 Profile Ignition Pickup Signal

EEC 4 Sequential Electronic Fuel Injection
Ford's SEFI Engine Management System utilises a Hot Wire MAF sensor. The Sequential Electronic Fuel Injection system switches the injectors individually rather than in banks. This promotes better performance, less pollutants and increased diagnostics capabilities by way of the Cylinder Balance Test.

The following signals/devices make up the SEFI inputs to the ECU:

- Fuel Pump Monitor

- Transmission Input Data

- Air Conditioner Clutch

- Air Charge Temp

- Engine Coolant Temp

- Mass Air Flow Sensor

- Barometric Absolute Pressure

- Neutral Drive Sensing Circuit

- EGR Valve Position Sensor

- Self Test Input

- Throttle Position Sensor

- Vehicle Speed Sensor

- Heated EGO Sensor

The following signals/devices make up the SEFI outputs from the ECU:

- Wide Open Throttle A/C Cutout Relay

- EGR Vacuum Regulator

- Self Test Output

- Data Output Link (for trip computer)

- Fuel Pump Solenoid

- Injectors 1 to 8

- Idle Speed Control

- Canister Purge Solenoid

Modifying the EEC 4 System for MAF Sensor

The following steps detail the process of converting a speed density 5.0L Ford to a MAF system. Before embarking on such a project, make sure the MAF sensor you use is matched for the injector size for your engine. For example, the Cobra MAF system EEC-4 and MAF have been recalibrated for #24 injectors rather than the #19 injectors on the standard Fords.

In addition to the MAF and injector selection, make sure the factory computer you are using is matched to the MAF you have chosen. For example, the Cobra system uses a Cobra computer, Cobra MAF, and #24 injectors.

Parts Required

You can source the parts for this conversion from wrecking yards and parts suppliers, but you can also get complete kits from various resellers like Summit.

Mass Air Flow sensor. Use a MAF sensor which is calibrated for the injector size you are using. The wrong sized injectors used with an after market recalibrated MAF can cause problems with ignition timing (leading to part throttle detonation) along with some driveability problems.

MAF mounting hardware. MAF bracket, mounting screws and sheet metal screws to mount the bracket to the shock tower, firewall or other suitable spot.

MAF power/signal harness. Consisting of the MAF connector, 4 wires that go to the EEC computer and EEC-IV connector pins for two of the wires.

MAF Air tubes. These are the tubes which go between MAF sensor, the engine and the air filter box.

VSS Hardware (Optional). If required, three EEC-4 pins and sufficient wire to hook up the VSS and Secondary Fuel Pump Monitor (FPM2) signals.

The following steps are a guide to this relatively simple conversion. All customisations are inherently different, so check your setup carefully and make the necessary adjustments accordingly. Consult factory manuals, particularly wiring diagrams, because installation processes differ.

Start with the EEC 4 computer:

1. Remove the speed density computer.

2. Remove the battery ground cable.

3. Remove the EEC 4 retaining screw to the lower right of the computer.

4. Remove the EEC connector using a 10mm spanner. Clear any wires/relays out of the way and slide the computer out.

Install the Mass Air Flow meter:

1. Remove the air snorkel and the air filter box cover.

2. Attach the MAF mounting bracket.

3. Attach MAF sensor to the bracket.

Wiring. There are 4 wires that need to be run to the MAF sensor;

•   2 signal wires; and

•   2 power wires.

Without a prefabricated harness to connect the MAF with the EEC 4, you will have to construct one from either of two types of factory connectors; a 4 pin or a 5 pin. The pins are marked A B C D (E) on the MAF sensor. Table 8 - Ford MAF/EEC 4 Connections shows which wires need to be connected to which pin number on the EEC connector.

Table 8 - Ford MAF/EEC 4 Connections

4 Pin		5 pin	
MAF	EEC 4	MAF	EEC 4
A	37 (Power)	A	37 (power)
B	40 or 60 (Ground)	B	No Conn.
C	9 (Signal Retn)	C	40 or 60 (Ground)
D	50 (Signal)	D	9 (Signal ret'n)
		E	50 (Signal)

1. Route the wires through the firewall.

2. Remove the Power and Ground wires from the EEC 4 connector by removing the red locking bar on the front of the connector and disengaging the wires. This is easily achieved with a jewellers screwdriver or a paper clip.

3. Tap into the wires in accordance with Table 8 - Ford MAF/EEC 4 Connections.

4. Solder the Signal Wires onto the new EEC 4 pins and insert them into the correct empty locations in the connector.

   Check your connections. If these are hooked up incorrectly, you will likely blow the electronics in the MAF and could also damage the computer.

The Thermactor pump wiring is next. Because the location of the pins for the Thermactor Pump Wiring differs between Speed Density and MAF systems, they will have to be relocated.

1. Move the wire currently in position 51 to position 38.

2. Move the wire currently in position 11 to position 32.

3. Splice in some extra wire for the pins to reach the new locations.

Hook up Vehicle Speed Sensor (VSS) wires (optional). VSS Sensors in US transmissions from 1986 - 1988 Speed Density cars were used for cruise control only. It may be necessary to install a VSS if your transmission has none. In MAF vehicles, the VSS output is used by the cruise control and the EEC 4. For speed density systems, leaving out this step will only cause a trouble code 29 (No VSS Signal) and nothing else. Alternatively, connect the VSS to the EEC 4 as follows:

1. Solder an EEC 4 pin onto the VSS Dark Green/White wire and connect it to pin 3 of the EEC 4.

2. Solder an EEC 4 pin to the Orange/Yellow wire and connect it to pin 6 of the EEC 4 connector.

Note: These are the colours for US 1988 models

3. Connect the cruise control module to the EEC 4 connector.

Connecting the FPM2 signal (optional). The Secondary Fuel Pump Monitoring signal monitors the voltage going to the fuel pump to test whether or not the fuel pump relay is operating correctly. Leaving out this circuit will only cause a code 95 to be generated in the EEC-4 self tests. Connecting pin 19 of the EEC-4 connector to the output of the fuel pump relay (pink/black wire) will stop the error code from setting.

Adding a "Check Engine" light (optional). The MAF engines have a 'Check Engine' light facility which is great to alert you to possible serious problems and it makes reading out self test codes much easier. Speed density cars don't have this, but in the MAF harness there is a tan and black/blue wire which connects the 'Check Engine' circuit on the instrument cluster to the EEC 4 connector. The tan wire connects the EEC STO/MIL line and the black/blue is for the lamp test when the engine is started. To fit the Check Engine lamp, do this:

1. With the MAF EEC 4 harness in place, cut the tan and black/blue wires from the pigtail connector and run a new circuit to the STO/MIL wire on the self test connector in the engine bay (you could also tap in by the EEC-4).

2. Install an after market bulb socket and a N194 bulb.

3. Connect your new wire to the socket and you now have a working check engine light.

Install the MAF computer and air hoses.

1. Put the locking bar back on the EEC connector if you haven't already done so. Reinstall the MAF EEC-4 and reconnect the connector.

2. Attach the hoses to the MAF sensor.

3. Attach the hose to connect the MAF sensor to the engine throttle body.

4. Attach the hose that connects the MAF to the air filter box cover.

5. Tighten all hose clamps.

6. Disconnect the vacuum hose going to the Manifold Absolute Pressure sensor.

7. Leave the vacuum port on the sensor open and plug the vacuum line from the engine.

Do not disconnect the electrical connector from the MAP Sensor.

8. Double check that all is in place and securely fastened.

Reconnect the battery and start the engine. Allow for a period of adaptive learning (refer Para). A few hours of normal stop and go driving will usually be enough. If the engine has extreme idle problems, then something is probably wrong. Check the wiring from the MAF to the computer and run KOEO and KOER tests and see what the problems are.

GM Engine Management System

The ECM (Electronic Control Module) can be described as a general purpose Engine Management System. In fact, a portable PC equipped with commonly available plug in cards can, and has been, used as an Engine Management System (EMS).

Like most computers, the ECM has a Central Processing Unit (CPU), memory (Read Only Memory (contained in the MEMCAL, see **Figure 67** MEMCAL, with cover removed), volatile (scratch) ram, and non-volatile ram contained on the main printed circuit board.

It also has a number of custom chips especially developed for automotive processing. It also has an Analog to Digital (A/D) converter (ADC), timers, pulse counters, and output drivers.

ECM Inputs

Voltage inputs, such as those from the MAP (Manifold Absolute Pressure), TPS (Throttle Position Sensor), CLT (Coolant Temperature Sensor), MAT (Manifold Air Temperature) and O2 (Oxygen) sensors are converted to bytes by the Analogue to Digital (A/D) converter. In digital form, the voltages can be read and processed as numbers by the CPU.

Pulse inputs, such as distributor reference pulses and speed sender pulses, are counted by pulse counters. A number representing the time between pulses is obtained, and this is divided by the counting period to give a number representing pulses per time unit. Engine and vehicle speed can be calculated from the pulses per unit time.

Inputs such as the P/N/Drive (Automatic Transmission) and AC (Air Conditioner) clutch are converted to bytes (on or off). Once converted to bytes, the CPU can process them and determine input states.

Figure 67 MEMCAL with cover removed

Conditions Monitored

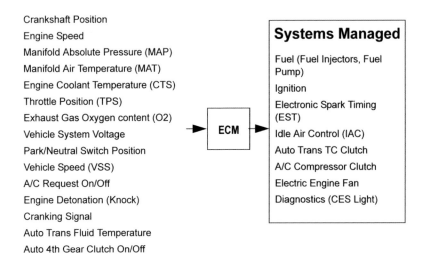

Crankshaft Position
Engine Speed
Manifold Absolute Pressure (MAP)
Manifold Air Temperature (MAT)
Engine Coolant Temperature (CTS)
Throttle Position (TPS)
Exhaust Gas Oxygen content (O2)
Vehicle System Voltage
Park/Neutral Switch Position
Vehicle Speed (VSS)
A/C Request On/Off
Engine Detonation (Knock)
Cranking Signal
Auto Trans Fluid Temperature
Auto 4th Gear Clutch On/Off

ECM

Systems Managed

Fuel (Fuel Injectors, Fuel Pump)
Ignition
Electronic Spark Timing (EST)
Idle Air Control (IAC)
Auto Trans TC Clutch
A/C Compressor Clutch
Electric Engine Fan
Diagnostics (CES Light)

Figure 68 ECM Inputs and Outputs

ECM Operation

When power is first applied, the CPU is reset, and then starts operating. On reset, the program counter is set to the beginning of the program. The program counter tells the CPU where to read the next program instruction.

The CPU reads a program instruction from the MEMCAL. When the Instruction Counter points to it, it is decoded internally. This instruction tells it what to do next.

This instruction can be one of several things, such as:

- read one of the input variables;

- read one of the calibration variables from the MEMCAL;

- read or write a value to internal memory;

- do a calculation like adding, subtracting, multiplying or dividing internal memory, input value, or calibration value;

- do a program related instruction, such as jump to a certain address on the MEMCAL and read the next instruction.

These instructions also force the program counter to switch to the address of the next desired instruction. Whenever the CPU has read and executed an instruction, it automatically reads the next instruction pointed to by the program counter. If the program counter has been modified by the previous instruction, it jumps to the modified address, otherwise it jumps to the address after the last instruction. In this way the CPU executes the program, fetching instructions from the program on the MEMCAL. This method of execution is the same for nearly all computer CPUs.

Outputs can be:

- Discrete (on/off) outputs, such as Torque Converter Clutch, Fan, AC Clutch or Engine Check Light;

- Pulse Width Modulated (PWM) outputs such as a Trip Computer;

- EST output, which controls Electronic Spark Timing (EST) operation;

- IAC output, which controls the Idle Air Control stepper motor;

- FUEL output, which controls the fuel injectors (Multi Port or Throttle Body).

Software

Any controller[1] needs two types of information to be able to run:

• PROGRAM. This is machine code or instructions which the controller reads so it knows what to do next.

• DATA. When the same program is used to control more than one drive-train, the data tailors the program so it works properly, regardless of whether it is a VN V8 Commodore, a Chev TPI or a 1.8L Camira. Same ECM, different data. The Data section comprises 300 or so variables.

MEMCAL

A Calibration is the combined Program and Data on a single EPROM housed in the MEMCAL (see FIGURE 67 MEMCAL, with cover removed). This is what gives the Delco ECM its flexibility, and means that one controller can be used for a large range of vehicles. All the information needed to adapt the controller is in the MEMCAL.

Both the program to control a drive-train and the data needed to customise it can be changed. Programs, however, can only be changed by programmers with an intimate knowledge of the behaviour of the controller. Thus, when a calibration is changed, it is nearly always the data that is altered.

A well written program can be adapted to different or modified drive-trains by changing just the data. The Delco factory program is designed to do exactly this. It can be viewed as a general purpose program which can be run on a standard or modified drive-train.

With the aid of KalMaker Street Pro 1. 2 or 3, and a sufficient knowledge of program operation, the GM system can be adapted to run on almost any engine.

Sensors and Actuators

The GM Engine Management System relies on data from various sensors (see Table 6 - **Common Sensors**) so that engine performance and efficiency is kept at a constant optimum. The system causes actuators to react accordingly. For example, if the Oxygen Sensor, located in the exhaust manifold, senses an incorrect Oxygen level, an electrical signal is sent to the ECM. The ECM processes this information and sends a command to the Fuel Injection System to change the air/fuel mixture. This constant activity ensures a predetermined, ideal air/fuel ration is maintained, no matter what the conditions.

1. The term "controller" is used by GM to mean an ECM without the MEMCAL. A replacement ECM (a controller) is sold over the counter with no MEMCAL.

The ECM receives information about the engine's operating conditions from various sensors and then calculates the optimum spark timing and fuel mixture according to preprogrammed values. The ECM controls the fuel mixture by varying the duration of time that the injector solenoid valves are open. This time period is referred to as the "pulse length" and is measured in milliseconds. General Motors "smart" ECMs have memory and learning ability and can remember changes that produce peak performance.

ALDL Connector

The ALDL (Assembly Line Data Link, or Diagnostic Link) connector comes in two different configurations:

- 12 pin. Used in US vehicles and the JD/JE Camira and LD Astra cars (see **Figure 69** ALDL Connector).

- 6 pin. Used in VN to VL Commodores. Later Commodores used a 16 pin OBD-II style connector.

Note: Because of the use of different intermediate plugs and harnesses between the ECM and the ALDL connector on different make and year vehicles, the colour codes on the wires attached to the ALDL terminals will not always match the codes on the appropriate wires from the ECM. Double check the connections to ensure the proper circuits go to the proper terminals.

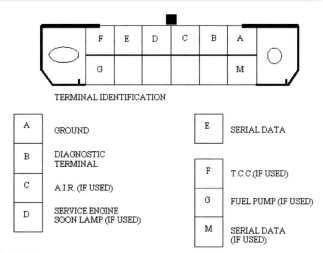

Figure 69 ALDL Connector

The following is a listing of the ALDL connector terminal locations and the circuits to which they are connected.

Table 9 - ALDL Connector Wiring

ALDL Terminal	Circuit	Description
TERMINAL A	GROUND	Connected to common ground circuit from ECM terminals A-12, D-1, D-3, D-6, and D-10 (refer SYSTEM GROUND on page 158.) which are, in turn, connected to a secure engine ground
TERMINAL B	DIAGNOSTIC	Connected to ECM Terminal A-9
TERMINAL E	Check Engine Soon lamp	Connected to ECM Terminal A-5
TERMINAL F	TCC	Connected to ECM Terminal A-7 (See A-7on page 157) if utilising an ECM controlled TCC system
TERMINAL G	FUEL PUMP TEST	Connected to fuel pump relay Terminal 87
TERMINAL H	12V	Battery Voltage

Electronic Spark Timing

All spark timing is controlled by the ECM. Electronic Spark Timing is the control of ignition advance by the ECM, and has the following components;

• Distributor;

• Electronic Spark Control (ESC) module; and

• Knock Sensor.

Distributor. The distributors used with TPI injector units are very similar to the HEI type distributors used on electronically controlled throttlebody injected, or carburetted V8 engines, in that they have no internal advance mechanisms or vacuum advance control canisters.

The distributor supplies reference signals to the ECM for spark timing and information on engine rpm. The 4-pin connector which connects these distributors to the basic wiring harness are similar in appearance but will not connect to a non-TPI distributor. The colour codes are the same and while there may be some minor internal electronic differences between the two, the non TPI distributors will work with the TPI system.

Knock Sensor. The knock sensor, located on the lower right side of the block, detects vibrations that are the acoustic signature of detonation and informs the Electronic Spark Control module which, in turn, directs the ECM to retard the timing in an attempt to eliminate the detonation. The combined effect of these two units can retard the ignition timing up to 20° to compensate for bad fuel, high engine temperature, or any other combination of factors that produce detonation.

Electronic Spark Control (ESC) Module. The Electronic Spark Control (ESC) has the capability of retarding the spark timing by up to 20° when the knock sensor detects detonation. This unit, which is slightly smaller and thinner than a pack of cigarettes and has a five pin wiring connector, is mounted by two small bolts, in most GM applications, in a group with the three relays that are used for the fuel pump and the MAF power and burnoff circuitry, on the cowl, on the right side of the evaporator blower or inner fender.

Electronic Spark Timing operation. To optimise engine performance, fuel economy and emissions, the ECM controls distributor spark advance (ignition timing) with the EST system. The ECM receives a reference pulse from the distributor, indicating engine RPM and crankshaft position. The ECM then sets the correct spark advance by way of the EST reference pulse to the distributor.

Relays
There are four ECM controlled relays which are an integral part of the GM system.

- Fuel Pump Relay;

- Fan Control Relay,

- Mass Air Flow Power Relay (Chev TPI); and

- Mass Air Flow Burnoff Relay (Chev TPI).

Fuel Pump Relay. The fuel pump relay is controlled by the ECM and acts as a remote switch to route power to the electric fuel pump. A relay is necessary in this application because most high pressure fuel pumps can draw up to approximately 10 amps of current. The fuel pump relay is backed up by an oil pressure activated switch which maintains +12 volts at the fuel pump power terminal as long as the engine has oil pressure. This will allow the vehicle to start and continue running in the event of a fuel pump relay or partial ECM failure. This oil pressure activated, fuel pump control switch is mounted (depending on the year and model), either in a threaded port on the left side of the engine block (just above the oil filter), or in conjunction with the oil pressure gauge sending unit in a fitting behind, and to the left of, the distributor assembly.

The first indication that the fuel pump relay has failed and that the backup switch has taken over fuel pump operation, would be extended cranking time before the engine eventually starts, accompanied by an illuminated "Check Engine/Service Engine Soon" light.

Mass Air Flow Power and Burnoff Relays. The Chev TPI system utilises two other relays. These twin relays supply current:

- through the MAF Power Relay, to provide power to the MAF sensor when the engine is running, and

- through the Burnoff Relay, to burnoff contaminants on the MAF sensor's hot wire when the engine is shut off.

Wiring

This section describes some details of the various electrical connections, wiring, components and related information to assist you in adapting a Delco ECM into a non-GM or custom environment. Every project is different, so not all of this information may be relevant.

If you are using a complete factory wiring harness that has been removed intact from the donor vehicle, you should find most of the connections listed in the following pages already in place. This will substantially simplify the rewiring process, and require you to merely thin out the wiring harness by removing unnecessary or unwanted wires, and make the few connections necessary to wire in the Delco ECM into your vehicle's existing wiring.

ECM Terminals

The following information is a listing of the 56 terminal locations (one 24 pin terminal, and one 32 pin terminal) in the two plastic connectors which attach the main wiring harness to the ECM. The listings are based on the JE Camira, VN Commodore V6 and V8 configurations. Other GM models are similar.

> *Note: Remove the ECM from the wiring harness connectors before doing any circuit testing or modifications.*

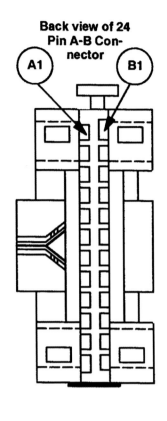

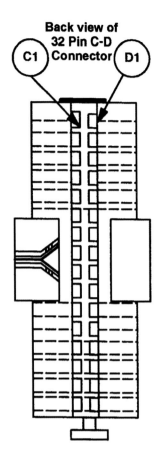

Figure 70 ECM Connectors

Terminal Listings

Each terminal will be dealt with individually to show more clearly its role in the overall installation.

Table 10 - ECM Connector Table

ECM	Wire Colour	Circuit Number	Description
a-1	DARK GREEN/WHITE	Circuit #465	FUEL PUMP RELAY CONTROL
a-2	Yellow/Black (VN) Dk Green (JE) Brown (TPI)	Circuit #463 (VN) #48 (JE) #436 (TPI)	Trip Computer (VN, JE) Air Switch, port solenoid (TPI)
a-3	Not Used (VN, JE) Dk Green/ Yellow (TPI)	Circuit #428 (TPI)	CANISTER PURGE CONTROL (TPI)
a-4	Not Used (VN, JE) Grey (TPI)	Circuit #435 (TPI)	EGR SOLENOID CONTROL (TPI)
a-5	BROWN/WHITE	Circuit #419	CHECK ENGINE/SERVICE ENGINE SOON LIGHT CONTROL
a-6	PINK (VN, JE) Pink/Black (TPI)	Circuit #439 (VN, TPI) #639 (JE)	+12V IGNITION supply
a-7	TAN/BLACK (JE, TPI) Grey/Red (VN)	Circuit #422	Automatic Trans TCC CONTROL
		Circuit #422	Manual Transmission O-D CONTROL

Table 10 - ECM Connector Table

		Circuit #456	Manual Transmission SHIFT LIGHT CONTROL
a-8	Not Used (VN) Orange (TPI)	Circuit #461	SERIAL DATA (TPI)
a-9	WHITE/BLACK	Circuit #451	DIAGNOSTIC TERMINAL
a-10	BROWN/YELLOW (VN) White (JE) Brown (TPI)	Circuit #437 (VN) 921 (JE)	VSS SIGNAL
a-11	BLACK	Circuit #469 #476 (TPI)	MAP, MAT Ground
a-12	BLACK (VN) Black/White (TPI)	Circuit #150 #450 (TPI)	SYSTEM GROUND
b-1	ORANGE (JE) Orange/Black (VN)	Circuit #540 (vn) #240 (JE) #340 (TPI)	+12V BATTERY supply
b-2	TAN/WHITE (VN)	Circuit #33 (VN) #120 (TPI)	Cranking Signal Input (VN) FUEL PUMP SIGNAL (TPI)
b-3	BLACK/RED (VN) Black (JE)	Circuit #453	EST REFERENCE
b-4			not used
b-5	PURPLE/WHITE	Circuit #430	DISTRIBUTOR REFERENCE
b-6	WHITE, PURPLE or DARK BLUE (TPI)	Circuit #963 (TPI)	VATS (Pass-Key)
b-7	Black (TPI)	Circuit #485 (TPI)	ESC SIGNAL
b-8	Brown (VN), GREEN or GREEN/YELLOW (TPI)	CIRCUIT #449 (VN) #59 (TPI)	A/C Request Input
b-9			
b-10	Grey (VN) ORANGE/BLACK (JE, TPI)	Circuit #434	PARK / NEUTRAL SIGNAL.
b-11	White/Red (VN)	#815	Knock Sensor Input. Connected to the knock sensor which is standard in the V6 and HSV V8. This is optional on std V8. The knock sensor is screwed into the water jacket drain plug on drivers side of engine bank. To function, a knock filter (SNEF) must be fitted either to Kalmaker Real time Board or in the Memcal.
b-12	DARK GREEN (TPI)	Circuit #998 (TPI)	MAF INPUT (TPI)
c-1	Blue/White (VN) Dark Blue (JE)	Circuit#304 (VN) #404 (JE)	FAN RELAY CONTROL
c-2	Lt Green/Black (VN) Light Blue (JE) Black/Pink (TPI)	circuit #366, #429 (TPI)	A/C Relay Control, AIR SWITCH (DIVERT SOLENOID) (TPI)
c-3	IAC lt green/black	Circuit #444	iac coil -B LO
c-4	IAC Lt green/white	Circuit #443	iac coil -B Hi
c-5	IAC lt blue/white	Circuit #441	iac coil -A HI
c-6	IAC lt blue/black	Circuit #442	iac coil -A LO
c-7	Lt Blue (VN) Black/Blue (TPI)	Circuit #446, Circuit #925 (TPI)	4th Gear O/Drive Temp, A/T O-D SWITCH SIGNAL (TPI)
c-8	Not Used (VN) black/lt blue (TPI)	Circuit #905	M/T OD Request (TPI)

Table 10 - ECM Connector Table

	DARK GREEN or LT.BLUE	Circuit #446	A/T O-D 4TH GEAR
	BLACK/BLUE or LIGHT BLUE	Circuit#902	M/T O-D REQUEST (4SPD Man w/OD)
c-9	Not Used		
c-10	YELLOW	Circuit #410	COOLANT TEMPERATURE SIGNAL
c-11	Lt Green	#432	MAP Sensor Input
c-12	TAN	Circuit #472	MAT SIGNAL
c-13	DARK BLUE	Circuit #417	TPS SIGNAL
c-14	GRAY	Circuit #416	TPS +5V REFERENCE
c-15	DARK GREEN (TPI)	Circuit #935 (TPI)	EGR DIAGNOSTIC SWITCH (TPI)
c-16	ORANGE/Black (VN) Orange (JE)	Circuit #540 (VN) #240 (JE) #340 (TPI)	+12V BATTERY supply
d-1	BLACK	Circuit#151	SYSTEM GROUND
d-2	BLACK	Circuit #452	TPS, CTS, MAT Ground
d-3	BLACK (VN)	Circuit #450	SYSTEM GROUND
d-4	WHITE	Circuit #151, Circuit #423 (TPI)	Engine Ground (VN), EST CONTROL (TPI)
d-5	TAN/BLACK	Circuit#424	DFI/HEI Bypass Control
d-6	Black	Circuit #150AA	OXYGEN SENSOR GROUND
d-7	PURPLE	Circuit#412	OXYGEN SENSOR SIGNAL
d-8			not used
d-9			not used
d-10	BLACK	Circuit #150, #450	SYSTEM GROUND
d-11	DARK BLUE or Dk Green or Grey(TPI)	Circuit #732 or #992 or #731	A/C PRESSURE, Fan Switch (varies between TPI models)
d-12	Black (TPI)	Circuit #900	H2O Injection (VN), MAF BURN-OFF RELAY CONTROL (TPI)
d-13	not used		not used
d-14	not used		not used
d-15	LIGHT BLUE or BLACK/PINK	Circuit #467	Injector Control
d-16	LIGHT GREEN or BLACK/ GREEN	Circuit #467	Injector Control

Each ECM Terminal is dealt with in the following text. Those terminals not in use are not shown here. Where necessary, reference is made to specific year/models and differences between wiring harnesses are indicated. Every attempt has been made to cover all models, but factory alterations, accessory installations and customizing techniques may cause different wiring source and destination locations than that which appears here. Always check carefully any ambiguous differences.

A-1   Circuit #465   FUEL PUMP RELAY CONTROL

Connected to Terminal 86 of the fuel pump relay.

This circuit allows the ECM to activate the fuel pump relay by supplying +12V through this terminal. The fuel pump power circuit is provided by a connection to relay Terminal 30 of the +12V wire directly from the Battery Fuse. In addition, Terminal 85 of the fuel pump relay should be connected to the common ganged ground circuit from ECM connector Terminals A-12, D-1, D-3, D-6, and D-10 which is, in turn, connected to a secure engine ground (See SYSTEM GROUND on page 158). A wire should be connected from the fuel pump relay Terminal 87 to the fuel pump positive terminal, and also to Terminal G of the ALDL connector. This connection will allow you to power up the fuel pump by supplying +12V to this terminal of the ALDL connector for test purposes.

A-2   Circuit #463   (VN) #48 Trip Computer
             (JE)

Connected to the Trip Computer Connector (Yellow/Black (VN) Dk Green (JE)).

Note: DELETE if not using a trip computer.

A-5   Circuit #419   CHECK ENGINE/SERVICE ENGINE
                                   SOON LIGHT CONTROL

Connected to the *Check Engine/Service Engine Soon* light.

This circuit allows the ECM to provide a ground to the Check Engine/Service Engine Soon Light, thus illuminating the light to alert the driver to possible problems with the ECM, individual sensors or wiring. Power for this light should be provided from the gauges supply. WE STRONGLY RECOMM-END THE INCLUSION OF THIS CIRCUIT in the re-wiring process as this light is an important part of the systems self-diagnostics.

A-6   Circuit #439 (VN) #639   +12V IGNITION circuit
             (JE)

Connected to a switched +12V source.

This circuit provides power to the ECM from a +12V switched source (the ignition switch) protected by a 10 amp fuse. Power should be available at this terminal when the ignition key is in the run and start positions. Depending on the type of wiring system that exists in the vehicle into which you are installing the ECM you will have to either tap into the appropriate wire in the ignition switch harness, or make the necessary connection at the main fuse block. For our rewiring purposes, this fuse will be referred to as the ECM fuse.

A-7   Circuit #422   Automatic Trans TCC CONTROL

Connected to the TH-700-R4 automatic transmission TCC Solenoid (Terminal D).

This circuit allows the ECM to control the TCC function by providing a ground through this terminal. This requires the inclusion of a functional VSS system. If you ARE using the ECM to activate the TCC function, a wire should be connected from this terminal to the ALDL connector (Terminal F). This connection allows you to activate the TCC function by supplying an external ground to this ALDL terminal to verify TCC operation.

A-9   Circuit #451   DIAGNOSTIC TERMINAL

Connected to Terminal B of the ALDL connector.

This circuit is referred to as the Diagnostic Test circuit. Terminal A of the ALDL connector should be connected to the ganged common ground circuit of ECM Terminals A-12, D-3, D-6, and D-10 which is, in turn, connected to a secure engine ground. Grounding Terminal B of the ALDL by jumpering it to Terminal A, with the ignition key turned to the ON position, engine NOT running, causes the ECM to enter the *Diagnostic Mode*.

A-10   Circuit #437   VSS SIGNAL

Connected to the Vehicle Speed Sensor (VSS).

Input from the VSS provides a reference to the ECM which it uses to control the TCC and other functions.

If the VSS is not used, ECM Terminal B-10 (the park/neutral switch connection) should be grounded to the ECMs ganged common ground wire circuit that is, in turn, connected to a secure engine ground. With B-10 grounded, the VSS system's self-diagnostics will not set a trouble code to indicate a VSS problem.

A-11   Circuit #476 or   ANALOG GROUND

Connected to Terminal B of the MAT and MAP sensors.

This circuit provides the analog ground for the MAT and MAP sensors.

Note: DO NOT connect to common engine/chassis ground.

A-12   Circuit #150   SYSTEM GROUND

Connected to Terminal 85 of the fuel pump relay and should also be connected to the ganged common ground wire circuit from ECM Terminals D-1, D-3, D-6, and D-10 which are, in turn, connected to a secure engine ground.

B-1   Circuit #540 (vn) #240   +12V BATTERY supply
              (JE)

This terminal should be connected through a 20 amp fuse to a constant NON-SWITCHED + 12V source (battery post on the starter motor, maxi-fuse for Painless Wiring systems, BAT connection on ignition switch, etc). The wire from this terminal can be ganged with the similarly coloured wire from ECM Terminal C-16, as is indicated by the same Circuit #540 (VN) #240 (JE). Also connected to this same +12V source should be fuel pump relay Terminal 30, and one side of the oil pressure activated fuel pump backup switch (if fitted).

B-3   Circuit #453   Crankshaft/Distributor
                                        REFERENCE

Connected to one of the four wires which run as a group to the four-pin distributor plug.

This circuit provides a reference ground between the ECM and the distributor ignition module, to assure there is no voltage drop between these two components.

B-5   Circuit #430   DISTRIBUTOR REFERENCE

Connected to one of the four wires which run as a group to the four-pin distributor plug. This circuit provides the ECM with rpm and crankshaft position input. Should this circuit become open or grounded, the engine will not run because the ECM will not pulse the injectors.

B-8   Circuit #449   A/C SIGNAL

Connected to the positive terminal of the AC compressor clutch wiring plug. Connected in this manner, this circuit will provide a +12V input to the ECM to inform it that the AC compressor clutch is engaged and the ECM will then proceed to adjust the idle speed, by controlling the IAC unit, to compensate for AC compressor clutch engagement.

> Note: DELETE if not using an air conditioning system.

B-10   Circuit #434   PARK / NEUTRAL SIGNAL

Connected to the park/neutral switch connector. Grounded in Park or Neutral. When the transmission selector lever is placed in the park or neutral position, this switch completes the circuit from this terminal to ground.

B-11   Circuit# 815   KNOCK SENSOR INPUT

The wire that connects the knock sensor to the ECM connects at terminal B 11 on the ECM.

C-1   Circuit#304 (VN) #404   FAN RELAY CONTROL
                 (JE)

Connected to Terminal 85 of the fan control relay.

This circuit allows the ECM to control the operation of the engine cooling fan relay by grounding this terminal, thus providing ECM control of the electric cooling fan operation. You should connect this circuit up when an electric fan is used.

> Note: If you are using an electric engine cooling fan in your installation, it should also be wired to run whenever the AC compressor clutch is engaged.

This can be most easily accomplished by adding a second fan control relay to the system. This second relay should be activated by the same circuit (Terminal B8) that provides the ECM with the AC on signal. A second relay is required because the stock fan relay is activated by supplying a ground, whereas the AC on signal is a + 12V input, thus requiring the use of a second relay, to allow either circuit to independently control the fan operation.

Note: DELETE if not using an electric fan.

C-3	Circuit #444	IAC COIL B LO
C-4	Circuit #443	IAC COIL B Hi
C-5	Circuit #441	IAC COIL A HI
C-6	Circuit #442	IAC COIL A LO

These four wires run directly, as a group, to the 4-pin IAC unit connector. It does this by sending voltage pulses referred to as counts, to the proper motor winding to either activate the in or out operation of the valve.

CAUTION: DO NOT, under ANY circumstances, apply +12V battery voltage across the IAC terminals! Doing so will permanently damage the motor windings!

| C-10 | Circuit #410 | COOLANT TEMPERATURE SIGNAL |

Connected to the coolant temperature sensor. This circuit provides coolant temperature input to ECM.

| C-12 | Circuit #472 | MAT SIGNAL |

Connected to the MAT sensor. This circuit provides inlet air temperature input to the ECM.

| C-13 | Circuit #417 | TPS SIGNAL |

Connected to terminal B of the 3-pin TPS connector. This circuit provides a TPS input voltage to the ECM, allowing the ECM to determine the amount of throttle opening, since the input voltage signal changes relative to throttle opening.

| C-14 | Circuit #416 | TPS +5V REFERENCE |

Connected to terminal C of the 3-pin TPS connector. This circuit provides the +5V reference signal to the TPS.

| C-16 | Circuit #540 (VN) #240 (JE) | +12V BATTERY supply |

This terminal should be connected through a 20 amp fuse to a constant NON-SWITCHED + 12V source (battery post on the starter motor, maxi-fuse for Painless Wiring systems, BAT connection on ignition switch, etc). The wire from this terminal can be ganged with the similarly coloured wire from ECM Terminal B-1.

Also connected to this same +12V source should be fuel pump relay terminal 30 and one side of the oil pressure activated fuel pump back up switch (if fitted).

D-1   Circuit #450   SYSTEM GROUND

Connected to the ganged common ground wire circuit along with ECM Terminals A-12, D-3, D-6, and D-10 (refer SYSTEM GROUND on page 158) which are, in turn, connected to a secure engine ground.

D-2   Circuit #452   TPS, CTS Ground

Connected to Terminal A of the 3-pin TPS connector. This circuit is the common +5V return line for the TPS and CTS.

D-3   Circuit #450   SYSTEM GROUND

Connected to the ganged common ground wire circuit together with ECM terminals A-12, D-1, D-6, and D-10, which are, in turn, connected to a secure engine ground.

D-4   Circuit #423   EST CONTROL

Connected to one of the four wires that run as a group to the 4- pin ignition module plug. This circuit allows the ECM to trigger the ignition module. This is also the circuit the ECM uses to actually control timing by advancing or retarding the spark, relative to the reference signal it gets from circuit #430 (Pin B5), which is the mapped timing data stored in the MEM-CAL.

D-5   Circuit #424   BYPASS

Connected to one of the four wires that run as a group to the 4-pin ignition module plug. At about 400 rpm, this circuit applies +5V to the ignition module which switches timing control from module's internal calibration (Module Mode) to the ECM.

D-6   Circuit #150AA   OXYGEN SENSOR GROUND

Connected to the ganged common ground wire circuit together with ECM Terminals A-12, D-1, D-3, and D-10, which are, in turn, connected to a secure engine ground. This circuit provides the ground for the Oxygen Sensor.

D-7   Circuit #412   OXYGEN SENSOR SIGNAL

Connected to the Oxygen Sensor signal wire. Ensure the connections for a heated O2 sensor are made correctly, with the heater connection going to an ignition supply.

D-10   Circuit #450   SYSTEM GROUND

Connected to the ganged common ground wire circuit along with ECM terminals A-12, D-1, D-3, and D-6, which are, in turn, connected to a secure engine ground.

D-15   Circuit #467   INJ 1-3-5-7

Connected to Fuel Injectors 1, 3, 5, and 7.

D-16   Circuit #467   INJ 2-46-8

Connected to Fuel Injectors 2, 4, 6, and 8.

Chapter 8

Custom Wiring

Designing a wiring system for custom applications is not difficult, but the approach is different for every job. For factory installations, factory harnesses are available which are routed through the car in the stock locations and use the factory connectors. The scratch built harness, however, is a different story. Each circuit must be carefully planned. The colour code for the wiring must be established in a logical manner, so that future modification and/or repair will be a simple task. There is nothing worse than chasing down a short when all the wires are the same colour!

The practice of cutting plugs from old wiring harnesses and soldering them into the new harness is not encouraged!

The solution for most custom wiring systems is to purchase one of the many wiring kits available from manufacturers in the US and Australia. Hot Rod Handbooks has worked with Painless Wiring for many years, and for good reason. Painless offers the highest quality products and a wide range of applications from factory replacement systems, factory and custom EFI harnesses, generic hot-rod systems and trunk mounted systems. While they are the leaders in their field, there are many other systems available that are of a high standard, such as Centech, E-Z-Wire and Just-a-Snap. In Australia, Ultimate Wiring Harnesses offer a high quality system specifically configured for carb engines, EFI or LPG.

WIth so many players in the field of custom wiring kits, it seems pointless describing a wire-by-wire wiring exercise. For those that prefer to create their own wiring system from start to finish, Skip Readio's book 'How to Do Electrical Systems: Most Everything About Auto Electrics' (ISBN: 1878772066) is probably the definitive text on this subject. For the rest of us, however, a wiring kit is economical, reliable and available in a configuration that will suit your project.

Each circuit in the wiring harness must be capable of supplying the component without overheating. The current carrying capacity of individual components is listed below.

Table 11 - Wiring Circuit Current Ratings and Gauge

CIRCUIT	CURRENT (Amps)	GAUGE (Imperial, Metric)	
Ignition	3.5	18	0.8mm
Starter Motor	up to 300	Battery Cable or Welding Cable	
Starter Solenoid	12	14	2.0mm
Horn	20	12	3.0mm
Headlights			
High Beam	15	14	2.0mm
Low Beam	10	14	2.0mm
Dipswitch	3	18	0.8mm
Dash Lights	3	18	0.8mm
Parking Lights	1.5	18	0.8mm
Dome Light	1	18	0.8mm
Back–up Lights	5	18	0.8mm
Tail Lights	1	18	0.8mm
Stop Lights	5	18	0.8mm
License Light	1	18	0.8mm
Electric Wiper	7	18	0.8mm
Heater/Defogger	10	14	2.0mm
Air Conditioner	20	12	3.0mm
Power Antenna	10	14	2.0mm
Power Windows	20	12	3.0mm
Power Seat	50	8	8.0mm
Power Door Locks	5	18	0.8mm
Radio/CB	5	18	0.8mm
Electric Clock	.5	18	0.8mm
Cigar Lighter	15	14	2.0mm

Note: The thicker the wire, the smaller its gauge number.

Multi-strand wire can carry more current for the same diameter than solid, single-strand wire. It's also a lot better at surviving the stress of flexing. Although it may seem like a good idea, don't use ordinary insulation tape to coat or insulate splices. The acetic acid corrodes the copper. Instead, use convoluted tubing to group your wire circuits together (see **Figure 71** Convoluted Tubing (split tube) and Insulated Clamps).

Figure 71 Convoluted Tubing (split tube) and Insulated Clamps

Steering Column. The connections to the steering column vary from make to make, depending on the number of circuits built in. You should have sufficient information from the donor car's wiring diagram to be able to established and tag all the circuits, so you can hook them in to your custom wiring system.

The circuits could be:

- Emergency Flashers

- Horn

- Wipers

- Washers

- Turn Signals

- Cruise Control

- Dip Switch

Because we cannot deal with all makes and models of factory steering columns, we will deal with the most popular ones here and leave it up to the individual to work out the connections and circuits via factory workshop manuals etc.

Planning

Proper Planning Prevents Poor Performance. Plan, note (that is, WRITE IT DOWN!) and establish all the required circuits and components first, then worry about hooking it all together! Some circuits, apart from the obvious ones, must be considered for their location. Others must also be considered for their current carrying capacity, such as the high performance electric fuel pumps for EFI and/or street/strip applications, high powered lights for off-road applications, hydraulic pumps, monster stereo systems - the list goes on.

- Fan. Is there a mechanical or Electric cooling fan?

- Fuel Pump. Is there a mechanical or electrical fuel pump?

- Dip Switch. Column or floor mounted?

- Neutral Safety Switch. Floor (shifter) mounted or mounted on transmission?

- Battery. Trunk, firewall, under seat?

- Is the horn switch ground activated (like in some Ford steering `columns) or 12V activated?

- Fusible Link/Maxi-Fuse. You MUST include one of these in your system where the main battery supply connects to the fuse panel.

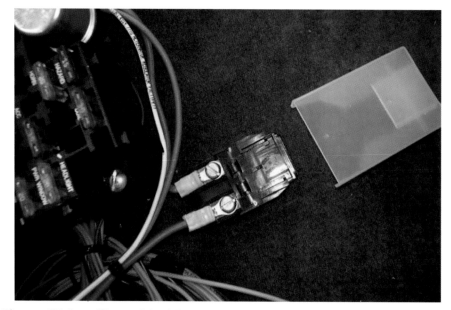

Figure 72 Installing a Maxi Fuse

Establish exactly where components are to be located, for example, fuel pump (electric), relay panel, battery, etc. Has the Alternator been mounted in its stock position? What about the Lights?

The Custom Wiring Harness described in this Chapter covers all the circuits that may be required in the design of our custom electrical system. To make the complete assembly easy to handle, it is divided into the following five sections:

- Front Lighting;

- Engine Bay;

- Dash;

- Rear Lighting;

- Extended System and Accessories.

Each of the harness sections contain wires terminating at elements which will vary from car to car. We shall use a typical GM wire colouring code as described in Table 13 - GM Wiring Colour Code.

Fuse Panel

The fuse panel contains enough fuses to protect each of the circuits described, although some may require doubling up. You can obtain these panels from a variety of suppliers such as Painless and Ultimate. Refer **Figure 73** Fuse Panels which illustrates the fuse centre.

In most quality wiring kits, the fuse panel is pre-wired into the harness. The fuse panel is supplied by the following three electrical circuits:

- Battery. Usually fed from the alternator Bat terminal or a 12 gauge wire from the starter solenoid. Supplies a continuous 12VDC supply, whether the ignition is on or off. Use a Red wire.

- Ignition. Fed from the ignition switch to handle circuits which must be isolated when the engine is shut off, such as ignition coil, radio, wipers. Use a Pink 12 gauge wire.

- Accessories. Alternative supplies which should be on when the ignition is on, off when the engine is shut off but supplying power from the ignition switch in the Accessory position for such things as the radio, engine cooling fan, heater fan, etc.

Figure 73 Fuse Panels

The Fuse Panel is the starting point for all the circuits in the Custom Electrical System. Table 13 - **GM Wiring Colour Code** lists the individual wires in their sections and describes the destination and source of each termination. The colour code for the wiring is based on the GM colour code, as described in the Painless Wiring instruction handbooks, however, it is not mandatory to reproduce this particular colour code in custom electrical systems.

Front Lighting Harness

The Front Lighting Harness supplies the following elements:

- Headlights
- Electric Cooling Fan
- Front Turn Signals and Emergency Flashers
- Horn

Light Switch. The GM type light switch is illustrated here. It is a robust, easy to find switch which costs a few dollars at a wreckers or auto parts store. For other types of switches, connect the wiring in accordance with the maker's specs.

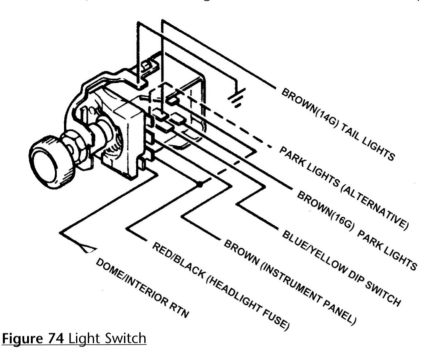

Figure 74 Light Switch

Dip Switch. The Tan and Light Green wires go to the dip switch (dimmer switch). A column mounted dip switch is a tidier option than a floor mounted type, however the wiring in the column contains all the other circuits such as horn, wiper, turn indicator etc and the factory wiring schematics must be consulted when hooking up your custom system. A floor mounted dip switch is easy - simply hook the high beam/low beam wires up to the switch and run the main lighting supply (from the light switch) to the centre connector (refer **Figure 75** Dip Switch Connectors)

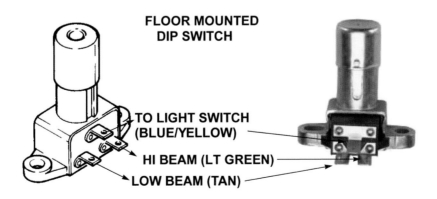

Figure 75 Dip Switch Connectors

Lighting Relays. This lighting setup is just fine for the old fashioned type of dip-switch and headlight switch combo. For many wiring projects, however, the steering column contains all the lighting controls (indicators, emergency flashers, lights on/off, hi/lo beam, turn indicators, emergency flashers), as well as the ignition switch, horn and windshield wiper/washer controls. Quite a common swap for any hot rod, as it keeps the dash clean and ensures the controls are in easy reach.

It is in this area that your wiring job will create the biggest problems. If your wiring kit caters for GM/Holden/Ford/Mopar wiring circuits that use a separate, heavy duty light switch and dimmer switch, then you'll need to do some re-working of the wiring yourself. Some wiring kits have all the necessary relays built in (such as the Ultimate Wiring harness) but you will still have to adapt the steering column wiring to the harness.

The cabling inside these steering columns is narrow gauge, designed to control external relays which will handle the high current drain of lighting circuits, horn, etc.

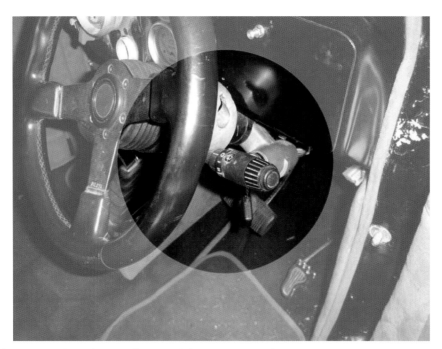

Figure 76 Steering Column Lighting Controls

Note: Make sure you have access to a correct wiring diagram for your steering column. To make your job even easier, try to get the lighting relay(s) from the donor car when you choose a steering column. You'll be glad you did!

Use 30Amp, good quality relays or use a proper headlight relay (which is actually two relays in one).

Your electrical system should supply lighting power on one main circuit (usually the thick red/black wire). The auxiliary circuit, (usually a thick orange wire) is meant for instrument panel lights, park lights and tail lights, but you can also used this circuit for the trigger supply for the hold on coil of the relays. We could have used the main circuit, but it is a good idea to keep the low current circuits separate from the high current circuits. Both circuits are fused.

Typically, the rotary switch on the stalk supplies grounds for the hold on coil of the relay for Park lights and Headlights On (see **Figure 77** Headlights On Relay).

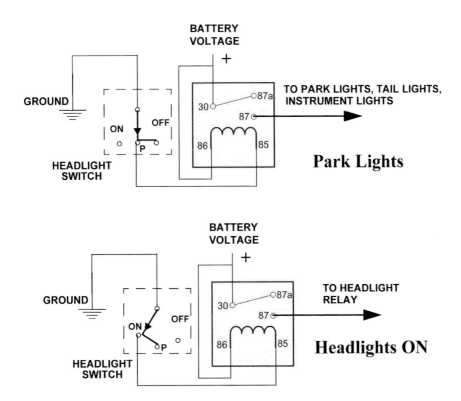

Figure 77 Headlights on Relay

In the Park lights position, the switch supplies a ground for the Park Lights relay. In the ON position, the switch supplies a ground for the Park Lights relay and the Headlights ON relay. The Headlights ON relay supplies the main headlight supply to the Hi Beam/Lo Beam relays.

The dip switch on the stalk grounds the control coils for the High Beam and Low Beam relays (see **Figure 78** High Beam/Low Beam). When the Headlights ON relay is energised (the headlight switch is turned ON) power to the headlights is via the Low Beam or High Beam relay: the dip switch will be in either one of those positions.

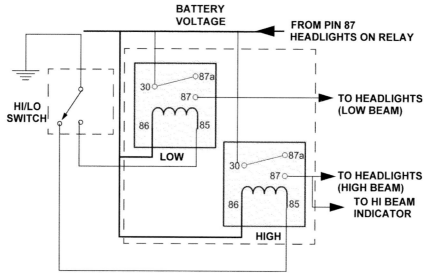

Figure 78 High Beam/Low Beam

To build our lighting circuit as described, we will need four relays. Using the relays and relay sockets described in Relays on page 26, our lighting circuit can be built as a unit that is compact and hidden away under the dashboard. Wire up all the relay sockets in accordance with the illustration, then plug in some good quality, 30 or 40 amp relays. See **Figure 79** Lighting Relays Configuration.

Cooling Fan. Included in the front lighting harness is the cooling fan. There are a number of different types of electric fans on the market, and they are a good option for non-factory installations where the mechanical fan won't fit. Electric fans are more efficient, take up less space and are not such a drain on engine power. What's more, the electric fan will come on when it is needed, either automatically from a thermostat, the engine management system or from a toggle switch mounted in the dashboard. Because they draw a LOT of current, you MUST use a relay. See **Figure 80** Cooling Fan Relay.

Whichever way you choose to go, ensure adequate grounding for the fan.

Note: Do not ground the fan motor to the radiator - ground it to the engine or chassis.

Engine Bay Harness

The Engine Bay Harness supplies the following circuits and elements:
- Coil
- Alternator
- Starter Solenoid
- Oil Pressure sending unit

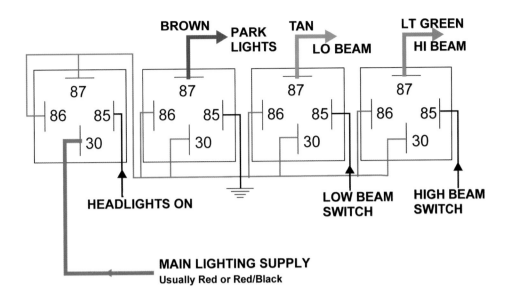

BROWN **PARK LIGHTS** **TAN** **LO BEAM** **LT GREEN** **HI BEAM**

87   87   87   87

86   85   86   85   86   85   86   85

30   30   30   30

HEADLIGHTS ON   **LOW BEAM SWITCH**   **HIGH BEAM SWITCH**

MAIN LIGHTING SUPPLY
Usually Red or Red/Black

 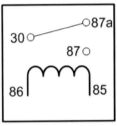

Figure 79 Lighting Relays Configuration

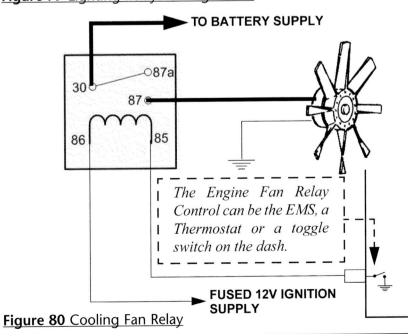

TO BATTERY SUPPLY

30   87a

87

86   85

The Engine Fan Relay Control can be the EMS, a Thermostat or a toggle switch on the dash.

FUSED 12V IGNITION SUPPLY

Figure 80 Cooling Fan Relay

- Engine coolant temp. sender
- Ballast Resistor
- Radiator Thermo Switch
- Brake switch

There are numerous combinations for alternators, starters and ignition components for the engine bay wiring. Custom wiring systems can utilise factory items and/or after market parts for their particular project, however, the popular combinations are illustrated.

Wiring the Alternator

There are many non-factory alternator configurations that will work well for custom electrical systems. The focus should be on functionality first. In other words, choose the alternator that is adequate for the job. With few exceptions, choosing an alternator from a home-grown, mass produced car will probably satisfy all but the most exotic combinations.

Because every car manufactured since the late 80s used a battery sensing, internally regulated alternator, we will assume that your project uses a similar configuration.

Some earlier internally regulated alternators require an excitation connection (usually the white wire). It must not be physically connected to the same terminal as the coil ignition, otherwise the engine won't shut off! Instead, use an ignition switch with the start/run ignition connections and install the idiot light. Alternatively, use an ignition relay, but why complicate matters unnecessarily? These days, most internal regulators are internally excited and require no link to the ignition circuit. The wire from the field is for the idiot light.

Check the wiring diagrams from the factory manual for the car that the alternator comes from The Remote Voltage Sensing feature is a big advantage when running a non-factory, custom built wiring system, but only works properly when a properly rated wire connects the battery to the junction. You should never connect the alternator directly to the battery.

Voltmeter and Alternator Warning Light. It is strongly recommended that your auto electrical system includes a VOLT gauge in the dash. It is also a good idea to have an alternator Warning Light to grab your attention the instant the alternator stops charging. With only the gauge in the dash, you might be in trouble before you notice an unusual reading.

Note: If the Warning Light comes ON while driving, watch the Water Temperature gauge. You might have thrown a belt, which will stop driving the water pump.

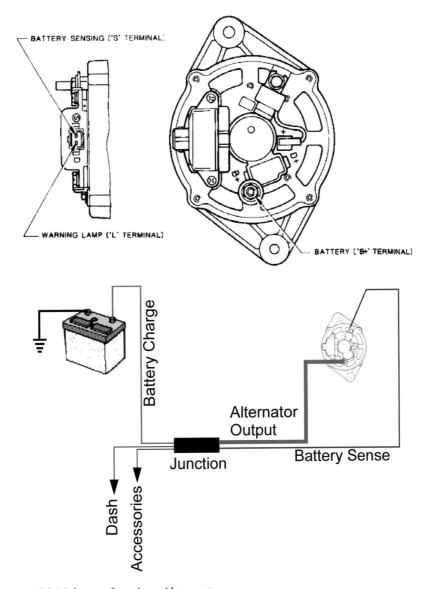

Figure 81 Voltage Sensing Alternator

If the ignition is switched ON without the engine running (for service work or for any other reason) the warning light is a good reminder that the ignition is ON.

The Charge light is linked directly to the alternator through its terminal (#1, I, L, D+, etc. see Table 12 - Alternator Terminals) and functions slightly differently on different manufacturers.

Alternator Terminal Identification
The following is alternator terminal identifications from different manufacturers. They often use different terms, but do the same thing.

Table 12 - Alternator Terminals

Terminal	Description
B+	Battery. Direct connection for charging current.
S	Sense. Sense battery voltage and determine output. Some are connected internally and are not suitable for connecting to an isolator for dual-battery systems.

Note: Battery Sensor connection is always at battery voltage.

Terminal	Description
L	Light. Usually from the diode stack (some use a transistor for light function) and will produce a counter voltage to cancel out the light. If 12Vdc is hooked to this, it must have a resistor or a diode so it doesn't try to charge the battery from this circuit.
P	Phase. One of the 3 phases of alternating current. Labelled stator on Fords, it is usually used for the electric choke to disable it if the key is on, engine off.
E	Earth or ground
R	Relay. The same as P or S, but is usually a relay to turn off a charge lamp (found on early GM externally regulated alterntors).
N	Neutral. Same as P but is usually found on remotely regulated alternators.
D+.	Dynamo. This is the ground on the armature of a generator. Grounding it will fully excite the generator.
F or FLD	Field. Rotor for alternators, armature for generators. Usually connects to the IGN or F terminal or an external regulator.
A	Armature (generator). The same as B+ on alternator. To add a light to a generator 'ground' the bulb circuit here.
F	Fault. Applicable to Delco CS series alternators. Do not full field this unit - it will damage the alternator.
I or Ind	Indicator, or Alternator Warning Light.

Coil and Starter Solenoid

Once again, there are numerous combinations of starter circuits, depending on the make and model starter system. Some use external solenoids (usually earlier models, as illustrated in **Figure 82** Start/Run Ignition System) but most solenoids are integrated with the starter motor. There is, however, a distinctive advantage with remote solenoids. They are unaffected by heat, as the solenoid can be mounted away from exhaust and hot engine blocks. If you have a high compression, hot running engine and the starter is giving you trouble when it's hot, this may be the solution. Check out **Figure 82** Start/Run Ignition System, which is typically early Ford but the same for most other similar systems.

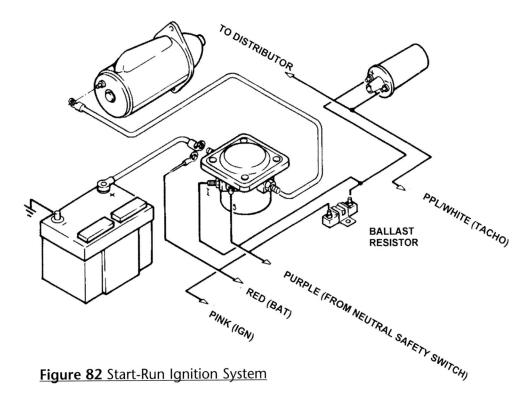

Figure 82 Start-Run Ignition System

Many coils these days do not need a ballast resistor. Check your system carefully and only include the ballast resistor if absolutely necessary. The job of the ballast resistor is to drop the ignition voltage down to about 8Vdc when the engine is running. For these systems, use an 8V coil and a suitable start switch. The full 12Vdc supply is sent to the coil to start the engine by bypassing the ballast resistor, then once the engine fires, the ballast resistor is brought back into the circuit to drop the voltage down for the coil. In non-ballast resistor systems (now the most popular) the coil is rated at 12V, for starting and running.

Dash Harness

The Dash Harness connects all the instruments and controls to their respective supplies and sensors.

In addition, it supplies accessories within the vehicle. Refer FIGURE 83 **Dash Wiring**. The following circuits and elements are covered:

- Gauges
  - Fuel
  - Temp
  - Speedo
  - Tacho
  - Oil
  - Volts
  - Amps

- Wiper Switch

- Wiper Motor

- Washer Switch

- Light Switch

- Hazard Light Switch

- Dip Switch

- Idiot Lights, as follows:
  - Left Turn Indicator
  - Rt Turn Indicator
  - High Beam Indicator
  - Charge Light

- Radio (Ign).

- Radio (Hot).

- Neutral Safety Switch

Wiring in an Ammeter. An ammeter is a gauge that will tell you if the charging system is working or not, but it must be wired in correctly or it will give a false reading. It can also be a battery fire waiting to happen if not installed properly!

The description given here is for a GM or Ford/Bosch single wire alternator.

The output of the alternator at the large stud should be run via a 10 gauge RED wire to the driver's side of the ammeter. Normally, this wire would run straight down to the starter solenoid where it connects to the battery

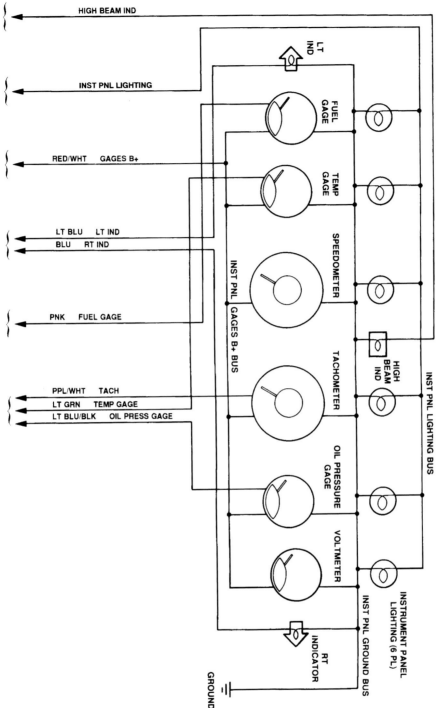

Figure 83 Dash Wiring

cable, but we need to wire in the ammeter so that it is electrically where the alternator output stud is located.

On remote sensing alternators (externally excited), a wire should be fed to the regulator in the alternator via the terminal furthest from the output stud. Run ALL of your feed wires off this post.

Note: It may be a good idea to mount an insulated stud on the firewall instead of mounting all your feed wires on the ammeter post.

The ONLY wire on the other ammeter post should be a 10 gauge wire running down to the starter solenoid where the battery is connected.

The other stud (usually a spade connector) on the alternator's regulator (closer to the output stud) goes to the idiot light then to the ignition switch.

Note: On GM alternators, You MUST wire this terminal in, or the engine will not shut off when you turn the ignition off!

The ammeter should run about 1 or 2 amps positive when the battery is charged.

Rear Lighting Harness

The Rear Lighting Harness supplies the following elements:

• Electric Fuel Pump

• Fuel Tank Sender

• Backup Lights

• Brake Lights

• Third eye Brake Light

Extended System and Accessories

The Extended System/Accessories harness supplies the following accessories:

• Dome Lights

• Power Windows

• Power Door Locks

• Extended Electrical System

The term "Custom Wiring" means that there will be deviations from the standard set of circuits and elements, dependant on the sophistication of the electrical system in the project vehicle.

The following circuits/elements will be covered in addition to the comprehensive circuitry already detailed.

- Washer Motor

- Battery isolation switch

- Accessories

- Transmission Kickdown

- Air Conditioner

- Cruise Control

- Electric Choke

- Anti-dieseling Solenoid

- Clock

- Cigar Lighter

- Trunk/Rumble Seat Solenoid

Table 13 - GM Wiring Colour Code

CIRCUIT	FROM	TO	COLOR
Front Lighting Harness			
High Beam	Headlight Connector	Dip Switch	Lt Grn
Low Beam	Headlight Connector	Dip Switch	Tan
Electric Cooling Fan	Fan	Switch or Thermostat	Gry/Wht
Left Front Turn Signals	Left Front	Indicator Switch	Lt Blue
Right Front Turn Signals	Right Front	Indicator Switch	Blue
Parkers	Park Lamps	Light Switch	Brn
Horn	Horn	Horn Relay	Green
Engine Bay Harness			
Coil	Coil +	Fuse Panel (optional via Ballast)	Pink
Alternator Exciter	Alt Field	Fuse Panel	Wht
Alternator Batt	Alt Bat+	Fuse Panel	Red
Starter Solenoid Relay	Solenoid	Start Switch via Neutral Safety	Purple

Table 13 - GM Wiring Colour Code

Oil Pressure sending unit	Sender	Gauge	Lt blu/Blk
Engine coolant temp. sender	Sender	Gauge	Lt Grn
Ballast Resistor	Ballast	Fuse Panel	Purple
Radiator Thermo Switch	Thermo Switch	Fan Switch	Gry/Wht
Brake switch	Brake Switch	Fuse Panel	Orange
Brake Switch Return	Brake Switch	Brake Lights	Wht
Dash Harness			
Gauges +	Gauge Supply	Fuse Panel	Red/Wht
Fuel Gauge	Fuel Gauge	Fuel Sender	Pnk
Temp	Temp Gauge	Temp Sender	Lt Grn
Tacho	Coil Tach	Coil -	Ppl/Wht
Oil	Oil Gauge	Oil Sender	Lt Blu/Blk
Volts	Volt Gauge	Fuse Panel	Red/Wht
Amps	Amp Meter	Alt Bat	Red
Wiper Switch	Wiper Switch	Fuse Panel	Blue
Wiper Motor	Wiper Motor B+	Wiper Switch	Blue
Light Switch	Switch Supply	Fuse Panel	Red/Blk
Indicator Switch +	Switch B+	Flasher Unit	Purple
Indicator Switch Left	Switch Left	Left Turn Lights front and Rear	Lt Blue
Indicator Switch Right	Switch Right	Right Turn Lights Front and Rear	Blue
Dip Switch Supply	Switch +	Headlight Switch	Blu/Yell
High Beam	Dip Switch	Headlights	Lt Grn
Low Beam	Dip Switch	Headlights	Brown
Idiot Lights, as follows:			
Left Turn Indicator	Lamp	Turn Switch	Lt Blue
Rt Turn Indicator	Lamp	Turn Switch	Blue
High Beam Indicator	Lamp	Dip Switch	Lt Grn
Charge Light	Lamp	Alternator	Brown
Radio (Ign)	Radio Switched	Fuse Panel	Red/Blk
Radio (Hot)	Radio Unswitched (constant)	Fuse Panel	Red
Neutral Safety Switch	Neutral Safety Switch	Starter Solenoid	Purple
Rear Lighting Harness			
Electric Fuel Pump	Fuel Pump B+	Fuse Panel	Ylw/Wht
Fuel Tank Sender	Sender Unit	Fuel Gauge	Pink
Backup Lights	Lamps	Backup Switch	Lt Grn
Brake Lights	Brake Lamps	Brake Switch	Orange
Third-eye Brake Light	Third Eye Brake Lamp	Brake Switch	Orange
Dome Lights	Lamp +	Fuse Panel	White
Power Windows	Power Widow B+	Fuse Panel	Yellow
Power Door Locks	Door Solenoid Switch	Fuse Panel	Yell/Blk

Installing an After market Wiring Harness

Today's wiring kits are user friendly, versatile and designed to be installed easily, even if the installer has no prior electrical experience. Whichever one you choose, most will be pre-wired and will have a central control unit or fuse panel from where all the groups of circuits originate.

What you need

You will need a crimping tool, wire strippers, wire cutters (side cutters) and convoluted tubing.

Figure 84 AMP Crimping Tool

Figure 85 Crimping Tool for Weatherpack Terminals

A good quality ratchet crimping tool is ESSENTIAL! DO NOT use those crappy little crimpers that come with the cheap terminal kits in auto-parts stores. Treat yourself to one of these (see **Figure 84** AMP Crimping Tool), or get someone to terminate the connectors for you.

You may also need a crimping Tool for positive lock connectors (sometimes called Utilux, or uninsulated terminals) and Weatherpack terminals (see **Figure 85** Crimping Tool for Weatherpack Terminals). This is not a ratchet tool, but is just fine for the soft brass terminals.

Fuse Panel. The Fuse Panel can be easily attached under the dash (refer **Figure 73** Fuse Panels) or, as a Painless Wiring option, in the trunk. All proper rated fuses, relays and flashers have been pre-installed and all wires are colour coded, allowing easy identification of circuits for future updating and/or modification. Fuse specifications and colour code designations are listed in Circuit Protection on page 16. Check that there is sufficient length in all wires and wire groups to the engine, dash and rear locations to complete the installation without splicing.

Wiring Groups
Most wiring kits can be divided into three major wiring groups:

Front Group. Includes:

- Low Beam/High Beam
- Left/Right Turn Signals;
- Starter Solenoid and Battery Supply;
- Alternator and Alternator Exciter;
- Water Temp;
- Air Conditioning.

- Park lights;
- Electric Fan;
- Horn;
- Distributor;
- Oil Pressure;

Dash Group. Includes:

- Wires to connect Gauges, Indicator Lights and Switches to their sources.

Rear Group. Includes:

- Tail Lights;
- Left/Right Turn Signals;
- Fuel Sender;
- Door Locks;
- Electric Fuel Pump

- Dome Lights;
- Brake Lights;
- Trunk Accessory;
- Power Windows;

Pre Installation, General Routing Guidelines

There are two phases of activity to wire in your kit:

- The physical routing and securing of the wiring harness, wires and groups of wires.
- The proper connection of the individual circuits and components.

Figure 87 Harness Routing in a Custom Installation (illustration courtesy of Painless Wiring) illustrates the suggested routing for the main groups.

Each custom application is unique, so each installation will differ in some way. There are some general instructions and guidelines, however, that cover all installations.

The following are a list of pre-installation checks and procedures:

1. Familiarise yourself with the wiring harness and all of the wire groups.
2. Decide on the mounting point for the fuse panel.
3. Decide where each of the wiring groups will be routed.
4. Lay the entire assembly out on the garage floor to help you identify all the groups of wires and spot any unusual routing 'challenges'. Pay particular attention to where the wires will pass sharp corners, exhaust pipes and other hazards.
5. Look for places to install harness supports (tie wraps, clips, clamps, etc). Allow enough slack for areas where movement will occur (body to frame, frame to engine, hinged openings, flip fronts, rumble seats, to name a few).

Figure 86 Lay the wiring out on the floor first

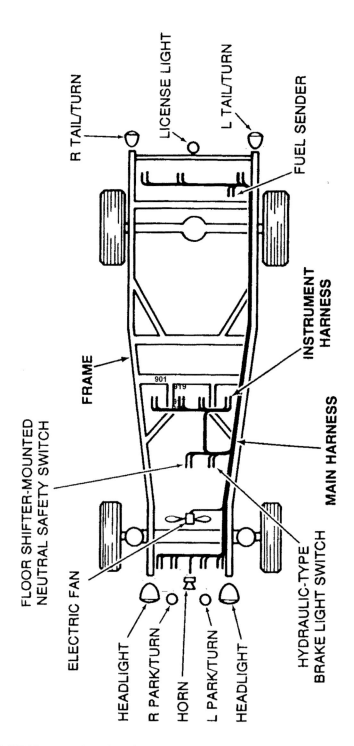

FIGURE 87 Harness Routing in a Custom Installation

Rough Installation

> **Disconnect power by removing the negative (black) battery cable from the battery. Make no connections at this time.**

Using cable ties, group all the wires into their respective sections, re-routing where necessary for your application (for example, you may have the electric fuel pump mounted on the passenger's side or the driver's side, or maybe you are using the trunk release circuit to activate the flip-front release solenoid or door solenoids for shaved door handles). Like any wiring installation job, you must TAKE YOUR TIME and DO NOT cut ANY wires or crimp any terminals until the entire system has been routed through the car.

1. Position the fuse panel.
    In most applications, the engine and headlight group wires will pass through the firewall. If there is no suitable hole, drill one near the fuse panel for these wires to pass through.

2. Install the firewall grommet.

3. Run the engine bay wires through the grommet and arrange them around their destination points.

4. Route the dash group wires upward to the rear of the dash and then temporarily secure them in place.

5. Position the rear group wires, the door groups, the speaker group wires and the tail section wires.

Harness Attachment

1. TAKE YOUR TIME

2. Permanently mount the fuse panel. Check to see if it needs to be grounded.

3. Starting from the fuse panel, mold each of the groups of wires along the floor pan, firewall, chassis, fender panels and other surfaces already decided upon. Secure every six inches or so. Route away from sharp edges, exhaust pipes, hinges etc.

Note: This is most important, as a steel panel will wear through the insulation very quickly, unless it is protected by a grommet.

There will probably be one or two circuits that are not used (the brake failure circuit, interior lights, fast glass, for example) but you should ` consider leaving them intact, just in case. Alternatively, cut the circuits out, secure them to the harness and insulate any bare wires. Roughly lay out the main sections of wiring, that is, engine, front and rear.

Make all these attachments loosely!

4.   Connect grounding straps or cables from the Negative battery terminal to the chassis.

5.   Connect grounding straps or cables from the engine to the chassis.

Do not rely on engine mounts for this connection.

6.   Connect grounding straps from the engine to the body.

7.   On fibreglass bodied cars, use a brass terminal block to ground all gauges and accessories.

8.   Ground the terminal block.

Household neutral grounding blocks are sufficient for the task of providing a ground source in fibreglass bodied cars.

Figure 88 Grounding Terminal Block

At this point, there will probably be a list of possible wiring alternatives for such things as windscreen wiper motors, ECU connections, different park/ neutral safety switch combinations, indicator connections and speedo sender configurations. Using factory wiring diagrams, check such things as headlight switch and relays, thermo fan configurations (including override switches) and idiot light connections (alternator, indicator – single and dual – brake fail light, check engine soon light, high beam indicator, etc). Connect these components using the configuration that is correct for your system.

Terminal Installation

The circuit connections are now about to be made. The routing and length of each wire should be checked and double checked before terminating. Turn signals, ignition switch and steering column connections are particularly troublesome, so ensure all doubt has been removed before proceeding with the following steps.

1. Have all the necessary tools at hand (crimping tool, connectors, wire strippers, side cutters, pliers, etc).

2. Select the correct size terminal for the wire.

> **Allow enough slack for movement in the harness and wire.**
>
> **Double check!**

3. Determine the correct wire length and cut to size. Strip insulation from end of wire using wire strippers (see **Figure 89** Use Wire Strippers). Don't rip the insulation off with side cutters, a box cutter or your teeth!

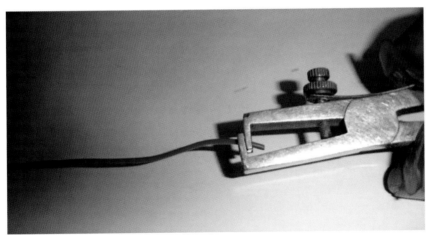

Figure 89 Use Wire Strippers

> *Note: Strip only sufficient insulation required for the type of terminal.*

4. Crimp the terminal.

> *Note: Do not overcrimp.*

5. Attach each wire after carefully routing it.

> *Do not attach first, then crimp.*

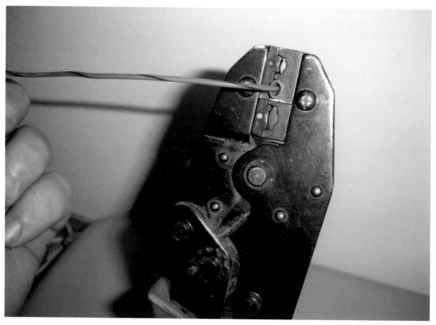

Figure 90 Crimp the Terminals

6.   When all wires are attached, tighten mounts and ties, permanently secure harness and re-check areas where the harness bends, goes through firewall/panels, etc.

Test the System

Now is the time to test the newly installed system. This is best done in a manner where the supply is too weak to cause permanent damage should there be a short in the system. The easiest method is to connect the new wiring system to a small battery charger which has an internal circuit breaker.

DO NOT CONNECT THE BATTERY AT THIS STAGE

1.   Connect the battery charger Negative output to the chassis or engine block.

2.   Connect the battery charger positive to the positive battery terminal.

3.   One at a time, turn on each light and check for proper operation.

4.   Turn ignition ON and check for Ignition voltage at the coil.

5.   Check for correct fuel pump operation, if applicable.

6. Turn on Wipers, Radio, etc and ensure proper operation.

7. Check for overheating of the RED Engine Section (#916) wire. If it is HOT, DISCONNECT IMMEDIATELY and re-check system.

8. When all circuits have been thoroughly checked and no fuses are blown, turn off all circuits and disconnect the battery charger.

9. Re-connect the Battery cables to the battery.

10. Re-check and test drive. If all fuses are intact and there are no malfunctions or incorrectly operating circuits, then proceed with confidence.

Chapter 9

Car Audio

In-car entertainment systems have come a long way in a short time. Aftermarket systems always seem to be streets ahead of everyday factory systems, and are only equalled by the factory installations in all but the most prestigious cars. Your custom auto electrical system should include the type of car audio/ entertainment system in the overall planning so that you are not tearing the system down later to make way for a new head unit or amplifier.

This section deals with the basics of installing and wiring a sound system in a custom vehicle, such as a Hot Rod or Kustom car, inasmuch as it fits in with the rest of your electrical system. If you are into full-on competition audio, then you should consult the appropriate industries, as we are dealing here with your basic head unit, amplifier and speakers. If all you are interested in is a cheap radio with, maybe, a cassette player built in, then you can skip this bit, too. If you like your music and like it crisp, clear and LOUD, then read on.....

Choosing your System

A good sound system is going to be expensive. If you are realistic, it won't come as a surprise that even a basic set up will come in at around $1500.00. You can, however, shop around for second hand components, use cheap stuff and upgrade later, or just start with something small and build it up over time. The way to do this is to use a head unit on its own and build in the amp and sub-woofers later. For the purpose of this Chapter, however, lets describe a good quality system and see how it all comes together in a custom installation. We'll keep its size down to a relatively sedate 60 Watts per channel, which means that the speakers NOMINAL INPUT should be rated at 60 Watts. At half volume, that's enough for the most ardent head-banger!

Main Components

Our sound system comprises the following major components:

- Head Unit. Our head unit will cost somewhere between $300 and $500. Look for a head unit that has controls that are easy to use. A remote control is essential for cars like T Buckets and coupes where the head unit may be mounted behind you or on the floor. Choose a CD Player that plays MP3 formats and may even come with a slot for a memory stick, USB drive (or "Thumb Drive") or iPod. Our head unit has a Line Out for driving an amplifier, and this is an ideal way to set up a sound system. The head unit's built-in amplifier can drive a set of small speakers, but the sound is nowhere as "clean" as the line out (or pre-amp) signal.

> **Note:** *Most factory OEM head units do not have a preamp output, and are not meant to drive an amplifier. You can use the speaker output to drive an amp, but the sound quality is compromised.*

- Amplifier. The amplifier takes the signal from the head unit and, well, amplifies it so that it will drive all your speakers. You can start off with an amp for the low frequencies (driving the sub woofer(s)) and use the head unit's built-in power to drive the high and mid-range speakers. This is adequate but the built-in power in a head unit is usually not strong enough for high volume listening and not clean enough for the discerning ear. Pick an amp that is powerful enough to drive all your speakers without having to turn the head unit's volume way up.

- Loudspeakers. Our system uses four speakers - one pair for the front, one pair for the rear. Loudspeakers are capable of reproducing sounds across the entire audio spectrum, but it is impossible to build one that reproduces all frequencies at acceptable levels. That's where tweeters, mid-range and woofers come in. Many tweeters are built in to a mid-range and woofer speaker - these are called combination speakers, and can work quite well. The deep bass sounds are handled by sub-woofers.

- Sub-woofers. You can run one sub-woofer in your system and it will work very well. If you really like your bass, get two. Subs come in various sizes, usual 10 inch, 12 inch and (gasp) 18 inch! Because they move a lot of air, subs need an enclosure. In some custom applications, the enclosure just won't fit, so you must choose a free air sub-woofer.

- Crossover/equalizer. An equaliser splits your sound system into frequency ranges. Speakers cannot reproduce sounds evenly over their range, so we use an equaliser to boost or cut certain frequency ranges to tailor the overall sound. A Crossover splits the output of our sound system into two (in the case of a two channel crossover) or three (three channel) frequency bands, and sends them to the speakers (or amps) so that the frequency bands are dedicated to a particular channel rather than being all mixed up together when they get to the speakers. Active crossovers use the pre-amp signal from the head unit and sends the output to the amplifier(s). Passive crossovers take the sound from the amplifier and sends the sound channels to the speakers. Active crossovers are the most efficient and popular. Many of today's amplifiers have the crossover built in.

Mounting the Car Audio Components

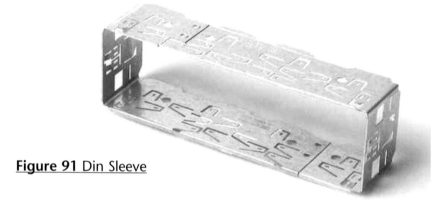

Figure 91 Din Sleeve

If your project car has a factory car audio system and you are upgrading it to include a late model system, it is simply a matter of fabricating the mounts or installing the DIN sleeve that comes with the after-market system.

Fit the DIN sleeve into the factory orifice by folding back the small tabs to hold it in place. It may be necessary to do some cutting and grinding, but once the DIN sleeve is in place, it is a simple job to slide the CD Player/ Receiver (the Head Unit) into the sleeve and plug in the car audio wiring harness.

Figure 92 Stereo Cradle

Alternatively, you can manufacture or buy a stereo cradle, like the ones sold in Australia by Simon Muntz's Street Rods and Accessories.

> *Note: You may need a backstrap to support the rear of your head unit. It is normally included in the installation kit.*

If you are installing an Amplifier and/or Sub Woofer combination, you should find a suitable location that is away from direct heat and not likely to be kicked or knocked when getting in and out of the car. For the amplifier, select a location that has good air circulation, such as in the trunk or under a seat. Installing sub-woofers correctly is a science in itself. The enclosure, the direction and configuration of one or two subwoofers and the type of vehicle that it is being installed in are all considerations that will make or break the system. You should consult the manufacturer's instructions, specialist publications and ask advice of the vendor before making any decisions.

Wiring Harness

Your car audio system should connect with your electrical system by way of its own wiring harness. The plug and wires (the pigtail) is normally supplied with the installation kit, but can also be purchased separately. The pigtail includes connections to the following sources:

- Power

- Ground

- Amplifier

- Speakers

Power

There are two power supplies that you need to connect to most later model after market car audio systems:

Switched. A switched power source is only on when the ignition is on. Connect the head unit's switched power lead to a switched power source (ignition source), so that it turns off when you turn off the car, and doesn't drain your battery.

Constant. A constant power source is always on. Connect your head unit's memory lead to a constant (battery) power source, so that you don't lose your radio presets, sound shaping, clock settings, etc every time you turn off the engine.

Some high-powered receivers and amplifiers require you to make a direct constant power connection at the positive terminal of your battery. This requires a heavier gauge power wire, an in-line fuse (usually included), and a ring terminal to connect the power wire to the battery clamp. Ensure you use a proper grommet when routing the power wire through the firewall or floor to make the connection at the battery.

Ground

A good ground connection is vital for proper receiver performance. If your ground wire doesn't contact bare metal, your head unit won't operate. A loose or weak ground connection can result in signal noise interfering with your cool tunes.

Amplifier

An Amplifier is required to run single or dual sub-woofers and/ or the pre-amplifier output of the head unit. There are too many configurations to list here, so it is important that you consult the installation instructions carefully. Generally, however, the following procedure will be common to most installations:

1. Check the owner's manual for the recommended gauge of the power and ground cables and connect the negative, or ground, power cables first. The ground cable should be kept as short as possible and should be bolted securely to a good, clean ground.

   Note: This must be done before connecting the RCA cables from the head unit to the amplifier. When you connect power to the system, you want the amplifier to find its ground through the ground cable, not the RCA cable.

2. Route the large diameter RCA cables (see FIGURE 93 **RCA Cables**) to connect the low-level output of the head unit to the low-level input of the amplifier.

   Note: If the head unit does not have a low-level output, you will need to use the high level, or speaker output. Generally, this is less desirable because of the noticeable increase in distortion and noise in such an arrangement. If your amp is for subwoofer only, this may be a less significant problem.

3. Connect the power antenna lead or the Amplifier ON lead from the back of the head unit to the amplifier remote turn-on (REM) input. When the

Figure 93 RCA Cables

radio is switched on, 12 volts should appear on the lead, which will connect the amplifier to the main power supply.

Note: Make certain that the power antenna lead stays on while the receiver is on. On some radios, power may be switched off from the lead when a CD or tape is played, so the power antenna will come down. If this is the case with your radio, it may have a separate lead coming out for the amplifier turn-on function.

4. Route the fused line between the battery and amplifier. Check your owner's manual for the proper rating for the fuse and cable if it is not supplied with the installation kit.

Note: Fuse your amplifier(s) as close to the battery as possible and ensure that power cables do not run next to RCA signal cables.

5. Connect the main power (+) for the amplifier directly to the battery using the same gauge cable for the amplifier ground.

6. Use 16-12 gauge speaker wire (depending on power output of your system) and connect the wire from the speakers to the amplifier.

Speakers

Note: You must ensure that you have correctly matched the speaker impedance with the amplifier/head unit. If you are not sure, consult the manufacturer's instructions and/or the vendor.

7. Connect speaker wires to the amplifier and/or head unit in their proper configuration - positive to positive, negative to negative.

Note: Keep speaker wires separate from power supply wires (particularly the big, heavy amplifier cables for larger systems) as the induced voltage creates noise.

Speaker wiring applications differ between Single Voice Coil (SVC) and Dual Voice Coil (DVC) speakers. A SVC speaker has one voice coil and one set of terminals (one positive and one negative). A DVC speaker has two voice coils, each with its own set of terminals. Because of this, DVC speakers (typically subwoofers) offer more wiring options than SVC speakers.

8.   Test your system

If your system works but your lights dim whenever heavy bass is output, you will probably require a higher rated alternator, and/or the installation of a stiffening capacitor (Cap). A Cap is less expensive than a replacement alternator, but will not substitute for one if it is needed.

Speaker Polarity

It is important to have the speakers connected correctly. There is a positive and negative side to the speakers and if connected incorrectly, a sound may come out but is out of phase with the other speaker. This will cause extra strain on the amplifier as well as a degradation of the stereo sound, to the point where it may reproduce a mono sound effect. To check speaker polarity, use the following simple technique:

1.   Connect one end of a jumper wire to the positive side of a 1.5Vdc battery (AA size) and the other end to a speaker connection.

2.   Connect another jumper wire to the negative side of the battery.

3.   Touch (quickly) the other speaker connection to the negative jumper wire.

The speaker will 'pop'. If it pops out, then polarity is correct. If the speaker pops inwards, polarity is reversed. Take note of the correct polarity and wire in the speakers accordingly.

Factory Car Audio Systems

How often have you headed back from the wrecking yard with a spunky looking factory stereo to put in your hot rod or custom, only to be confronted with an array of wires with such diverse colours that you don't know where to start? Buying a good, late model factory sound system is a good idea, and cheaper than most after-market systems. This section attempts to cover most of the major car manufacturer's standard wiring installations to assist you with your project.

Note: Wire colours vary greatly. Your car might not even have the colours described here.

Before we get into the colour codes and circuit diagrams, let's take the installation of a typical GM late model radio one step at a time. The following is an example only, and is used as a generic guide. Refer to the colour code tables for specific make/model radio wiring information.

The typical GM radio wiring harness is made up of three 4-wire bundles. The first bundle is for the rear speakers, the second, similar bundle is for the front speakers. Check the colours of the wires, and keep an eye out for the "tracer". An example is the GM colour code, as follows:

- Light green: right speaker +

- Dark green: right speaker -

- Tan: left speaker +

- Gray: left speaker -

- Dark Blue: right rear +

- Light Blue: right rear -

- Brown: left rear +

- Yellow: left rear -

The third bundle is for power, as follows.

- Yellow: 12V power when the ignition switch is turned to ON or ACC. This is the main power for the radio.

- Black: Negative-ground.

- Gray: 12V illumination power. When you switch the headlights on, the face lights up.

- Pink: Power antenna.

- Orange: Memory. Remembers the station settings you input and the clock (if included).

Using this example, you can figure out which wires in your custom system go to which connections in your factory stereo. Remember to cap the wires that are not used (for example, the power antenna if you don't have one) to prevent the wire from shorting to ground.

Use the colours for reference purposes only and always test wires to make sure they are correct. To check hot, ignition, lights, dimmer, use a test light or voltmeter. To check speakers use a test radio or follow the procedure for Speaker Polarity, as described below.

Table 14 - Factory Audio Colour Code

Circuit	Color code
BMW	
Power	
Memory (+12v Constant)	Grey/Red
Ignition (+12v Switched)	Violet
Ground (-)	Brown
Illumination	White/Blue
Dimmer	(none)
Power Antenna	White
Speakers	
Right Front (+)	Gray/White
Right Front (-)	Gray/Brown
Left Front (+)	Gray/Red
Left Front (-)	Gray/Violet
Right Rear (+)	Black/White
Right Rear (-)	Black/Brown
Left Rear (+)	Black/Red
Left Rear (-)	Black/Violet
DODGE/CHRYSLER	
Power	
Memory (+12v Constant)	Red/White
Ignition (+12v Switched)	Red
Ground (-)	Black or Braided Silver Wire
Illumination	Orange
Dimmer	(none)
Power Antenna	Yellow
Speakers	
Right Front (+)	Violet
Right Front (-)	Blue/Red
Left Front (+)	Green
Left Front (-)	Brown/Red

Table 14 - Factory Audio Colour Code

Circuit	Color code
Right Rear (+)	Blue/White
Right Rear (-)	Blue/Red
Left Rear (+)	Brown/Yellow
Left Rear (-)	Brown/Red
FORD	
Power	
Memory (+12v Constant)	Green Yellow
Ignition (+12v Switched)	Yellow/Black
Ground (-)	Black or Fat Red
Illumination	Orange
Dimmer	Orange/White
Power Antenna	Blue (varies greatly)
Speakers	
Right Front (+)	White/Green
Right Front (-)	Green/Orange
Left Front (+)	Orange/Green
Left Front (-)	Light Blue
Right Rear (+)	Pink/Blue
Right Rear (-)	Green/orange
Left Rear (+)	Pink/green
Left Rear (-)	Pink/Blue
GENERAL MOTORS	
Power	
Memory (+12v Constant)	Orange
Ignition (+12v Switched)	Yellow
Ground (-)	Black
Illumination	Gray
Dimmer	Brown
Power Antenna	Pink
Speakers	
Right Front (+)	Light Green
Right Front (-)	Dark Green
Left Front (+)	Tan
Left Front (-)	Gray
Right Rear (+)	Dark Blue
Right Rear (-)	Light Blue
Left Rear (+)	Brown
Left Rear (-)	Yellow
HONDA/ACCURA	
Power	

Table 14 - Factory Audio Colour Code

Circuit	Color code
Memory (+12v Constant)	Blue/White
Ignition (+12v Switched)	Yellow/Red
Ground (-)	Black
Illumination	Red/Black
Dimmer	(none)
Power Antenna	Yellow/White

Speakers

Right Front (+)	Red/Green
Right Front (-)	Brown/Black
Left Front (+)	Blue/Green
Left Front (-)	Gray/Black
Right Rear (+)	Red/Yellow
Right Rear (-)	Brown/White
Left Rear (+)	Blue/Yellow
Left Rear (-)	Gray/White

ISUZU

Power

Memory (+12v Constant)	Red/White
Ignition (+12v Switched)	Orange
Ground (-)	Black/Yellow
Illumination	Green/Red
Dimmer	Red/Green
Power Antenna	(none)

Speakers

Right Front (+)	Grey
Right Front (-)	Grey/Green
Left Front (+)	Yellow
Left Front (-)	Blue/Yellow
Right Rear (+)	White
Right Rear (-)	Red/White
Left Rear (+)	Orange
Left Rear (-)	Black/Orange

JEEP

Power

Memory (+12v Constant)	Pink
Ignition (+12v Switched)	Violet/White
Ground (-)	Black
Illumination	Orange
Dimmer	Blue/White
Power Antenna	None

Table 14 - Factory Audio Colour Code

Circuit	Color code
Speakers	
Right Front (+)	White
Right Front (-)	Black
Left Front (+)	Green
Left Front (-)	Black/Yellow
Right Rear (+)	White/Black
Right Rear (-)	Brown
Left Rear (+)	Green/White
Left Rear (-)	Brown/White
MAZDA	
Power	
Memory (+12v Constant)	Blue/Red
Ignition (+12v Switched)	Blue/White
Ground (-)	Black
Illumination	Red/Black
Dimmer	none
Power Antenna	Blue (some have a (-) trigger, need relay)
Speakers	
right Front (+)	Blue/Red
right Front (-)	Blue/Orange
left Front (+)	Blue
left Front (-)	Blue/White
right Rear (+)	Blue/Orange
right Rear (-)	Blue/Black
left Rear (+)	Blue/White
left Rear (-)	Blue/Green
MAZDA RX-7	
Speakers	
right Front +	Red
right Front -	White
left Front +	Blue
left Front -	Green
front Tweeter crossover	Gray/Black
right Rear +	White/Blue
right Rear -	Blue/Yellow
left Rear +	Yellow/Green
left Rear -	Yellow/Blue
rear Tweeter crossover	Black/Red
Illumination	Red/Green

Table 14 - Factory Audio Colour Code

Circuit	Color code
Ground	Black
Built in antenna	Small socket
Retractable antenna	Large socket

MERCEDES BENZ

Power

Memory (+12v Constant)	Red
Ignition (+12v Switched)	Black/Yellow
Ground (-)	Brown
Illumination	Grey/Blue
Dimmer	(none)
Power Antenna	Blue

Speakers

Right Front (+)	Black/Green
Right Front (-)	Black
Left Front (+)	Black/Red
Left Front (-)	Black
Right Rear (+)	Black/Green
Right Rear (-)	Black
Left Rear (+)	Black/Red
Left Rear (-)	Black

MITSUBISHI

Power

Memory (+12v Constant)	Red/White or White/Green
Ignition (+12v Switched)	Blue/White
Ground (if fitted)	Black
Illumination	Green/White
Dimmer	Black/White or Black/Yellow
Power Antenna	White/Black

Speakers

Right Front (+)	White/Red
Right Front (-)	Black/Red
Left Front (+)	White/Blue
Left Front (-)	Black/Blue
Right Rear (+)	Yellow/Red
Right Rear (-)	Grey/Red
Left Rear (+)	Yellow/Red
Left Rear (-)	Grey/Blue

NISSAN

Power

Table 14 - Factory Audio Colour Code

Circuit	Color code
Memory (+12v Constant)	Red
Ignition (+12v Switched)	(varies) Brown or Green
Ground (-)	Black (varies - most don't have one)
Illumination	Red/White
Dimmer	Red/Black
Power Antenna	Green
Speakers	
Right Front (+)	Brown
Right Front (-)	Brown/White
Left Front (+)	Black
Left Front (-)	Black/White
Right Rear (+)	Blue
Right Rear (-)	Pink
Left Rear (+)	Red
Left Rear (-)	Green
SAAB	
Power	
Memory (+12v Constant)	Grey
Ignition (+12v Switched)	Red
Ground (-)	Black
Illumination	Brown/White
Dimmer	(none)
Power Antenna	Green
Speakers	
Right Front (+)	Blue
Right Front (-)	Red
Left Front (+)	Green
Left Front (-)	Brown
Right Rear (+)	White/Blue
Right Rear (-)	White/Red
Left Rear (+)	White/Green
Left Rear (-)	White/Brown
SUBARU	
Power	
Memory (+12v Constant)	Red/Green
Ignition (+12v Switched)	Blue/Yellow
Ground (-)	Black
Illumination	Dimmer
Power Antenna	Red/White

Table 14 - Factory Audio Colour Code

Circuit	Color code
Speakers	
Right Front (+)	White
Right Front (-)	Blue/Black
Left Front (+)	Yellow
Left Front (-)	Blue/Red
Right Rear (+)	White/Blue
Right Rear (-)	Blue/Black
Left Rear (+)	Yellow/White
Left Rear (-)	Blue/Red
TOYOTA	
Power	
Memory (+12v Constant)	Blue/Yellow
Ignition (+12v Switched)	Gray
Ground (-)	Brown
Illumination	Green
Dimmer	White/Green
Power Antenna	Black/Red
Speakers	
Right Front (+)	Light Green
Right Front (-)	Blue
Left Front (+)	Pink
Left Front (-)	Violet
Right Rear (+)	Red
Right Rear (-)	White
Left Rear (+)	Black
Left Rear (-)	Yellow
VOLVO	
Power	
Memory (+12v Constant)	Green
Ignition (+12v Switched)	Black
Ground (-)	Fat Black
Illumination	Yellow (not on plug)
Dimmer	(none)
Power Antenna	Red
Speakers	
Right Front (+)	Gray/White
Right Front (-)	Gray
Left Front (+)	Blue/Yellow
Left Front (-)	White
Right Rear (+)	Green/Brown

Table 14 - Factory Audio Colour Code

Circuit	Color code
Right Rear (-)	Green
Left Rear (+)	Yellow/Brown
Left Rear (-)	Yellow/Green
VOLKSWAGEN	
Power	
Memory (+12v Constant)	Red
Ignition (+12v Switched)	Black (not available in most cars)
Ground (-)	Brown
Illumination	Grey or Grey/Blue
Dimmer	(none)
Power Antenna	White
Speakers	
Right Front (+)	Red
Right Front (-)	Brown/White
Left Front (+)	Blue
Left Front (-)	Brown/Blue
Right Rear (+)	Red/Green
Right Rear (-)	Brown/Black
Left Rear (+)	Blue/Green
Left Rear (-)	Brown/Red

Chapter 10

Tools and Test Equipment

You cannot 'see' Electricity. To test for the presence of Electricity and to diagnose the behaviour of this invisible energy, the proper use of tools and test equipment is necessary. The average Hot Rodder needs to know what he/she is looking at and then be able to interpret test equipment readings which will assist in the auto electronic/electrical system diagnosis. To diagnose and repair electrical circuits correctly, a number of common tools and instruments are used. The most common tools are:

- jumper wires,
- test lights,
- voltmeters,
- ammeters,
- ohmmeters
- Circuit Breaker.

Jumper Wires

Connecting one end of a jumper wire to battery positive provides 12Vdc power for testing a component (refer **FIGURE 94** Jumper Wire). Jumper wires can be used to check the load components (in this case, a lamp) by short-circuiting switches, conductors, and connections in the circuit. Jumper wires can also be used to provide the ground to test that portion of the circuit.

Never connect a jumper wire across the terminals of the battery. The battery could explode, causing serious injury.

Test Lights

A test light consists of a transparent handle which contains a light bulb. A pointed probe extends from one end of the handle and a ground wire with an alligator clip extends from the other end. If the circuit is operating

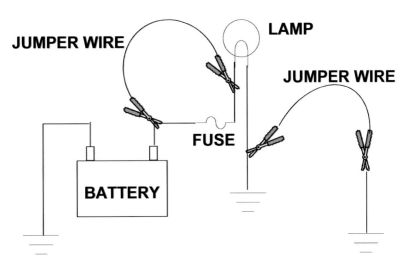

Figure 94 Jumper Wire

properly, clamping the ground wire of the test light to ground and probing the live circuit should light the lamp (refer **Figure 95** Test Light).

A test light only indicates the presence of a voltage, not how much voltage is at the point of the circuit being tested. However, the effects of voltage drops will enable the user to compare the brightness of the test light to that which would be expected in a good circuit. If the test light is connected after a voltage drop, the lamp will be dim. Connecting the test lamp before the voltage drop and the test light will be bright. The light should not illuminate at all if it is probing for voltage at the return side of the circuit. In the example shown in **Figure 95** Test Light, the connector has broken and is open circuit. The test lamp shows a voltage on one side of the connector, but not the other.

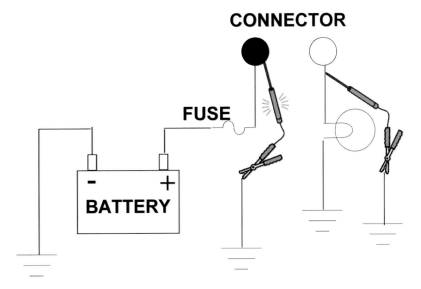

Figure 95 Test Light

It is not recommended that a test light be used to probe for power in a computer-controlled circuit. The increased draw of the test light may damage the system components.

Another type of circuit tester is the self-powered continuity tester (see **Figure 96** Continuity Tester). The continuity tester has an internal battery that powers a light bulb. If the circuit is complete between the probe and the ground wire, the bulb illuminates. With the power in the circuit turned off or disconnected, the ground clip is connected to the ground terminal of the load component. By probing the feed wire, the light will illuminate if the circuit is complete (has continuity).

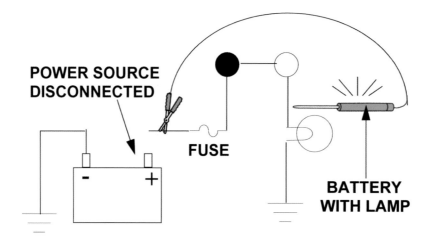

Figure 96 Continuity Tester

Do not connect a self-powered test light to a circuit that is powered. Doing so will damage the test light.

Multimeter
The Voltmeter, Ammeter and Ohmmeter are almost always combined in a handy little gadget called a Multimeter. There are two types of Multimeter:

- Analog Multimeter; and
- Digital Multimeter.

The Analog Multimeter is a "seat of the pants" device which presents the user with a scale and a moving pointer. A Digital Multimeter has a Liquid Crystal Display (LCD) window which reads out the value of the reading numerically. The Analog multimeter is fine for general purpose, non-computer controlled engines and vehicles, but for any car using electronic ignition, engine management or any other electronic devices, the Digital Multimeter is the way to go (see **Figure 102** Digital Multimeter).

Voltmeter

A voltmeter does not interrupt the circuit, but connects in parallel with the circuit being measured to read the voltage across it. A voltmeter has a high resistance, which prevents it from disrupting the circuit. **Figure 97** Voltmeter shows how to check for voltage in a closed circuit.

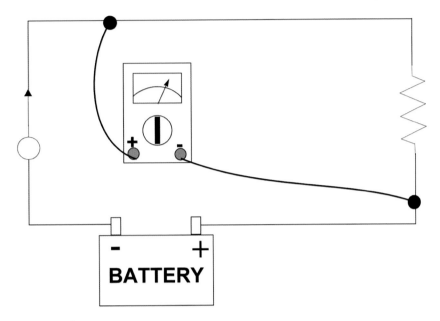

Figure 97 Voltmeter

Voltmeter - Normal Circuit Readings

Figure 98 Voltmeter Readings in Normal Circuit illustrates the various readings which can be expected within a closed circuit. The voltage at the source (battery, point A) is 12Vdc. There is a drop of 6 Vdc across the 1-ohm

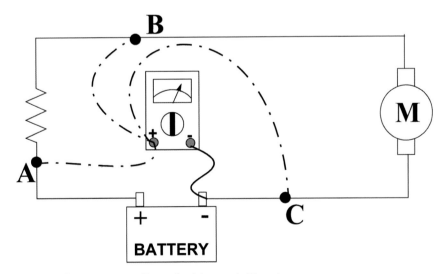

Figure 98 Voltmeter Readings in Normal Circuit

resistor. The reading on the voltmeter is 6Vdc (positive) at point B. The remaining voltage drops in the load (resistance) and the voltmeter reads 0Vdc at point C, indicating that the motor circuit is operating normally.

Voltmeter - Open Circuit Readings

When reading the voltage in the same circuit that has an open (refer **Figure 99** Voltmeter Readings in Open Circuit), 12Vdc will be indicated at any point in the circuit which is more positive (closer to the battery + terminal) than the ground (-) point in the circuit. This is indicated at points A, B, and C, but not at point x. The circuit is open, therefore there is no electrical flow, so no voltage is dropped across the resistor (load).

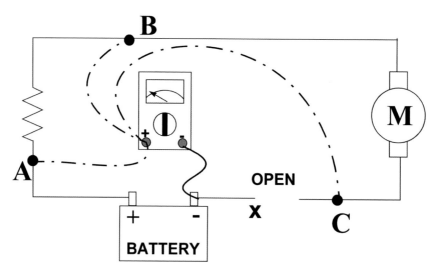

Figure 99 Voltmeter Readings in Open Circuit

Voltmeter - Measuring Voltage Drops

Before the voltage drop across each load can be measured, it must be determined which side of each load is positive and which side is negative. A point in the circuit is either positive or negative, depending on what is being measured. To measure the voltage across R1 (refer **Figure 100** Voltmeter Readings Across Loads), the positive lead of the Voltmeter is placed at point A and the negative lead at point B.

The voltmeter will measure the difference in volts between these points. To measure across R2, the positive probe of the Voltmeter is placed on point B and point C is the negative end. We determine this because point B is more positive than point C for R2. To measure across R3, the positive probe of the Voltmeter goes to point C, and point D is negative.

> **Note:** *The positive lead of the voltmeter should be placed as close as possible to the positive side of the battery in the circuit.*

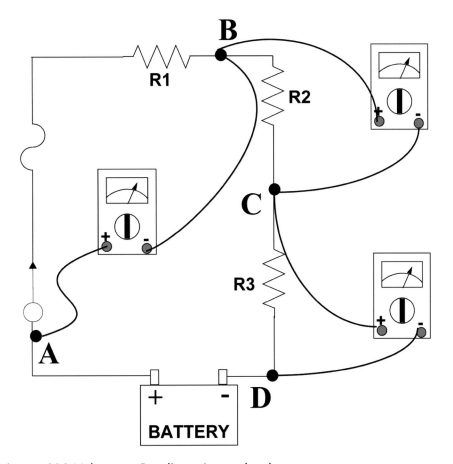

Figure 100 Voltmeter Readings Across loads

Ohmmeter

For troubleshooting automotive electrical/electronic problems, an Ohmmeter is an extremely useful piece of test equipment. Connecting the ohmmeter between either end of a conductor, an open circuit or excessive resistance can be measured. The meter should read 0 ohms if the conductor is good. If the meter indicates an infinity (maximum resistance), this usually indicates an open circuit.

> **The Ohmmeter is self-powered.**
> **Do not use an Ohmmeter on a powered circuit.**

The test chart shown (refer Table 15 - **Test Chart**) illustrates the readings that may be expected from an ohmmeter or voltmeter under different conditions. It is important to become familiar with these examples in order to analyse circuits.

Table 15 - Test Chart

Type of Fault	Test Equipment	Expected Results
Open Circuits	Ohmmeter	Infinite resistance between conductor ends.
	Test Light	No light at termination
	Voltmeter	0Vdc at termination
Grounds	Ohmmeter	0 ohms resistance to ground.
	Test Light	Illuminates when connected across fuse holder with fuse removed.
	Voltmeter	Not used to test for grounds.
Short Circuits	Ohmmeter	Lower than specified resistance through component (eg ignition coil). No resistance to an adjacent conductor.
	Test Light	Light illuminates at shorted conductors.
	Voltmeter	A voltage can be read on both conductors.

Ammeter

An Ammeter must be connected in series with the load to measure the amount of current being drawn in the circuit (refer **Figure 101** Ammeter). In order to make a series connection, disconnect the load (turn the switch OFF) and reconnect it with all of the current going through the ammeter. Polarity is the same as for a Voltmeter, ie the positive side of the Ammeter must coincide with the positive end of the circuit.

> **Do not connect an ammeter in parallel with the circuit because this can cause damage to the circuit or the meter.**

To prevent damage to the computers on modern engines, use only an induction-type ammeter which clamps around the conductor. The ammeter measures current by the strength of the magnetic field that is created by the current flowing through the wire.

> **Always use an ammeter that can handle the expected current. Excessive current can damage the meter.**

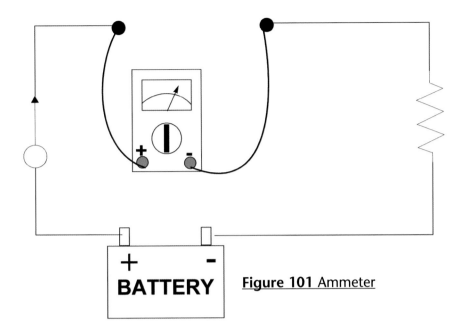

Figure 101 Ammeter

Digital Multimeter

Computer-controlled systems require high impedance multimeters for measuring voltage, resistance and current in the circuits. Computer systems have integrated circuits operating on very low current levels, and analog meters will load down these sensitive computer circuits and burn out the IC chips. The advantage of the digital multimeter (DMM, see **Figure 102** Digital Multimeter) is its very high input resistance (impedance), which prevents the meter from drawing too much current when connected to a circuit. Most DMMs have at least 10 megohms (10 million ohms) impedance, which reduces the risk of damaging computer circuits and components.

> **Not all digital Multimeters are rated at 10 megaohms impedance. Be sure that the mweter you are using is rated accordingly.**

DMMs will indicate polarity with the reading, so the user need not be concerned with polarity, however, it is still good practice to use the correct polarity probe in the circuit under test.

Reading the Digital Multimeter

When using a DMM, it is important for the user to be able to accurately read the meter. It is important that users of these devices have confidence in their conclusions drawn from the readings they have observed on the test equipment. This will reduce instances where parts that were not faulty get replaced due to inaccurate diagnosis of test equipment readings. Although

Figure 102 Digital Multimeter

there are deviations between the different DMMs as to the way the display is presented, most follow the method described here.

Meter Scaling. The meter displays values in different scales. The most common scale graduations are 200, 2K, 20K, 200K, 2M, and 20M. Table 16 - **Meter Scales** refers.

Table 16 - Meter Scales

Scale	Reading	Measure
2	0 to 2	Volts, Amps
20	0 to 20	Volts, Amps, Ohms
200	0 to 200	Volts, Ohms
2K	0 to 2,000	Volts, Ohms
20K	0 to 20,000	Ohms
200K	0 to 200,000	Ohms
2M	0 to 2,000,000,	Ohms
20M	0 to 20,000,000	Ohms

Continuity. When continuity is good, the DMM, switched to resistance, will read 0 or close to 0 even on the low ohmmeter scale. If continuity is very poor, the DMM will display an infinite reading. This reading is usually shown as a blinking '1.000,' a blinking '1,' a blank reading or an 'OL.'

Resistance. It is important that the correct scale be used to obtain an accurate reading. When the DMM is connected to a circuit to test its resistance, begin with the lowest (20) scale, then scale up until the infinite indicator is no longer displayed. This is true unless the lowest scale does not produce the infinite reading. In this case, stay on the lowest scale. Also, if the DMM indicates an infinite reading on the highest scale, there is an open circuit. This method of scaling up will ensure the DMM is set to the lowest scale possible and still be capable of reading the resistance of the component or circuit.

The number that represents the scale reading is the potential number of units that can be read on that particular scale, before the infinite indicator is displayed. Any letter suffix represents the multiplying factor. On the 20 scale and the 200 scale, there is no multiplying factor and the meter reads up to 20 ohms or 200 ohms before the infinite indicator is displayed. On the 2K scale the multiplying factor is 1,000. This scale can read up to 2,000 ohms before an infinite indicator is shown.

The 20K scale reads up to 20,000 ohms before the infinite indicator is shown. The 20M scale has a multiplier factor of 1,000,000 and reads up to 20,000,000 ohms of resistance before the infinite indicator is shown.

If the resistance reading is on the 200 or 20 scale, simply read the level directly from the display. If the display shows 154, the resistance is 154 ohms. If the display shows 104.4, the resistance is 104.4 ohms. If the resistance value of the component or circuit is over 200 ohms, the display would show the infinite indicator. If the infinite indicator is shown, then scale up to the next range.

If the meter is set on the 2K scale, the resistance is read by placing the decimal point three places to the right. For example, if the resistance value is 450 ohms the display will read 0.450. If the resistance value was 1,230 ohms, you would see 1.230 on the display. If the resistance was over 2,000 ohms, the display would show the infinite indicator - go to the next highest scale.

If the DMM is on the 20K scale, move the decimal point three places to the right. Do this regardless of whether or not all three places are actually shown on the display. For example, if the display showed 15.00 this would indicate 15,000 ohms of resistance. A reading of 50 ohms would be indicated by 0.05.

The 200K scale is read the same way as the 20K scale. Move the decimal point three places to the right. If the display shows 150.0 the resistance value is 150,000 ohms.

On the 20M scale move the decimal point six places to the right. A display of 20.00 would actually be 20,000,000 ohms, and a display of 1.456 would be 1,456,000 ohms. If the amount of resistance is higher than 20M ohms, the display will show the infinite indicator. This usually means there is an open in the circuit.

Voltage. A voltage reading on the DMM is very simple. The scales are usually 2V, 20V and 200V. The 2,000 scale is usually reserved for Vac, although some DMMs differ. On the 2Vdc scale the display would show up to 2.000Vdc. On the 20Vdc scale the display will be up to 20.00Vdc and on the 200Vdc scale the display will be up to 200.0Vdc. Be sure the meter is on the appropriate DC or AC voltage to test the circuit, and if you are unsure of the level of the voltage to be tested, start at the highest end (200Vdc) and work down. If you try to measure 200Vdc on the 2Vdc scale, you may damage the meter.

Circuit Breaker

A circuit breaker, fitted with alligator clips, is useful to bypass a fuse that keeps blowing. The circuit breaker will keep the current flowing through the circuit so that it may be checked for the cause of high current draw while protecting the circuit by cycling on and off.

Chapter 11

Crimping and Crimping Tools

Factory wiring harnesses take advantage of production-line manufacturing processes that the hot rodder does not have access to. In addition, the factories manufacture thousands of the same electrical system to fit a variety of models. Despite these advantages, a well thought out custom system will be far superior to a factory one for a number of reasons. By taking your time and working through each individual circuit, your system will be neat, easy to install and far easier to maintain than a factory harness that has been "customised" to fit your project. In so doing, you will need to make many connections and terminations, even on the various kits that are available in the market place. The most important of those tools is the crimping tool.

Soldering

Although soldered connections may seem the best for conductivity and strength, the electrolytic action of DC (the DC voltage reacting with chemicals, such as soldering flux), there are drawbacks. Besides time and inconvenience, the wire at the soldered end tends to crack under prolonged vibration. A better idea is a quality crimping kit, available from most auto parts stores.

Note: Don't try to insulate splices with ordinary plastic insulation tape. The acetic acid vapours corrode the copper wire. Use heat-shrink tubing.

Crimping Tools

There are two types of crimps and their associated crimping tool that are fundamental to most custom auto electrical systems and cost effective enough to include them in your inventory of tools:

- The AMP Terminal Crimper. This is a ratchet crimping tool available at most specialist auto parts outlets. They are for the insulated terminals, or

Pre Insulated Diamond Grip (PIDG) commonly known as AMP or Tyco Ring, Spade and Splice Terminals (**FIGURE 103** AMP Terminals and Ratchet Crimper).

Figure 103 AMP Terminals and Ratchet Crimper

• The Utilux/Positive Lock/Weatherpack Crimper. There are ratchet types and good quality hand crimpers for use with Weatherpacks and Utilux connectors, also known as Faston tabs and uninsulated connectors,

Crimping Insulated Terminals

To ensure your termination is strong, insulated and likely to stay that way, you not only need to know how to use the tools correctly, but you need to be able to recognise a good crimp. If you can reproduce one that looks like the ones that are on the factory wiring harnesses, you will have a good head start.

1. Strip the insulation. Don't strip away too much insulation and USE WIRE STRIPPERS (see **Figure 105** Wire Stripping).

2. Using the guide in Table 3 - **Wire Terminal Colour Codes**, you should be able to slip the stripped end of the wire into the insulated barrel of the terminal.

3. The bare end of the wire should slip nicely into the metal part of the terminal until the wire's insulation stops you from going any further.

tabs and uninsulated connectors,

The Ratchet Crimper is recommended, but the hand crimper will suffice for these kinds of terminals.

Figure 104 AMP Utilux (Positive Lock or Series 68) and Weatherpack Crimpers

4. Match the colour of the crimping jaws with the colour code in Table 3 - **Wire Terminal Colour Codes**.

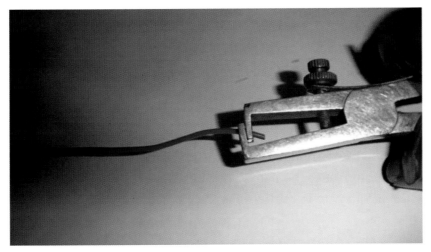

Figure 105 Wire Stripping

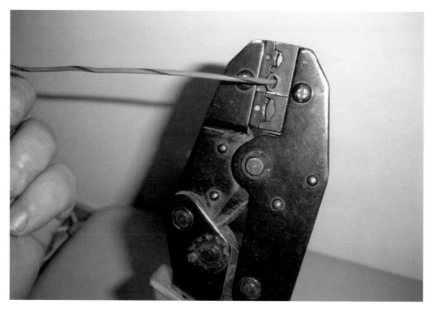

Figure 106 Match the Crimp Jaw with the Terminal

Crimping Uninsulated Terminals

Utilux, Positive Lock and Weatherpack terminals are more delicate than the insulated AMP type. Use these terminals and connectors in conjunction with an insulated carrier, such as relay sockets, one pin and multiple pin plugs and sockets and single or multi-pin weatherpacks.

WEATHER PACK CONNECTORS

CRIMP THE WEATHER SEAL TO THE INSULATION

YOU'LL NEED THE WEATHER PACK EXTRACTION TOOL

Figure 107 Uninsulated Terminal Carriers

The stripped wire should lay in the terminal barrel so that the bare end sits in the bottom half of the barrel and the insulation sits in the top half (see **Figure 108** Sit the Wire in the Terminal).

5. Selecting the correct size jaw, make the crimp in the bottom (uninsulated) half.

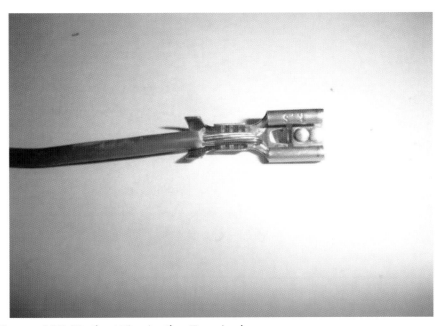

Figure 108 Sit the Wire in the Terminal

6. Make the crimp on the insulated part of the wire (top half of the terminal) then the uninsulated section.

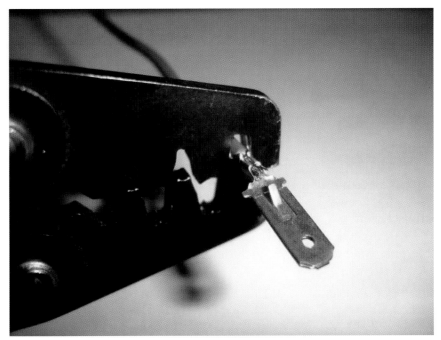

Figure 107 Make a Crimp on the Insulated Section for Grip

Chapter 12

Troubleshooting

The following paragraphs describe various troubleshooting techniques for different sections of your auto electrical project. The descriptions are of a technical nature, and are described here to give you some food for thought should there be a potential problem with a hybrid/custom auto electrical/ electronic system. Most of the descriptions have been sourced from professional automotive technicians, automotive workshop manuals, on-line discussions and information made available on various Internet sites dedicated to automotive topics. It is divided into these broad sections:

• Wiring Problems, including:

• Isolating Wiring Problems

• Circuit Defects

• Starting System Problems, including:

• Battery Failure

• Charging System Problems, including:

• Symptoms

• System Checks

• Diagnosing Electronic Ignition Systems

• Engine Management Systems, including:

• Preliminary Checks and Engine Preparation

- Trouble Codes

- Sensor Troubleshooting

Wiring Problems

Automotive wiring problems can be difficult to diagnose given the over-whelming complexity of today's automotive electronic systems. This section takes a generic look at all cars except for those with positive grounds.

Wiring problems almost always are due to two things:

- You forgot something

- You got careless

If you suspect a wiring problem, go over your system and check that the following applies:

- No wires have been run through a metal hole without some sort of insulator between the metal and the wire's insulation. If not, check to see if the wire has chaffed and shorted to ground.

- All wires are correctly sized for the circuit.

- No wires have been twisted together to form a connection, especially component power wiring.

Wire nuts are a LAST RESORT or EMERGENCY!

- Wires have not been routed close to a heat source such as the exhaust.

- Wires have not been routed close to turning hardware like fans or drive shafts.

- Your wiring is neatly bundled with cable ties and convoluted (split plastic) tubing and secured with insulated clamps.

- Grounds. You have a grounding strap from the engine to the chassis to the body to the battery negative.
  Some devices in your car such as lights and dashboards will have a separate ground wire. Trunk mounted batteries have the battery cables

(both of them) extending all the way to the engine (starter motor for the positive, ground point on the engine for negative).

- You have a fuse for each circuit and at least one fusible link or maxi fuse for the main supply to your fuse panel. If you have all these things in place, you will be able to easily diagnose wiring problems, find the problem quickly and fix it.

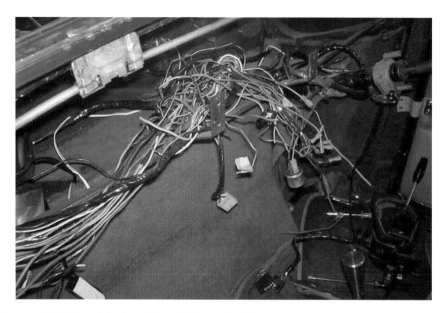

Figure 110 Troubleshooting Wiring Problems

Isolating Wiring Problems

Every custom wiring job is different, but there are a few standard procedures that you can follow to isolate a problem to a particular area. It may not be the wiring at fault, but a fan motor, switch, relay, or some other component that has failed. Nevertheless, you can easily establish which circuit is at fault by pulling one fuse at a time until the symptoms disappear.

Once you have established which circuit is at fault, and you have determined that it is in the wiring, conduct continuity and insulation tests on the wires supplying power and grounds in accordance with the tests described in **Chapter 10** Tools and Test Equipment

Circuit Defects

This section describes the defects which may occur in electrical circuits in a car. Although there are many different defects which may arise as a result of a diverse combination of criteria, they are all derived from the basic defects described here.

Circuit Defect Descriptions

Electrical circuits problems are a result of the following defects:

• open circuits;

• short circuits;

• grounds; or

• excessive voltage drop.

These will cause the circuit to operate improperly. Understanding the different types of circuit defects will allow the user to isolate the problem quickly and make the necessary decisions to effect the repairs to the circuit.

Open Circuit. If the continuity of the circuit is broken, the circuit is open. An open circuit is like turning off the switch, and no current flows (refer **Figure 111** Open Circuit). The open can be on either the live (positive) side or the ground side of the circuit.

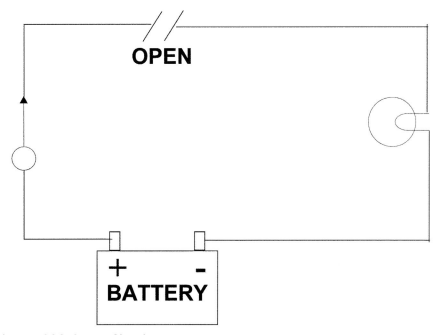

OPEN

+ −
BATTERY

Figure 111 Open Circuit

Short Circuit. An example of a typical short circuit can often be found in a well used ignition coil. The windings within a coil are insulated from each other. If the insulation breaks down, a conductor-to-conductor contact is made between the turns. This results in some of the windings being bypassed, reducing the number of windings in the coil through which electricity would normally flow. The efficiency of the coil is decreased and, because the current bypasses a portion of the normal circuit resistance, current flow increases and excess heat is generated.

Another example of a short circuit is if the insulation of two adjacent wires breaks down (refer **Figure 112** Short Circuit Problems). If the short is between points A and B, light 1 would be on all the time. If the short is between points B and C, light 2 would illuminate with light 1 when the switch for light 1 was closed.

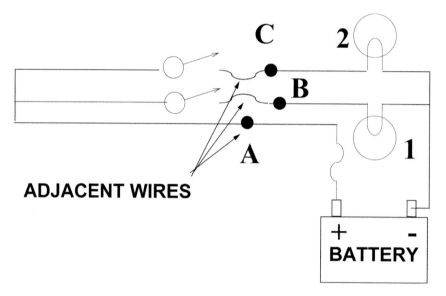

Figure 112 Short Circuit Problems

Grounds. A grounded circuit is much like a short in that the load component is bypassed. In a grounded circuit (see **Figure 113** Grounds), an insulation breakdown occurs (or, in this case, some idiot dropped a spanner across the conductors) that allows the current to flow to ground before reaching the load component, in this case, a lamp. For example, if the wire leading to the tail light has an insulation breakdown that allows the wire to touch the body or frame, current will flow to ground at this point and return to the source. A grounded circuit may cause excessive current to be drawn from the battery, and has the potential to be very damaging to many components in the electrical system. If the correct fuse is installed in the circuit of the system, the excessive current draw will cause the fuse to blow. The open fuse will prevent the flow of electricity, protecting the circuit from the increased current.

A grounded circuit can be checked by removing the fuse and connecting a test lamp in series across the fuse connections. If the lamp lights, the circuit is grounded.

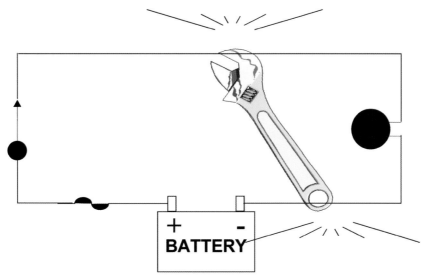

Figure 113 Grounds

The first ground point in any car is the alternator, because every car's electrical system 'sees' the alternator first. Be careful that there are more ground paths to the block or head than through the adjustment bolt of the alternator. It there are none, the ground is through the adjustment bolt, the fixed bolt and the screws through the front half of the casing. Any corrosion on the bolts that hold the alternator together, or anything else that interferes with contact between the halves is a potential for some serious grounding problems. Watch for sparks when connecting a jumper from the engine to the back of the alternator. This is a sure fire test that there needs to be some more work done to eliminate grounding problems around the engine bay.

One of the biggest problems for customisers is add-on accessories. For example, it would be catastrophic to locate a ground for the fog lights at the oxygen sensor wire. It is a black wire, and it is not unusual to assume it is a ground. This will throw the whole system off.

Never ground an accessory to the computer

Excessive Voltage Drop. Voltage drop occurs across load components in electrical circuits, and this includes places where it is not required. Corrosion, poor grounding and defective components causes the applied voltage to be used up in other points of the circuit rather than that required by the load component. The effect is that the load component, with reduced voltage applied, operates less efficiently. An example would be a tail light circuit with a load component (light bulb) rated at 50 watts. To be fully effective, this bulb must draw 4.2 amperes at 12 volts, so the full 12 volts must be available to the bulb. If resistance is present at other points in the circuit, some of the 12 volts will be dropped. With less voltage being available to the light bulb, the bulb will illuminate with less intensity.

The maximum Voltage drop across any connection in a points/carburettor powered vehicle is about 0.2Vdc (200 mV). For computer controlled (ECM) installations, there should be no more than 0.1Vdc per individual wire, ground, connection or switch. The following upper limits are recommended:

- 200mV for a length of wire or cable,

- 300mV for a switch,

- 100mV for a ground, and

- 50mV for a sensor connection.

Excessive voltage drop may appear on either the insulated or grounded return side of a circuit. It may also be present in both. To test for voltage drop, the circuit must be active (current flowing).

The source voltage must be correct before voltage drop readings can be valid. Whenever voltage drop is suspected, both sides of the circuit must be checked.

Poor grounds and bad connections cause voltage drops. At 90% of rated voltage, an electric motor produces only 81% of its normal power output, a lamp a mere 70% of its candlepower.

Voltage is always looking for an easy way out!

Doubling the current without increasing the wire diameter increases heat by up to four times. The potential energy that each electron loses by travelling across the voltage drop is expended from the conductor in the form of heat.

There can be a big difference between hot resistance and cold resistance in metal conductors. Resistance rises with temperature, so a lamp measuring one ohm may have many times that when the filament is glowing. If you had used one ohm in your calculations, the current reading you actually got would not be consistent with the formulas. Alternatively, the resistance of non-metallic conductors (such as carbon) falls as temperature rises. This is the basic principle behind thermistors, among other things.

Starting System Problems

This section deals with starting system malfunctions, from a total lack of rotation to slow cranking. All cases must be treated immediately, because the entire electrical/electronic system will not tolerate these conditions for very long. The actual replacement of the parts involved doesn't require any special skill, but finding the exact cause of the problem can sometimes be difficult. It is not uncommon to incorrectly diagnose a starting system problem and replace perfectly serviceable components unnecessarily. This section is intended to protect the user against embarrassing and expensive mistakes.

No Cranking. If the engine does not crank over, turn on the headlights. If they're dim or don't go on at all, the battery and/or the connections are probably at fault. The same is true in cases where the lights get noticeably dimmer when the ignition switch is turned to the Start position. If the headlights continue to shine brightly when you turn the key, there's an open circuit in the starting system somewhere.

Starting System Sounds. The first indication of starting system trouble is unusual noises during engine cranking. If the solenoid clicks once, but the starter doesn't turn, the battery and its cables should again be suspect, but a jammed engagement mechanism or a seized engine could be the problem. A chattering solenoid is either not getting sufficient current, or has a faulty hold-in winding.

Slow cranking may be the result of a high electrical resistance, a low battery, a bad starter motor or a tight engine. If slow cranking is accompanied by spurts of life, incorrect valve timing (caused by a broken or jumped camshaft drive belt, chain, sprocket, or gear) is a possible suspect.

If the starter motor spins freely but doesn't turn the engine, or there is an unpleasant grating, grinding noise, the starter has to come out so you can examine the pinion and flywheel/ flexplate teeth and the engagement (bendix) mechanism.

If you haven't isolated the offending component yet, it's time to check the battery.

Starter Drain Test. The best test for the condition of the starter motor is a starter current drain test. The simplest way to do this is to ground or disable the spark, then use an inductive ammeter around the cable.

Load Tester. A more comprehensive procedure, for those with access to the proper test equipment, involves a load tester, as follows:

1. Run the engine until it reaches normal operating temperature.

2. Disable the ignition.

3. Connect the Load Tester (load off). If using separate meters, put the carbon pile in series between the ammeter's negative lead and the battery.

4. Crank the engine for 10 seconds and note the battery voltage reading just before you stop.

5. Turn the variable resistor/carbon pile knob until you get the same voltmeter reading obtained in step 4.

6. At this point, the ammeter will indicate the starter's current draw.

If more than the specified current is being drawn, the possible trouble could be as follows:

*   a bad starter motor,

*   a cable shorting to ground or

*   high internal engine drag (if there is slow cranking when hot, the lube oil may be draining from the cylinder walls, possibly because flooding caused the fuel to wash the oil film away).

If the current drain is below specifications and the engine cranks slowly, the following are likely causes: high resistance in the cables (insufficient cable thickness, poorly done cable repair), poor engine ground, worn or pitted solenoid contacts, or the starter motor itself (slow hot cranking with low current drain may due to a missing starter/solenoid heat shield).

A related indication is a battery voltage reading that stays high (11Vdc or more) while the starter engages.

Voltage Drop. While the engine is cranking, voltage at the starter motor's + terminal should be the same as that at the battery + terminal. If not, there is an unwanted voltage drop between the battery and the starter motor. For example, if the battery dips to 11Vdc while the starter turns but only 7Vdc appears at the starter motor connection, there is a voltage drop of 4Vdc. The maximum allowable loss is 0.5Vdc.

Voltage Drop Testing. Further voltage drop testing in the starter circuit will detect unintended load in the form of resistance. The resultant voltage drop will show up on a DMM by detecting an electrical potential across the resistance (while the starter is cranking). Connect the DMM, scaled to accurately read up to 20Vdc, across the following points, in turn, and record any readings:

- Between the battery's positive post and the solenoid's battery terminal;

- Between the negative post and the starter motor housing;

- Between the solenoid's battery and motor terminals.

Any reading of over 0.3Vdc indicates excessive resistance somewhere in the circuit between the two points.

Starter Control. If, after the process of elimination has not solved the problem and the solenoid won't engage, check the voltage drop between the solenoid battery supply and the start switch terminals. If it's over 3.5Vdc, there is a starter control circuit problem. Isolate the problem area with the aid of a jumper wire to bypass the neutral or clutch safety switch, ignition switch, or related wiring. If the problem disappears when one of these components is taken out of the circuit, it's more than likely that the problem has been found.

Solenoid Failure. Measuring the voltage available at various points in the system is another important diagnostic procedure. For instance, at normal temperatures a typical solenoid will operate when it receives 8Vdc at its input terminals, or somewhat more if it's very hot. If more voltage than that is present, but the solenoid still fails to engage, the solenoid is the most likely component to have failed.

Starter Armature. It shouldn't take more than 8Vdc at the starter motor armature terminal to make the starter run. If more than that amount of voltage is present, but the motor won't spin, the most likely causes are bad brushes, windings or maybe the engagement mechanism is jammed. Either way, the starter must be removed for further examination.

Final Cause. Unfortunately, there's another possibility: a seized engine. Try to rotate the crankshaft using a socket and bar at the pulley or damper bolt. If it won't budge, the car is suffering from a much more serious ailment than a problem in the starting system.

Battery Failure
Whenever battery failure is suspected, perform some simple visual inspections as follows:

1. Check the case for cracks.

2. Check the electrolyte level in each cell.

3. Check the terminals for corrosion.

Corrosion
The action of the sulphuric acid reacting with the lead and copper leaves lead sulphate and copper sulphate deposits on the battery terminals. These deposits are an electrical resistance and cause voltage drops. If the deposits are bad enough, the resistance can increase to a level where there is insufficient voltage available for the starter motor to crank the engine.

Overcharging
One of the most common causes of early battery failure is overcharging. If the charging system is supplying a voltage level over 15.5Vdc, the plates may become warped from the excess heat that is generated because the charge rate is too high. Overcharging also causes the active material to precipitate and fall from the plates.

Undercharging
On the other hand, if the charging system does not produce enough current to keep the battery charged, the lead sulphate can harden. Remember, the recharging process converts the sulphate on the plates, so if there is an undercharging condition, the sulphate is not converted and it will harden. If this happens, the hardened lead sulphate acts as a resistance to the flow of electricity trying to charge the battery.

Vibration
Vibration is another common cause of battery failure. If the battery is not secure and there is excessive vibration, the plates will shed their precipitant before the electrical charge can convert it. If enough material is shed, the sediment at the bottom of the battery can create an electrical connection between the plates. The shorted cell will produce no voltage, resulting in a battery that will have only 10.5Vdc across the terminals, not enough voltage, in most cases, to drive the starter motor. To prevent this problem, make sure the battery is securely clamped using proper hold-down fixtures.

Capacity Test

To conduct a quick and simple Battery Capacity Test, carry out the following steps:

1. Connect a voltmeter across the battery.

2. Disable the ignition. For a points/coil system, remove the coil wire from the cap and ground it. For electronic systems, locate the wire which will stop the primary voltage feed when disconnected, or disable the fuel injection.

3. Crank the engine for 15 seconds.

4. If the voltage stays above 9.6Vdc, the battery is good.

WEAR YOUR GOGGLES OR GLASSES!

Charge Level. The charge level is determined by the concentration of acid inside the battery. The stronger the concentration of acid in the electrolyte, the higher the specific gravity of the solution and the higher the state of charge.

Checking State of Charge. On batteries with removable caps, state of charge can be checked with a "hydrometer". Some hydrometers have a calibrated float to measure the specific gravity of the acid solution while others simply have a number of coloured balls. On the kind with a calibrated float, a hydrometer reading of 1.265 (corrected for temperature) indicates a fully charged battery, 1.230 indicates a 75% charge, 1.200 indicates a 50% charge, 1.170 indicates a 25% charge, and 1.140 or less indicates a discharged battery. On the kind that use floating balls, the number of balls that float tells you the approximate level of charge. All balls floating would indicate a fully charged battery, no balls floating would indicate a dead or fully discharged battery.

Some sealed batteries have a built-in hydrometer to indicate the state of charge. The charge indicator only reads one cell, and does not necessarily indicate the average charge for all battery cells. Typically, a green dot means the battery is 75% or more charged. No dot (a dark indicator) means the battery is low and should be recharged before it is returned to service or tested further. A clear or yellow indicator means the level of electrolyte inside has dropped too low, and the battery should be replaced. On sealed batteries without a built-in charge indicator, the state of charge can be determined by checking the battery's base or open circuit voltage with a digital voltmeter or multi meter. This is done by touching the meter leads to the positive and negative battery terminals while the ignition key is off. A reading of 12.6Vdc to 12.7Vdc indicates a fully charged battery; 12.45Vdc is 75% charged, 12.24Vdc is 50% charged, and 12.06Vdc is 25% charged.

Recharging the Battery

Do not attempt to recharge a battery with low (or frozen) electrolyte! Higher levels of hydrogen are produced inside the battery and may be ignited by a spark.

The charging system should be capable of recharging the battery if it is not fully discharged. Thirty minutes or so of normal driving should be sufficient to bring the charge level up to normal. If the battery is completely dead or extremely low, it should be recharged with a fast or slow charger. Driving with a fully discharged battery will cause the charging system to work over-time to fill the battery with volts, which will increase the risk of overtaxing and damaging your vehicle's charging system. Disconnect one or both battery cables from the battery before charging it with a charger. This will eliminate any risk of damage to your vehicle's electrical system or its onboard electronics.

Positive (red) to positive and negative (black) to negative

Jump Starting Procedures

To minimize the risk of damage to your car's electrical system, carry out the following procedure when jump starting.

Do not smoke. Wear eye protection

1. Make sure the vehicles are not touching (contact could provide an unwanted electrical path).

2. Turn the engines off.

3. Connect the red jumper cable from the positive (+) post or terminal on the "good" battery to the positive post or terminal on the low or dead battery in the other vehicle.

4. Connect the black jumper cable from the negative (-) post or terminal on your good battery to a solid ground on the other vehicle.

> **DO NOT make the final jumper connection directly to the low or dead battery itself**

The reason for not doing this is because the final jumper connection usually produces a spark. Making the final connection away from the battery will minimize any danger of an explosion by keeping the spark well away from the battery.

5. Make sure the ground connection on the vehicle with the low or dead battery provides a good electrical contact. Use an unpainted metal surface like an engine bracket or a frame member.

6. Make sure the cables do not touch each other and that the cables are clear of the fan and pulleys on both vehicles.

7. Start the engine in the vehicle with the good battery.

8. Run the engine at fast idle for several minutes before attempting to start the vehicle with the low or dead battery. This will allow the charging system to pump some life into the other battery lessening the drain on the good battery and charging system.

9. As soon as the vehicle with the dead battery starts, disconnect the battery cables. The vehicle should then be run or driven at least thirty minutes to recharge the low or dead battery. Additional charging time may be required depending on the battery's condition and state of charge.

If the vehicle does not crank or cranks slowly, recheck the jumper connections. If it still doesn't crank, the problem may be something other then the battery (such as a bad starter, solenoid, battery cable connection or internal engine problem). If the vehicle cranks normally, but refuses to start, it may have an ignition, fuel or mechanical problem.

Do not crank the starter more than thirty seconds at a time. Allow the starter to cool for about two minutes before cranking the engine again. Continuous cranking of the starter motor causes overheating of the windings and subsequent failure. Continuous cranking will also drain power from your good battery and possibly damage the charging system.

Many battery problems are a result of failure of the Charging System.

Charging System Problems

This section deals with the problems and cures for the Charging System circuitry. For details of what components make up the charging system, refer Chapter 4 **The Charging System**.

Symptoms

Symptoms of charging system illness include the following:

- a low or dead battery.

- alternator noise.

- dim bulbs, and

- a charge indicator light that shines at the wrong time.

When any of these symptoms are present, it only makes sense to check the simplest things first. The fan belt, for instance. Do-it-yourselfers sometimes replace alternators and/or regulators when the problem was simply that the alternator wasn't getting sufficient mechanical input. Suspect slippage if the trouble only occurs when it's raining or at high speeds. Check belt tension - it shouldn't flex more than 1/2".

Next, check for corroded battery terminals, broken wires and evidence of short circuits (burnt insulation, hardened or crystalised grommets, discoloured insulation etc). Don't burn out several alternators in a row because a missing grommet or a gap in insulation made them work themselves to death.

The main fusible link is sometimes overlooked (refer **Fusible Links** in Chapter 2 **Custom Auto Electrical - the Basics**). If it's blown, find out what caused the short, correct the problem, then replace the link.

Don't use ordinary wire.

Note: Be alert for bad grounds and other potentially troublesome connections.

If you suspect that a short circuit is draining the battery, make sure all accessories are off (remember to close the doors so the courtesy light won't be on), remove the negative cable from the battery and connect a test light between the battery post and the cable clamp. If the light glows, remove fuses until it goes out, which will isolate the leaky circuit.

In the case of a no-charge condition, touch a screwdriver blade to the back of the alternator with the key on. Since there's no residual magnetism as in an old-fashioned DC generator, a strong attraction will let you know right off that the field circuit is complete.

Before you go any further, make sure the battery is in a reasonable state of health so you can trust the results of your investigations.

See what the idiot light or ammeter tells you. In a basic design, the charge indicator light circuit supplies the alternator with initial field current when the key is turned on, so the bulb glows. Once the engine is started, the field circuit is completed, and it winks out. If the light doesn't go on with the key, suspect a bad bulb or socket, an open in the regulator or field circuit, or maybe a shorted positive diode. If the bulb is lit with the ignition off, it's a good bet that one of the positive rectifiers is shorted, which will allow the battery to discharge to ground.

The most common problem indication you'll get, of course, is when it stays lit with the engine running, which should start you on the search for the component that's interfering with the charging system.

System Checks

Using a voltmeter, perform a basic quick check to find out for sure if the system is charging or not. Simply connect the leads to the alternator output stud and ground or across the battery terminals, check the reading with the engine off, then start it up and see if it rises (with some regulators, you'll have to rev it to 1,500 rpm or so to get the regulator to kick in). Readings will vary, but expect to see somewhere between 13.5Vdc and 14.5Vdc.

Note: If voltage continues to rise above the upper limit, the regulator is faulty.

Testing Alternator Charge Rate

If you suspect there is a problem in the charging system of your project, there are a few simple tests that can determine the source of your problem.

Charge rate at idle:

1. With the engine off, measure the battery voltage AT THE BATTERY with a DMM.

2. Discharge the battery a little by turning on the headlights, fans, etc to draw a large load from the battery.

3. Let the voltage drop to just below 12V, for example, 11.6V. Turn off everything and let the battery settle to 12V.

4.   Start the car.

5.   Turn all accessories (loads) on again and give the motor a short rev to ensure the regulator is turned on and charging.

6.   Measure battery voltage again. There should be at least 13V at idle.

Charge rate at cruise:

7.   Hold the revs a little higher and the voltage should rise to 13.8V to 14.8V maximum. This indicates regulation and a peak current output at off idle/cruise engine speeds.

Peak Voltage regulation:

8.   While holding a high idle, get an extra pair of hands to turn off all accessories.

9.   The voltage should not rise beyond 14.8V. This indicates peak voltage regulation.

If the charge rate in the above tests is poor, conduct the test again, but measure the voltage AT THE ALTERNATOR. You may find 14V at the alternator B+ output but there may only be 12.8V at the battery positive. You will get some loss over the wire from the alternator to the battery, but it should me no more than 1 volt maximum.This difference should reduce as the battery charges and draws less current but if the test fails, it indicates a poor connection. Check the following:

•   Fusible link to the battery from the alternator.

•   Connectors. Plastic connectors become brittle with age and may crack and let in moisture. A bad connection creates resistance which creates heat.

•   Charge cable heat. High rating alternators (85A +) will typically have a warm charging cable, but should not get hot. Replace the cable if it is discoloured or the insulation is brittle.

•   Check the battery terminals. The voltage drop may be at the point where the wire attaches to the battery terminal or at the starter motor.

•   Alternator ground. Check the alternator's ground and the engine to chassis to battery negative cable(s).

Ripple Voltage

Ripple voltage is the leakage of Alternating Current (AC) into the electrical system due to a faulty diode, field winding or a combination of minor defects. While unnoticeable in points/ carb systems, ripple voltage can have a catastrophic effect on solid state devices. Modern electronic devices such as computers, ECMs and ECUs need a straight, flat DC level or they will exhibit some very strange symptoms. It's a good idea to check for ripple voltage whenever you're presented with a problem that seems to have no answer. Opinions vary as to the maximum acceptable AC in the charge circuit. If possible, look up the manufacturer's recommendation.

Of course, you have to know how to ascertain the amount of ripple present, and there are several ways. High-tech alternator testers include a ripple measurement feature or you can use your Digital Multi-Meter (DMM) across the battery terminals and simply switch to the AC volts function.

Internal Checks

If your tests prove that the alternator is the problem, you can either replace it with a new or remanufactured unit, or disassemble it to find out what's wrong.

If the alternator has seen many miles of service, this may be a simple matter of worn-out brushes. They should have at least 0.2" of carbon left. Test stator resistance by connecting an accurate ohmmeter between two of the three leads, switching between leads until all the leads have been tested against each other. A typical Bosch unit should produce a reading of about 0.15 ohm. Stator insulation should be checked by looking for continuity on the 1,000 ohm scale between any lead and the metal ring. Resistance should be infinite. Rotor resistance is taken across the slip rings. Expect a reading of 3.4 to 3.75 ohms. To check rotor insulation, connect the meter between one of the slip rings and the claw poles. Again, you should get a reading of infinity.

Sometimes alternators can partially fail. In the back of every alternator is the diode stack which converts the alternators AC output to DC. If one or more of these diodes fail, the alternator's capability to output sufficient current will be reduced. It may continue to produce some current, but not enough to keep the battery fully charged, especially at idle or low speed. Diodes are checked by looking for good continuity in one direction and none in the other, or by the use of a special tester.

> **Always disconnect the battery before unhooking the wiring on the alternator.**

Diagnosing Electronic Ignition Systems

The complexity and delicacy of many Electronic Ignition systems means that some tests can only be carried out with sophisticated test equipment. In addition, a greater understanding of electronics will be required in order to chase down a fault to component level. Fortunately, these systems are extremely reliable and rarely need such treatment. With this in mind, the systems we will deal with here will be the Pulse Generator type (refer **Magnetic Pulse**, Chapter 5 **Ignition Systems**) and **Hall Effect** type (refer **Hall Effect Distributor**, Chapter 5 **Ignition Systems**).

There are many different species of Electronic Ignitions and Electronic Ignition Conversion Kits available. To provide details of troubleshooting techniques for all of them would require several volumes, therefore we will restrict ourselves to the basics and assume the reader will identify the appropriate connections from their workshop manuals, installation instructions and/or owner handbooks.

Testing Ignition Hall Sensor

In order to test the output of the Hall Sensor, a good DMM is required so that the sensor output of between 400mV (0.4Vdc) and 11.0Vdc can be accurately read. The procedure is fairly simple, and requires some knowledge of the wiring between the ECU and the Distributor, which can be easily obtained via the installation manual or factory service manual. The procedure is as follows (refer **Figure 114** Hall Sensor Connections):

1. Unfasten clips and remove distributor cap.

> **Do not allow clips to fall back into the distributor where they may damage the Hall Sensor**

2. Visually inspect rotor trigger vanes, Hall sensor and ECU cable for evidence of any damage or crimping of wires.

3. Turn distributor shaft by hand and ensure vanes do not come into contact with Hall sensor.

4. Connect a Voltmeter between the Hall Output connection and chassis ground.

5. Switch Ignition ON.

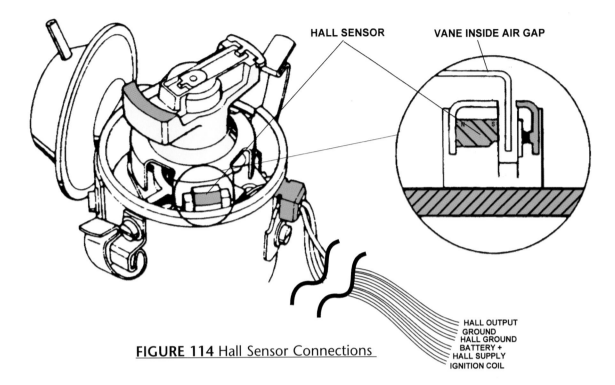

HALL SENSOR   VANE INSIDE AIR GAP

HALL OUTPUT
GROUND
HALL GROUND
BATTERY +
HALL SUPPLY
IGNITION COIL

FIGURE 114 Hall Sensor Connections

6. With the Vane inside the air gap (as illustrated in Figure 114 - **Hall Sensor Connections**) the Voltmeter should read approximately 11Vdc.

7. Switch Ignition OFF.

8. Turn the distributor shaft until the Trigger Vane is OUTSIDE of the air gap.

9. Switch Ignition ON.

10. The Voltmeter should measure approximately 500mV (0.5Vdc) or less.

11. Switch Ignition OFF.

Should the Voltmeter readings fall outside of these measurements, the Hall Sensor cannot be considered reliable, and should be replaced.

Testing Magnetic Pulse Generator

There are many varieties of Pulse Generator type ignition systems and conversion kits. As with the Hall Effect type, all makes and models cannot be covered in this book, so a generic application is described here. Armed with the appropriate user manuals, installation instructions and workshop manuals, the average automotive enthusiast should be capable of testing their Electronic Ignition system for serviceability.

Preliminary Checks.

When ignition system problems are suspected, the following procedures should take place:

- Visual Check

- Reluctor Air Gap Check

- Voltage Supply Test

- Pulse Module Test

Visual Check. Visually inspect all cables and wires at the coil, distributor and spark plugs for cracks, damage and discoloration.

Reluctor Air Gap Check. Carry out the Reluctor Air Gap Check and Adjust as follows:

1. Check the air gap between the reluctor tooth and the pick up coil (refer FIGURE 115 **Reluctor/Pick-up Air Gap Adjustment**). The correct gap should be in accordance with the manufacturer's specifications (approximately 0.006" to 0.009" or 0.15mm to 0.25mm).

2. If gap is inconsistent with the specifications, loosen the pick-up coil hold down screw.

3. Insert a non magnetic feeler gauge of the correct thickness between the reluctor tooth and the pick-up coil.

4. Adjust the air gap until the feeler gauge is snug.

5. Tighten down hold down screw.

6. Rotate reluctor at another point around its peripheral and adjust gap again.

7. Ensure the vacuum advance mechanism does not interfere when engaged.

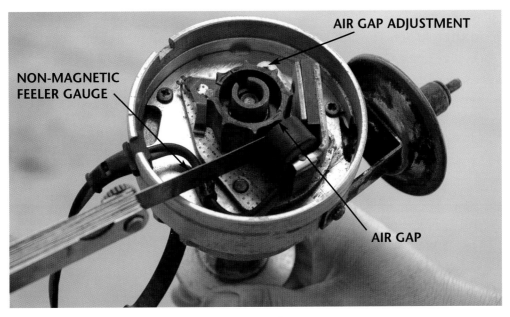

FIGURE 115 Reluctor Pickup Air Gap Adjustment

Voltage Supply Test. Electronic Ignition systems require stable voltage supplies with good grounding in order to function properly. If the supply to the ECU is intermittent or subject to high resistance due to corrosion, then the trigger pulse to the coil will be weak and of no use. To test for adequate voltage to the ECU, carry out the following measurements:

1. Ensure ignition is OFF.

2. Unplug connector from the ECU.

3. Connect the Negative lead of the Voltmeter (set to read Battery Voltage) to a good ground.

4. Connect the Positive lead of the Voltmeter to the supply lead (usually a RED wire).

5. Switch Ignition ON.

6. The Voltmeter should indicate Battery Voltage (give or take 1.0Vdc). A correct reading indicates that the supply for the ECU is sufficient. An abnormal reading MUST be corrected before resuming. Check the ignition supply circuits, battery terminals, connectors, grounds etc.

7. Switch Ignition OFF.

Pulse Module Test. The Pick-up Coil in the Distributor can be tested with a good Ohm Meter. The test which follows checks insulation of the Pick-up Coil. Proceed as follows:

1. With the connector from the distributor to the ECU unplugged (a two wire connector) ensure ignition is OFF.

2. Connect one lead of the Ohm meter to Ground.

3. Connect the other lead of the Ohm meter to one of the connectors coming FROM the distributor.

4. Observe a reading of INFINITY (an Open Circuit, or maximum resistance).

5. Measure the resistance of the other connection. Observe a reading of INFINITY. Any deviation from the readings indicates that the magnetic pick-up is unserviceable and must be replaced.

Any further testing of the ECU and the Pick-up and Reluctor may be necessary if problems still exist. These further tests should be carried out in accordance with the appropriate manuals, as they are more specific than that which could be detailed in this book.

Engine Management Systems

Transient voltages from early style timing lights and battery chargers may destroy delicate semi-conductors in the ECU/ECM. Always disconnect battery terminals when charging the battery. Check with the manufacturer of the timing light to ensure compatibility with electronic ignition systems. Transient voltages may also trigger the ECU at random.

Sensors inform the ECM (Electronic Control Module) of the engine's digital environment. Based on this input and the commands embedded in the EPROM, the computer makes decisions and issues commands to various actuators, such as solenoids, injectors, stepper motors, etc., which make adjustments to such things as a/f mixture, spark timing, idle speed, and other settings to ensure maximum operational efficiency. ON/OFF functions such as canister purge and torque converter clutch lockup are also controlled. If the information received is faulty or interrupted, engine efficiency and performance deteriorate rapidly.

For the most part, self-diagnostics, a scan tool, or an engine analyser can identify a faulty sensor that maybe out of range or entirely inoperative, but the problem may be elsewhere in the circuit or a related condition could return false readings. Replacing the sensor without ensuring that the old one is faulty is wasting time and money. This section intends to include tests and clarify operational parameters to minimise such "seat-of-the-pants" troubleshooting. The focus is on sensors, actuators and all points in between, however a full system check is necessary to provide a starting point in the evaluation of electronically controlled engine diagnostics.

Preliminary Checks and Engine Preparation

To make an accurate diagnosis of performance problems on electronically controlled engines, it is necessary to approach the procedure as if the engine were not equipped with such a system. In the days before electronic engine management systems, it was routine to perform some basic tests and observations before determining a diagnostic routine. The arrival of engine management systems has not changed the basic structure of the engine, so all the old basic checks and inspections still apply. Also, the self test diagnostics do not have the ability to locate problems not directly involving the electronic engine management systems.

Visual Checks

Perform the following visual checks before running any diagnostics:

1. Turn OFF all electrical loads (radio, lights, air conditioning etc) and close doors.

2. Check that the air cleaner and ducting are free of obstructions. Remove, if necessary, to perform this step.

3. Check all engine vacuum hoses for correct routing.

4. Ensure all engine vacuum connections are clean and tight. Check also for cracked, pinched or broken hoses and fittings.

5. Inspect all electrical/electronic system wiring harnesses, terminals and connections. Push, pull, shake, or wiggle the harness while making these checks.

6. Check for proper matching of male/female harness connectors.

7. Check all connectors and terminals to ensure they are all properly seated.

8. Check for corrosion in connector terminals.

9. Check for partially broken or frayed wires, particularly at the connectors.

10. Check for shorting between wires.

> *Note: It may be necessary to disconnect or disassemble a connector to carry out some of these checks*

11. Check distributor cap, rotor and internal components for damage, wear or corrosion.

12. Shake the PCV valve to make sure it is still operational.

13. Examine all sensors and actuators for signs of physical damage.

14. Ensure oil filler cap is secure (some turbo charged engines will run rough if the oil cap is loose).

15. Check engine coolant level and condition.

Engine On Checks

The following diagnostic routines will be necessary before running any further on board diagnostics:

1. Check spark plugs for correct heat range and wires.

2. Start the engine.

> **Apply parking brake, transmission in park (or neutral) before running the engine.**

3. Check that fuel system delivery pressure is within specifications.

4. Verify that base ignition timing (timing without the engine management system) is in accordance with recommended specifications.

5. Test the ignition coil output (ensure there is a spark).

6. Check for manifold vacuum leaks.

7. Carry out the procedures, where possible, to check for camshaft timing, lifter and valve operation, piston and rings operation.

8. Bring the engine up to normal operating temperature until the thermo stat opens.

9. On engines so equipped, ensure the electric fan comes on.

10. Check upper radiator hose pressurises and heats up.

11. Check exhaust manifold for leaks.

12. Check O2 sensor and vacuum connection for leaks.

If the engine is mechanically sound and the sensor itself checks out, the source of the complaint is most likely grounding, a broken or frayed wire, a loose or corroded connection, or, on rare occasions, a faulty computer.

A variety of symptoms can be expected when one of the sensors or its wiring breaks down. GM troubleshooting guides available to service technicians and published in workshop manuals say the engine will stall and die. Bosch systems issue documentation to suggest ailments such as starting problems both hot and cold, hesitation, stalling (especially under load),
rough idle, and low power output are reasons to suspect sensors. Nissan gives stalling, poor idle, black smoke, and switching to the fail-safe mode (or limp back mode) as evidence of air flow meter problems (in some models, this mode will be manifested by the inability to exceed 2,000 rpm).

Generally, contamination of the sensing element, which slows response, will result in stumble. Regardless of those corporate opinions, the most logical effect of a bad signal (or no signal) is stalling, sagging, or miss-firing at transient throttle. If the sensor is too far out of range, it may cause the computer to go into limp-back mode, also known as Limited Operating Strategy (LOS). In other words, driveability and performance will be adversely affected.

Diagnosis of the exact cause can be difficult because there are many things which can cause those same symptoms. Ignition problems, compression, fuel pressure, etc. Something often overlooked is a ripped duct between the sensor and the throttle body, which admits unmeasured or "false" air and leans out the mixture. A PCV system with a valve that's stuck wide open or a
cracked hose can do the same thing, and a plugged air filter can cause trouble, too. Engine Management systems, fuel injection systems and the associated electronics are tardy and robust, and should never be the first areas to test when there is a problem. The trouble is most likely elsewhere because these systems are generally quite dependable.

That's not to say you'll never encounter a failed sensor. For instance, older GM MAF Sensors have a poor reliability record (the higher-frequency 10kHz Hitachi unit used on late model GM cars has a much lower failure rate).

Trouble Codes
In cases where the basics have checked out and you suspect the EMS, use the OBD (On-Board Diagnostic) function (if available) as your first step in

determining if the air flow/mass meter is the culprit. Until such time as Trouble Code standards are set, trouble codes will vary between different engine manufacturers, so the specific service information and trouble code listing for the engine you are working on will be a necessary tool to pinpoint problems and effect repairs.

It is important to realise that trouble codes alone will just point your diagnostic efforts in a general direction. They are not the final word on what is wrong. Some further troubleshooting will be required at component level before you can confidently replace the sensor or component and expect a repair to be successful.

Scan tools are expensive, but streamline the troubleshooting process. Errors in sensor calibration are magnified as air flow increases, so being able to test during road load can be helpful. In some cases, both the air flow value the ECM is using and the actual signal from the sensor can be displayed. If these two numbers don't match, the computer is probably reverting to a substitute value from memory because the MAF Sensor information is faulty.

Sensor Troubleshooting

Some sensors produce a voltage for use in the ECM (for example, O2 sensor, Coolant Temp Sensor, etc). Others act as a variable resistor (TPS, Powered O2 sensor, Neutral Safety Switch, etc), and require a supply from the ECM to modify and send back. The ECM compares the signal from the sensor with what it sent out and issues commands to actuators accordingly. There are three types of these sensors:

- potentiometers,

- thermistors, and

- pressure sensors.

Throttle Position Sensor

The TPS informs the ECM of throttle activity. The correct response to a signal which indicates a quick transition from cruise to wide open throttle, for instance, is to issue a command for a richer a/f mixture.

Inside the TPS, a potentiometer varies in resistance as the throttle is opened or closed. It is usually a three-wire device with terminals for supply voltage (connected to one end of the resistance element of the potentiometer), output to the ECM (the wiper of the potentiometer), and ground (the other end of the resistance element).

The most common symptom of a TPS problem is probably off-idle stumble, but other driveability troubles are common. If the TPS is sticking, it can cause high idle speed. The ECM will read a higher voltage than the specified minimum in the return wire. Because vacuum is high, the ECM reacts in accordance with a decelerating condition, enabling the Automatic Idle Stabilizer (AIS) motor. Hard starting is another symptom. If the TPS doesn't return to the 0Vdc (throttle OFF) position, the ECM will read it as full throttle and engage the clear-flood mode when cranking the engine. The injector pulses will be issued from the ECM to provide an a/f ratio of 20:1 to clear the flood condition that doesn't exist.

To test the TPS using a DMM, carry out the following steps:

1.   Disconnect the TPS connector.

2.   Re-connect all three terminals to the harness again using jumpers.

3.   Connect the DMM across the output and ground wires.

4.   Switch on the ignition.

5.   Observe the voltage reading. It should show approximately 0.25Vdc (typically) at curb idle.

6.   Open the throttle slowly.

7.   Observe an even rise in voltage to approximately 5Vdc.

The rise in voltage should be smooth and free of jumps. Any sudden dives in voltage also indicate a faulty TPS. If the test indicates anything but a smooth rise, replace the TPS.

Some TPSs are adjustable. Consult the workshop manual to ensure the TPS is adjusted correctly. Differences of 0.2Vdc will cause problems.

Engine Coolant Temperature Sensor

All Engine Management Systems include a Engine Coolant Temperature Sensor (CTS). The CTS is actually a thermistor, a resistor which changes resistance with temperature. There are two varieties:

• Positive Temperature Coefficient. In the Positive Temperature Coefficient (PTC) version, resistance increases as temperature increases.

• Negative Temperature Coefficient. The Negative Temperature Coefficient (NTC) version (the most common), works just the opposite - resistance decreases as heat increases.

Note: common GM range is 25,000 ohms at 0° F to 185 ohms at 210°f

For the NTC version, low coolant temperature produces a high resistance in the order of 100,000 ohms at -40° C while high temperatures cause a low resistance (around 70 ohms at 130° C/266°F). The ECM supplies the ECT sensor with 5Vdc and measures the voltage coming back. This tells the ECM what the engine's coolant temperature is. This information is used to control fuel management, idle air control, spark timing, EGR, canister purge and other engine operating parameters.

Note: it is easy to mistake the CTS for the thermoswitch controlling the radiator fan.

The ECT Sensor can lie. With a NTC version, too high a resistance will prevent the system from going into closed-loop or may cause the engine to run rich because the computer will believe the engine is colder than it really is. Too little resistance will cause lean stumble and surge problems.

If you should happen to have access to a scan tool, you can read coolant temp directly. A cold engine should obviously show about ambient, and a hot engine should produce a display of between 190 and 220 deg. F.

To test the ECT Sensor, check the actual coolant temperature with a thermometer or digital pyrometer then measure the resistance across the sensor's terminals with the DMM on Ohms. Check the reading against the manufacturer's specifications for resistance vs temperature. Typical readings are listed in Table 17 - **ECT Resistance Readings**.

Table 17 - ECT Resistance Readings

F	C	OHMS
210	100	185
160	70	450
100	38	1800
70	20	3400
40	4	7500
20	-7	13500
0	-18	25000
-40	-40	100700

Alternatively, start the engine and watch the reading. If you don't see at least a 200 ohm change within a minute, unscrew the sensor, clean it of the rust and scale which tends to accumulate in automotive cooling systems and try again. If you don't get that rapid resistance change, or your readings don't match specs, replace the ECT Sensor.

If the ECT Sensor checks out, but the symptoms are still present, find out if the system is responding to ECT input. With an NTS unit, you can unplug the sensor's lead to simulate the high resistance of super low temperatures. This will richen the mix, so idle should speed up. Jumping the two connector terminals should trick the computer into responding to high temperature conditions. The lean blend it commands may make a cold engine's idle roughen, or stall it out altogether.

If idle quality seems a little too obscure to base troubleshooting procedures on, you might want to read injector pulse width. This is easy with a scanner or oscilloscope, but you can do pretty well with the six-cylinder scale of a digital dwell meter tapped into an injector's ground wire. Pulse width should increase with the ECT Sensor disconnected and decrease with the terminals shorted.

Air Charge Temperature Sensor

Similar to the ECT the ACT can be checked in the same way. The following table (Table 18 - **ECT/ACT Measurements**) refers to the Ford ACT/ECT Temp vs Voltage vs Resistance readings for EEC 3, 4 and 5 systems.

Table 18 - ECT/ACT Measurements

F	C	V	K Ohms
248	120	0.28	1.18
230	110	0.36	1.55
212	100	0.47	2.07
194	90	0.61	2.80
176	80	0.80	3.84
158	70	1.04	5.37
140	60	1.35	7.60
122	50	1.72	10.97
104	40	2.16	16.15
86	30	2.62	24.27
68	20	3.06	37.30
50	10	3.52	58.75

Mass Air Flow Sensors

The Mass Air Flow Sensor (MAF, refer **Figure 116** Mass Air Flow Sensor) measures the weight of the air entering the engine. This information is used by the computer to supply the correct amount of fuel. Failure symptoms include hard starting, hesitation and stalling.

Figure 116 Mass Air Flow Sensor

Troubleshooting. On the vane type, reach inside the air box and move the flap through its range by hand. You should feel no binding or roughness. If it's a version that incorporates a fuel pump switch, make sure you hear the pump start when you push the vane (key on). Look for reference voltage input (that's 5Vdc) at the connector. Switch to the output contact and you should see the reading change smoothly as you push the flap to the fully-open position (in most cases, this will be a falling reading, but on Ford EEC-IV units it will rise. Look for 0.25Vdc closed and 4.50Vdc open).

Check for trouble codes and tap the sensor lightly. Replace the MAF Sensor if the engine stumbles when tapping the sensor. It makes sense to follow that with another quick check. Unplug the MAF sensor harness connector, then start the engine. If the engine runs appreciably better now, the sensor is faulty.

Some carmakers supply direct resistance specifications, too. As with a Throttle Position Sensor (TPS, refer **Figure 58** Throttle Position Sensor), you can check the condition of the potentiometer and any jumps in either voltage or resistance readings will mean replacement of the MAF sensor is necessary.

If you are fortunate enough to have a Digital Storage Oscilloscope, set it for two volts and 200 milliseconds per division, then tap into the sensor's signal wire. Any spikes or jagged areas in the pattern as you move the vane are cause for replacement.

With a Bosch hot-wire air mass sensor, make sure you have battery voltage at the appropriate terminal, then measure output. A reading of 2Vdc at idle that rises to almost 3Vdc at 3,500 rpm is typical. If you blow compressed air through it, you should see the voltage change.

If your DMM can measure frequency, you can use it to check AC, Hitachi, and any other MAF sensor unit which produces a signal based on frequency. Set the meter to read Hz or kHz, and connect its leads to the sensor's signal and ground wires. An ordinary AC MAF as found on a 2.8L Chevy V6 should show you about 45Hz at 1,000 rpm and 72Hz at 3,500. The high-frequency MAF Sensor of a late-model 3800 will read 2.9kHz and 5.0kHz at those same speeds. Record the readings at various rpm and compare them to the manufacturer's specifications. You should see a linear frequency rise with no dips or jumps as speed increases.

These high-frequency sensors may emit frequencies too high to read on a DMM, and the only alternative is to use an oscilloscope. Start out by setting amplitude to 5V per division. Changing the amplitude to one volt per division will give a different view of this signal. The timebase setting varies according to the range of the MAF Sensor (eg 0.1 milliseconds per division for a 10kHz Hitachi unit). You should see a square waveform with even frequency pulses. As engine speed and load is varied, the voltage and pulse width frequency should change smoothly and evenly. If you see any gaps in the pattern while tapping the sensor or driving the car, a new MAF Sensor is in order.

You can measure a Toyota/Lexus Karman-Vortex signal using an oscilloscope set at 1V and 10 milliseconds per division. At idle, you should get a nice even rectangular waveform.

Another test, which Lexus gives in the 1990 service manual, is that of resistance compared to temperature. Disconnect the sensor from the harness, then check the resistance between terminals THA and E2 of the meter's connector. At 68 deg. F., you should see 2-3 ohms. This should fall to 0.9-1.3 at 104 deg., and 0.4-0.7 at 140 deg. At the other end of the scale, 10-20 ohms is specified at -4 deg., and 4-7 ohms at 32 deg.

Mass Air Flow Sensor Diagnostic Sequence. When stalling, hesitation, missing on transient throttle or poor idle quality causes you to suspect the MAF Sensor, the diagnostic sequence can be summed up as follows:

1.   Ensure the basic preliminary checks have been carried out in accordance with the procedures outlined in Preliminary Checks and Engine Preparation.

2.   Get the trouble codes from the self-diagnostics, then erase the codes.

3.   Tap the MAF sensor to see if the idle changes (refer FIGURE 61 **Mass Air Flow Sensor**).

4.   Disconnect the MAF Sensor (key off) then see if the engine runs better.

5.   For Vane type MAF Sensors, move the flap to feel for binding and roughness.

6. Use a scan tool, Oscilloscope or DMM to catch any steps or jumps in the reading of the voltage, resistance or frequency signal.

7. Make the repairs, clear any new codes, and take a test drive to verify that the symptoms have been eliminated.

Manifold Absolute Pressure Sensor

Generally, MAP sensors can be checked using jumpers with contact taps so the component can stay in the system. On a typical application, there are three terminals;

*   ground (terminal A);

*   sensor output voltage (terminal B); and

*   reference voltage (terminal C).

After identifying the terminals, carry out the following steps:
1. Switch the ignition to ON (do not start).

2. Connect the DMM, switched to DC Volts, across terminals A and C.

3. Observe a reading of approximately 5Vdc.

4. Apply 10 in/Hg of vacuum to the MAP Sensor with a vacuum pump.

5. Observe a reading of approximately 2.3Vdc.

6. Apply 20 in/Hg of vacuum to the MAP sensor.

7. Observe a reading of approximately 1.0Vdc.

On a typical EFI system, 23 in/Hg or so at idle will kill the engine because it simulates decel, a mode in which the computer shuts down the injectors. Sometimes engines cut out intermittently while idling because of this function. This happens when the timing has been advanced so far that the throttle opening has to be smaller than normal to maintain proper idle speed. That, in turn, produces enough vacuum at idle to trigger injector cut-off.

Ice and condensation in the vacuum line can interfere with the MAP signal. Route it as necessary to eliminate low spots.

Detonation (Knock) Sensors

The Detonation Sensor (or Knock Sensor, as it is more commonly known) is screwed into the block or intake manifold where it listens for detonation (or "pinging"). When it detects detonation, it sends a warning signal to the computer, which responds by retarding the spark. As soon as this abnormal combustion condition subsides, the sensor stops generating the signal, and timing is once again advanced to the optimum setting. The most obvious problem is continuous pinging. You should never hear more than a momentary trace of this sound, however, problems such as reduced performance and poor fuel mileage could result if a false detonation signal is fooling the ECM into retarding the spark advance for no real reason.

A simple test can confirm that the Knock Sensor is doing its job. The test simulates the sound of detonation while observing the timing. Carry out the steps as follows:

1.   Connect a timing light.

2.   Start the engine.

3.   Shine the timing light at the timing marks

4.   Hold the engine at about 2,000 rpm (this is necessary because the system is disabled at idle).

5.   Tap on the area nearest the sensor with a wrench or extension bar.

6.   Observe that the timing retards. If no change occurs, change to a different tool and modify the force you're using. If that still doesn't make the spark advance drop back, check the wiring and connections before deter mining that the knock sensor itself or the ECM is at fault.

In cases where timing is retarding all the time, check for an over sensitive knock sensor or an internal engine noise that mimics engine spark detonation.

Oxygen Sensors

These procedures are described for self powered conventional sensors. Some new cars are using a heated O2 sensor (or 3- or 2-Wire O2 Sensor) that requires a 12Vdc supply for a heating element. In the case of these O2 sensors, ensure that the sensor output wire (usually the black wire) is used for the test, and the 12Vdc supply wire is untouched.

Many Oxygen sensors are replaced that are good to excellent. They routinely last 50,000 or more miles, and if the engine is kept in tune, can last the life of the car. Of course, there's always the possibility of mechanical damage such as a broken element or wire, but contamination is the primary cause for failure. Contamination is in the form of carbon, metals from burned lubricating oil or silicon introduced via gasket sealers or anti-freeze. These can all coat the platinum, which will make the sensor sluggish or altogether inoperative.

Testing O2 sensors in the engine. The engine must first be fully warm. If you have a defective thermostat, this test may not be possible due to a minimum temperature required for closed loop operation.

Proceed as follows:

1.   Attach the positive lead of a high impedance DC voltmeter to the Oxygen sensor output wire.

Analog voltmeters will not gve accurate results.

This wire should remain attached to the computer. You will have to probe the connection or use a jumper wire to get access.

2.   Attach the negative lead to a good clean ground on the engine block or accessory bracket. Heated sensors will have 12Vdc on one lead, ground on the other and the sensor signal on the third. If you have two or three wires, use a 15Vdc or higher scale on the meter and check the voltage on each connection until you know which is the sensor output wire.

3.   Turn the ignition key to ON

Do not start the engine.

4.   Observe a change in voltage on the meter. If not, check your connections.

5.   Check all leads to make sure they are not fouling any moving parts (fan, belts, pulleys, etc).

6.   Start the engine.

7.   Run the engine above 2000 rpm for two minutes to warm the O2 sensor and try to get into closed loop. Closed loop operation is indicated by the sensor showing several cross counts per second. It may help to rev the engine between idle and about 3000 rpm several times. The computer recognizes the sensor as hot and active once there are several cross counts.

8.   Observe the voltage oscillate above and below 0.45Vdc, usually between 0.2Vdc and 0.7Vdc - the O2 sensor is good.

A steady reading around 0.45Vdc indicates that the engine (and the O2 sensor) is not yet warm enough. Run the engine above 2000 rpm again and recommence the test.

Rich or Lean Mixture. A steady high above 0.45Vdc or a steady low below 0.45Vdc indicates a rich or lean mixture condition. If the reading is a steady low, richen the mixture by partially closing the choke (for carburettor engines) or feeding propane from an unlit propane torch into the intake (for injected systems). Alternatively, pull the vacuum hose to the fuel pressure regulator, which will increase pressure and richen the mixture. If the voltage now rises above 0.7 to 0.9, and you can change it at will by this method, the O2 sensor is usually good and something else is causing a lean mixture condition.

If the voltage is steady high, lean the mixture by creating a vacuum leak. Pull the PCV valve out of its hose or disconnect the power brake booster vacuum supply to allow air to enter. If this drives the voltage to 0.2Vdc to 0.3Vdc or less and you can control it at will by opening and closing the vacuum leak, the sensor is usually good. Find the cause of the lean mixture condition and re-connect all vacuum lines. If no variations to the voltage readings can be made, carry out the following steps:

1. Stop the engine.

2. Disconnect the sensor wire from the computer harness.

3. Re-attach the voltmeter to the sensor output wire.

4. Repeat the procedure.

If the sensor voltage does not change and the sensor and ground connections are good, heat the engine again. Repeat the test. If still no voltage or the voltage remains fixed, the O2 sensor is faulty or fouled.

A fouled O2 sensor will cause the engine to run rich. If no voltage is present and the engine has been running rich, carbon fouling is a possible cause. Run the engine at 3000 rpm for a few minutes, then carry out the procedures from Testing O2 sensors in the engine. If this fails, fix the cause of the rich mixture, replace the O2 sensor and re-test.

> **If the cause of the rich mixture problem is no rectified, the new sensor will fail.**

Testing O2 sensors on the workbench. With the O2 sensor removed from the engine, carry out the following test procedures:

1. Clamp the sensor in a vice, pliers or vice-grips.

2. Clamp the negative voltmeter lead to the case, and the positive to the output wire.

3.   Using a propane torch set to high, aim the inner blue flame tip to heat the fluted or perforated area of the sensor.

4.   Observe a DC voltage of at least 0.6Vdc within 20 seconds. If no voltage is present, the most likely cause is an open circuit internally or lead fouling. Replace the O2 sensor.

5.   Remove from flame.

6.   Observe a drop in voltage to under 0.1Vdc within four seconds. If the voltage does not drop within this time frame, it is likely that the O2 sensor is silicone fouled. Replace the O2 sensor.

7.   Re-apply heat for two full minutes

8.   Observe that there is no significant drop in voltage. Sometimes the internal connections will open circuit under heat. This is the same a loose wire and the O2 sensor must be replaced. If the sensor quickly switches from high to low as the flame is applied and removed, the sensor is good.

Ford Oxygen Sensor Test. This test can be carried out using a digital Voltmeter. Proceed as follows:

1.   Hook the DMM to the sensor's signal wire.

2.   Set the voltage scale to read around 1.0Vdc Max.

3.   If the oxygen sensor is heated (has more than one wire), make sure that battery voltage and ground are available for the heater element.

4.   Warm the sensor by running the engine at about 2,000 rpm for a couple of minutes.

5.   Create rich and lean conditions, and monitor the sensor's response. This can be done by adding fuel (propane works well) to cause a rich condition, and creating a large vacuum leak to cause a lean condition.

6.   Look for the oxygen sensor voltage to go above 800mV when a rich condition is present, and below 150mV when lean. Maximum voltage should never be above 1.1Vdc.

The minimum voltage should never go negative by more than a few mV. Transition time from lean to rich and rich to lean is also important. The oxygen sensor should be capable of switching from below 250mV to above 750mV (and vice versa) in less than 100 mSec. Using a good digital voltmeter, however, can't tell you transition time. Instead, look for transitions from rich to lean and lean to rich to appear instantaneously on the meter. If the sensor fails any one of these tests, it should be replaced.

Cam/Crank Position Sensors

The Cam/Crank Position Sensor indicates the position of the crank- (or cam-) shaft to enable the ECM to maintain optimum engine efficiency. The information is used to time injector opening and ignition timing.

Failure symptoms include no start, extended cranking and backfire on start up. Check the trouble codes and diagnose as necessary.

Intake Air Temperature Sensors

The Intake Air Temperature Sensor or Manifold Air Temperature (MAT) Sensor is a thermistor, similar to the ECT Sensor (refer **Engine Coolant Temperature Sensor**). It measures air temperature in the intake manifold and signals the ECM to adjust air/fuel mixture to compensate for variations in engine temperature.

Failure symptoms include "Check Engine" light is on continuously, hesitation, poor mileage, rich exhaust odour, poor performance and poor economy. Inspect for damage or corrosion on terminals when trouble codes indicate a problem in this circuit. Check the sensor for carbon accumulation or contaminants which can cause false readings.

If the MAT Sensor is suspected, refer Engine Coolant Temperature Sensor and carry out similar tests.

ECM Failure

Although a very reliable piece of equipment, it can sometimes happen that the ECM suffers a complete, catastrophic failure, especially if it is immediately or shortly after initial installation. There are two main conditions that could cause this situation:

- An intermittent short to ground or a Battery Voltage short overloading the ECM. If the short is not properly diagnosed and corrected, replacing the ECM will provide only a temporary remedy before it fails again.

- An overload to the ECM may occur in a circuit unrelated to the problem being diagnosed.

Because different systems share common circuitry with the ECM, a short to ground or a voltage short in one system may appear to be a malfunction in another system.

An ECM malfunction may indicate an existing problem somewhere else. Therefore, care should be taken in the diagnosis of ECM/Sensor/Actuator problems in order to avoid unnecessary damage to replacement ECMs.

The ECM should never be used as a diagnostic tool.

Certain circuits should be double checked before replacing the ECM. Coming up with a suspect ECM is suspect in itself - it does not often happen that the ECM fails. What may have caused the problem is any one of a number of solenoids and related circuits. The following examples (they are GM specific, but apply to any make) should be re-examined to eliminate possible disaster. All of the solenoids can be checked at the ECM feed circuit to component return circuit or they can be removed and tested individually.

- Torque Converter Clutch Solenoid (TCC) located in the transmission. If this solenoid is found to be inoperative, remove the solenoid and check its resistance. Replace if necessary.

- Early Fuel Evaporation Solenoid (EFE). Resistance out of the circuit must be above 20 ohms.

- Air Injection Reaction Solenoid (AIR). Resistance out of the circuit must be above 20 ohms.

- Exhaust Gas Recirculation Valve Solenoid (EGR). Resistance out of the circuit must be above 20 ohms.

- Canister Purge Solenoid. Resistance out of the circuit must be above 20 ohms.

- Mixture Control Solenoid on carburettor-equipped vehicles must measure at least 10 ohms resistance.

- If the vehicle is equipped with cruise control, cruise control solenoids measuring below 20 ohms of resistance can also cause the ECM to fail.

Never disconnect or connect any ECM or component part of the ECM with the ignition in the 'on' position. This will cause voltage spikes that could damage the ECM.

When it is absolutely necessary to work on the ECM, ensure you are properly grounded. Failure to do so could cause static electricity from your body to adversely affect the ECM circuitry.

Large surges of voltage from the alternator can also cause electronic circuits to fail prematurely, including the ECM. Alternator output should always be checked on the problem vehicle. Readings should be stable between 13.8Vdc and 14.2Vdc. Shorts to ground from the alternator feed terminal can also cause the ECM to destroy itself.

The idle speed control motor on carburettor-equipped vehicles can cause ECM failure by drawing too much current. If the ISC motor is retracted for too long a period of time, current drain can become excessive. Current should not be any more than 3 amps and retract time should be no longer than 10 seconds.

When the feed circuit from the ECM to the fuel pump relay becomes shorted to ground, it can burn out the ECM in a fraction of a second. The proper diagnostic procedure is as follows:

1.   Attach a fuel pressure gauge to measure fuel pressure at the injector rails

2.   Switch ignition ON.

3.   Note fuel pressure.

4.   If fuel pressure is zero, listen for a relay click when ignition is in the ON position and then turned OFF. If no noise is heard, check the fuel pump relay circuit from the ECM relay.

Engine Analyzer Test Results

Ever had your car into a shop and had an electronic tune up by one of them fancy engine analysers? Ever wondered what all the numbers mean? The following is an example of what the print out from an engine analyser test will reveal. All the measurements are explained and the diagnosis examined. The first listing (Table 19 - **Primary Ignition Results**) is fairly straightforward and requires no explanation.

Table 19 - Primary Ignition Results

Test	Idle	Cruise
Engine Speed	927 RPM	2196 RPM
Battery Voltage	13.79 Volts	13.80 Volts
+ Coil Input	11.91 Volts	12.07 Volts
- Coil Input Initial	1.03 Volts	1.02 Volts
- Coil Input Final	2.02 Volts	1.99 Volts
Average Dwell	20.00°	40.80°
Dwell Variation	5.80°	2.60°
Dwell On Variation	6.12°	2.73°
Dwell Off Variation	5.76°	2.52°

The second reading is a little more complex (Table 20 - **Secondary Ignition Results**) and is explained in detail.

Table 20 - Secondary Ignition Results

Cyl	Av Kv	Delta Kv	Burn Time	Burn Kv	Burn Slope	Coil Oscill	Snap Kv	Circuit Gap
1	6	4	1.3	1.1	0.2	6	14	3
3	8	3	1.2	1.0	0.1	5	13	4
4	6	4	1.3	1.1	0.2	6	13	4
2	7	2	1.3	1.0	0.2	4	13	4

Kv= kilovolts (1,000 Volts).

Average kv for cyl #1 is 6000 volts. This is the total energy in Kv required to establish a complete circuit in the secondary. It is the voltage required to jump all the plug gaps, overcome all the resistances and create the spark. Once this happens the demand drops and is measured as Burn Kv. Delta Kv is the highest to lowest variation, that is, it was firing from 4-8kv, or 6Kv average. Burn Time is the time in milliseconds (thousandths of a second) that the spark bridged the spark plug gap. Burn Kv is the voltage that was maintained during the burntime measurement. Burn slope is the variation in the Burn Kv. Coil oscillations is an indicator of what happened once the coil's energy depleted such that it could NOT sustain a spark across the gap. The residual energy shows up as decreasing oscillations or cycles. Too few oscillations might indicate a short in the coil windings. Snap Kv is the voltage measured when the throttle is snapped open. It goes up because there is more pressure in the cylinder when the throttle is opened quickly. This raises the energy demand, so if it doesn't go up either the spark is finding an easier path to ground (burn hole in rotor or plug wire) or there is not enough air reaching the cylinder (eg carbon fouled intake port). Too much Snap Kv might indicate a lean fuel mixture. Circuit Gap is a measurement of the rotor air gap usually taken right after the snap when the engine is under deceleration and high manifold vacuum. This makes the plug very easy to bridge so the rotor air gap is the biggest resistance in the circuit.

The third listing is detailed in Table 21 - **Cylinder Efficiency Results** and explained in detail.

Table 21 - Cylinder Efficiency Results

Test	Result			
Cyl Number	1	3	4	2
RPM Drop	8	20	12	28
Rel Compress	96	97	97	100
Amp Draw	8.4	8.5	8.5	8.7

Most engine analysers measure relative compression by measuring the current (amps) flowing through the starter motor during the test. The ignition circuit is disabled by the analyser to prevent the engine from starting. The engine is cranked over continuously (about 15-20 seconds) by the analyser, which synchronises the firing order by pulsing the #1 plug wire briefly to identify #1 cylinder. From there it's a simple job for the analyser to measure current drain in amps when each cylinder is going through its respective compression stroke. The specific numbers are meaningless, it's the relative variation between them that is of value. If, for example, #2 was 50 instead of 100, it would indicate that #2 was weak on compression. A much higher reading on a particular cylinder might indicate a build up of carbon or a mechanical problem such as a piston seizing in it's bore. The test is only as good as the starter motor. A faulty starter would affect the engine's operation and the readings would be misleading.

The RPM drop test is carried out by the analyser, which kills spark to one cylinder at a time and measures how much the RPM drops (which it should). If a cylinder doesn't drop off then it isn't working or contributing any power.

Common Faults

Table 22 - Fault Location Table

Fault	Solution/Suggestion
My car keeps blowing fuses. Should I install a larger fuse?	Not unless you are willing to risk electrical damage or a fire! A fuse is a protection device that is designed to blow if the current in a circuit exceeds the "safe" limit for that circuit. Fuses are built with a specific current rating which is marked (in Amps) on the fuse. The wiring and design load of the circuit dictates the size of fuse that's required to protect the circuit. When the current in a circuit exceeds the normal limit for whatever reason, the metal element in the fuse melts and opens the circuit stopping the flow of current. A short, for example, causes a runaway electrical current flow. If not stopped, wires will melt and an electrical fire will result.
What happens if you install a fuse with the wrong current rating?	If you install a 20 amp fuse in a circuit designed for 10 amps, you're asking for trouble. A difference of 10 amps might not sound like much, but it may be enough to fry a sensitive electronic component or to overheat wires to the point where the insulation may start to melt.
	WARNING: Under no circumstances should you ever bypass or eliminate a fuse. No electrical circuit should ever be operated without fuse protection. This is extremely dangerous, especially if you've had problems with a fuse blowing before.
What is the problem when a fuse keeps blowing?	If a fuse keeps blowing, it usually means something is amiss in the circuit. The wiring should be checked along with the components in the circuit to determine if there's a short or other problem.
The fuse keeps blowing in the wiper circuit.	The fuse for the windshield wiper circuit, for example, may blow if ice or debris builds up in the cowl areas and interferes with the movement of the wiper arms.
A fuse keeps blowing in a motor circuit.	If a fuse blows in a motor circuit (heater blower motor, cooling fan motor, power seat or window, electric fuel pump, etc.), it often indicates a shorted motor.
A fuse keeps blowing in a lighting circuit.	If a fuse in a light circuit blows, look for wiring or connector shorts. Adding driving lights may also overtax the headlight circuit unless a separate circuit is provided for them.
The Air Conditioning fuse keeps blowing.	An A/C fuse will blow if the system is low on refrigerant, is working unusually hard, or if the compressor is hanging up.
Could my stereo system be blowing fuses?	Stereo systems with high amp boosters should also have their own electrical circuit with fuse protection to avoid overloading the normal radio circuit.
Today I was driving down a very rough road. A few miles later, I realised that my car's left signal light stopped blinking, though it still comes ON when the signal stick on the steering column is pushed down. Any ideas what is wrong and where to look for?	The first clue would be to look for the flasher unit that is about the size of a large bottle cap. This unit can be unplugged and a replacement unit installed. Visit your local auto parts store for this. Remember exactly where the old one was plugged in - this is not always easy! Also check to see if the other bulbs on that side of the car are good. A burned out bulb can sometimes stop a flasher from flashing.

Table 22 - Fault Location Table (continued)

Fault	Solution/Suggestion
Some wires are getting hot.	Three important things to remember on any troubleshooting job, electrical or electronic: grounds, grounds, grounds. Is there corrosion under that screw? Has a strap or cable been left off? Wires shouldn't get hot. You've got a problem.
How can I tell if my battery is low and needs to be recharged?	The first and most likely indication of a low battery would be a hard starting problem caused by slow cranking. If the battery seems weak or fails to crank your engine normally, it may be low. To find out, you need to check the battery's "state of charge".
Can I use filtered water instead of distilled water in my battery?	You need to use pure water. Whether you get this by living in an area where tap water is pure enough, or by buying bottled water, is up to you. The problem is dissolved minerals, so filtration isn't going to help. Water is rarely distilled to purify it these days, it's usually de-ionised water, made by pumping it through an ion-exchange column, which is cheaper than distillation. You can buy bottles of this cheaply from almost anywhere - it's even sold for use with steam irons. Melted ice from the freezer is not pure enough.
My battery keeps running down. Does that mean I need a new battery?	To determine whether the battery is faulty, carry out the following steps: 1. test the condition of the battery to see if it is capable of holding a charge, 2. check the output of the charging system to see if it is functioning properly, and 3. if the battery and charging system are okay, check for a possible current drain on the battery when the key is off. In other words, if the battery is good and the charging system is doing its job, then something is draining voltage from the battery and running it down when the key is off. One way to check the battery is to recharge it, then let it sit for a day with both battery cables disconnected. If the battery holds the charge and doesn't run down, it's probably good, and the problem is in your charging system or wiring.
My car has had a new battery 6 times in the 8 years that I've owned it. The people replacing the battery say that the battery has a "dead cell" and has to be replaced. After the first two or three changes, the dealer did an "electrical systems check" and found no problems. Whenever the battery "dies," the symptoms are as follows: • Dome light fine, dash lights dim. • No battery indicator on dashboard (leading up to failure). • No cranking sounds, just "click" when you turn the key. • It starts with a jump, and if the battery is replaced, it will be reliable for at least 6 mths. The car runs great and is in very good condition.	Overcharging can shorten the life of batteries. It warps the plates and/or the electrolyte boils with the high levels of hydrogen gas produced as a result of the overcharging. The voltage regulator in the alternator would be the cause of overcharging.

Table 22 - Fault Location Table (continued)

Fault	Solution/Suggestion
My battery builds up a blue/green corrosion on the +terminal.	The powder or residue can be removed by vinegar. After drying the terminals apply a thin coat of vaseline over the terminals. This will stop the corrosion. On old cars the battery terminal clamps eventually disappear after turning into the powder. Don't get the powder on you or your clothes. It stings and will leave holes in your clothes.
How do I check to see if the charging system is performing adequately?	To see if the charging system is working properly, start the car and turn on the headlights. If the headlights are dim, it indicates the lights are running off the battery and that little or no juice is being produced by the alternator. If the lights get brighter as you rev the engine, it means the alternator is producing some current, but may not be producing enough at idle to keep the battery properly charged. If the lights have normal brightness and don't change intensity as the engine is revved, your charging system is functioning normally. You can also check the charging system by connecting the leads of a voltmeter to the battery. When the engine starts, the charging voltage should jump to about 14.5Vdc or higher. If the reading doesn't change or rises less than a volt, you have a charging problem that will require further diagnosis. If the battery and charging system seem to be working normally, the only thing that's left is the electrical system. If the battery runs down overnight or when the vehicle sits for several days, it means something is remaining on and drawing current when the ignition is turned off. It may be a trunk light or cigarette lighter that remains on all the time, a fuel pump relay or other relay with frozen contacts that's drawing current, a rear window defroster that doesn't shut off, or a short in the radio or other electrical accessory. All vehicles draw a little current from the battery when the key is off to run the clock, keep the memory alive in a digital radio (so it doesn't forget the station settings) and the engine computer. Alarm systems need current to keep their circuits armed as do cellular phones.
How can I test for excessive current drain from the battery when the engine is off?	Current drain on the battery can be checked with an ammeter. Make sure the ignition is off, then disconnect one of the battery cables. Connect one ammeter lead to the battery and the other to the cable. The normal current drain on most vehicles should be about 25 milliamps or less. If the key-off drain exceeds 100 milliamps, there's an electrical problem that requires further diagnosis.
How do I isolate the cause of unwanted current drain?	Finding the hidden current drain can be time consuming. The easiest way to isolate the problem is to pull one fuse at a time from the fuse panel until the ammeter reading drops. This will tell you which circuit is draining the battery. Then you have to check the wiring and each of the components in that circuit to pinpoint the problem. Check the trunk light if the car has one. They used a mercury activated switch, and if it is mispositioned the light may be on all of the time. This could be your problem.
Yesterday when I got out of my 1988 Ford Bronco 5.0L I noticed smoke coming out of the grill. Smoke and flames were pouring out of the alternator. Should I just replace it, or look for trouble elsewhere?	Alternator fires are a known concern on some Ford models (yours is one of them). The cause is excessive resistance in the wire terminal crimp in the alternator power harness connector. You should buy the readily available repair kit that includes a new harness connector and instructions for proper installation. Of course you will also have to replace the burnt alternator.

Table 22 - Fault Location Table (continued)

Fault	Solution/Suggestion
I have an electrical problem. When the ignition key is turned to "start", the engine fires up OK. When I let go of the key it dies! Hold the key to start and it runs. Let go and it dies. I've tightened, disconnected, reconnected every thing. I've checked fuses and links but I'm baffled.	Cars with ballast resistors do exactly this when the ballast resistor is faulty. Check to see if there is 12Vdc at the coil when the ignition is on.
Strange electrical problem. The trunk opens automatically whenever it feels like it. Door locks unlock themselves overnight, or locking themselves erratically whenever they feel like it. I've taken it to two dealerships and they can't find any problems. Of course when I get it home the neighbour phones to tell me the trunk is open or making funny clicking noises.	Probably a faulty keyless entry module. If the car was purchased used, it may be equipped with Keyless Entry but you never received the remote. If it ONLY happens when at home there could possibly be some kind of radio interference causing it (cordless phone, ham radio etc). If so, try reprogramming the remote. If it does it everywhere, check for any loose/dirty connections. If you are handy with a soldering iron, you may want to disassemble it and resolder all the contacts. Failing that, have the module replaced or disconnected.
I see sparks on the sparkplug wires, especially on the rubber cover of the distributor rotor (running between the bottom one and the central one). Is this normal?	It's not normal, but it's a common fault. It's called "tracking". There are two causes, either a failure of the insulation on the distributor cap or plug wires (pretty rare these days, with better plastics and insulation than in the old days), or more commonly due to some surface contamination. Wet or oily dust settles on the outside and then starts to conduct electricity. Eventually it conducts so much that it may affect the engine's running, especially in damp weather. You should fix it now, it's not going to get any better. The problem is that as tracking takes place, it tends to build up a line of burnt carbon on the surface of the distributor cap. While it's just wet dust you can clean it, but a burn mark can't be wiped away. Take off your distributor cap and wires, having first noted how to put the wires back in place. Take them inside to a well lit workplace and use lint free cloth and maybe a little WD40 to polish them clean. The surface should be clean, smooth, shiny and polished. If you find thin black lines or cracks, then you need a new cap. Polish the spark plug insulators and ignition coil too. Put the cap and wires back in place, making sure that they go to the right plugs.

Table 22 - Fault Location Table (continued)

Fault	Solution/Suggestion
I've picked up a Nippondenso alternator from the wreckers. The alternator carries the following identification: 27060-87701 100211-1400 12v 7C14 There is a stud on the end of the rectifier pack which I'm sure is the alternator output (thick brown cable fitted). There is also a 2 pin connector built into the regulator (1/4" push on type). This connector is labelled "L" on one terminal and "IGN" on the other. The IGN connection (white cable/red tracer/brown bands) is the connection to the ignition light (the other end of which goes back to the alternator output terminal). It's the other connection labelled L that I'm unsure of. It has a yellow cable with a white tracer and brown band. What does this connection do?	The IGN is ignition (12Vdc with the key ON) the other is a light, rated at 12V. Once excited the diode pack will produce a counter voltage and cancel the light. You do not need both of these to make it work, only one or the other. The "L" is all that is needed, "IGN" is a backup to excite the alternator in case the bulb fails. IGN will work fine if your system has no light but may require a snap of the throttle to get it going, especially if its been setting awhile.
Does a replacement battery have to be the same size as my old one?	No. If your old battery has reached the end of the road and needs to be replaced, or if you think you need a battery with a bigger amp capacity for easier cold weather starting or to handle added electrical accessories (such as a killer stereo system, driving lights, etc.), then there's no reason why you have to install a battery that's the same size as your old one. The word "size" may be a bit confusing here because what we're really talking about is the battery's amp or power rating, not the physical dimensions of its case. A battery with a bigger case is not necessarily a more powerful battery. Battery manufacturers can cram a lot of amps into a relatively small box by varying the design of the cell plates and grids. So two batteries with identical exterior dimensions may have significantly different power ratings.
Is there any danger to me or my vehicle if I give someone a "jump" start?	Yes. The danger to you is a battery explosion. Batteries contain hydrogen gas, which can ignite and explode if a spark occurs anywhere near the battery. Batteries also contain acid which may be splashed on you if the battery explodes. The danger to your vehicle is if someone reverses the jumper connections or touches the jumper cables together. The voltage surge that results may damage your charging system and/or other electronic components in your vehicle.
Does High Octane fuel help?	Maybe, maybe not. Some cars have knock sensors and can adjust the engine timing or turbocharger boost to suit the octane rating of the fuel being used. On most cars, however, you should use the cheapest fuel that makes your engine run well. Check your owner's manual for details on what your engine needs.

Table 22 - Fault Location Table (continued)

Fault	Solution/Suggestion
My GM Mass Air Flow Sensor is suspect. I get a code 34 and 44 - MAF signal low/no go and Oxygen Sensor.	Unless it is totally dead, try tapping on it with a screwdriver handle while the car is idling. If the engine stumbles, replace it.
My GM TPI has been throwing intermittent Code 43 messages over the last year. This translates to knock sensor circuit. After finding the original plastic connector to the knock sensor almost completely disintegrated from heat stroke, I replaced the connector. Let us assume that I spliced the new one in correctly (I know this may be a big assumption). I still get the code, not as often but almost always at idle or no throttle decel. Questions for the more astute: How does one test the knock sensor as a component? How does one test the circuit itself? Any hints?	Although it's not very common, it sounds like you've got a classic case of a worn out knock sensor. The only definitive way to test for this condition is to monitor the amplitude on the KS line using a digital oscilloscope (DSO)while the engine runs. Unfortunately, even if you did find a shop with a DSO it's unlikely the tech(s) would know what thecorrect amplitude range should be. Without such test equipment, the answer is to go ahead and replace the sensor. Make sure you use a torque wrench when installing the replacement. Proper torque is essential to KS function - not too loose and not too tight.
My engine seems to "skip" as you drive, as if the ignition shuts off for a second, then turns back on. It does not appear to follow any pattern, and at other times it runs perfectly. Whenever the problem appears, there are two solenoids under the hood that click on and off rapidly. I have replaced the fuel filter, cap, rotor, wires, ignition coil and distributo pickup coil. I suspect that the problem is in the electronic ignition computer, but this part costs over $100.00 so I hesitate to replace it on a guess.	Could just be looking at a new battery here. What may be happening, is an internal intermittent short, due to sulphation. A battery which is sulphated generally starts with a good fast charge then falls off quicker than it should do. If the internal resistance increases, the charging current will be severely hampered, this in turn may make the plates buckle slightly, and maybe the sulphated plates touch. Check to see if the battery is becoming hot. Check the electrolyte is not below the plates Check the wiring to the alternator for poor connections. Poor connections will be hot to the touch.

Table 22 - Fault Location Table (continued)

Fault	Solution/Suggestion
I am having a problem with the Throttle Body injection system on my car. Upon turning the key in the ignition to ON (not START), a squirt of fuel is deposited (not sprayed) from the injector and then stops. When the engine is cranked there are four deposits of fuel leaving the injector and going into the throttle body. If I continue to crank, I'm sure that the crankcase would fill up with fuel. I stopped after seeing this happen because the vehicle was obviously flooded. I have had intermittent starting problems over the last few months, and I suspect that this was the cause. It would seem to be electrical, but I do not have any documentation that would help me diagnose such a problem. I really don't want to swap the computer blindly and end up not accomplishing anything.	It sounds like it's actually the injector that's defective. Even if you had an electrical problem which was commanding too much fuel, it should still come out in a conical spray pattern. Also, when you turn on the ignition but leave the engine off, the fuel pump is energized for a second or two before the ECM shuts it down. A bad injector which cannot hold full pressure may leak at this time.
Periodically my ignition abruptly cuts out. No hesitation, no shudder, no rough running. It just stops getting spark (Ford EEC 4).	Next time it loses spark pull the SPOUT connector. If it then has spark, the problem is in the ECU. If it still doesn't have spark replace the hall effect (pick-up in distributor).
Driving at freeway speed I noticed the voltmeter slowly dropping; at idle the charge light, brake light, and check engine light all came on and the voltmeter was barely at 12V. Lights dimmed etc. The warning lights go off at above 3000 rpm or so. The belt is tight, the battery is old but the terminals seem clean and the electrolyte level is low but adequate. How do I proceed?	It sounds as though your regulator or diode stack is shot. Most cars are wired so that when there's no alternator output (like pre-start), all idiot lights come on as a lamp test.
Can I test my alternator by disconnecting the battery while the engine is running and if the engine stops, the alternator is good?	**DON'T DO THIS.** If you have a battery sensed alternator, there's a large risk of damaging the alternator. This test also tells you very little, as most faulty alternators are still capable of keeping the engine running.

Table 22 - Fault Location Table (continued)

Fault	Solution/Suggestion
I am having trouble with the spark from number 6 cylinder. The car runs rough no matter what temperature or how long it has been running. No codes show on the computer and so far we have replaced the following: KNOCK SENSOR, CAM SENSOR, CRANK SENSOR, ECM MODULE (computer) & EPROM, MODULE & COIL PACK, PLUGS & WIRES, OIL PRESSURE SENSOR, FUEL PUMP,CATALYTIC CONVERTOR. Have checked and followed all service notices and suggestions and still no luck.	Check manifold vacuum, or for vacuum leak on the intake runner.
I have replaced a 30amp ignition fuse several times. The engine will run for a brief period, sometimes days at a time then the fuse will blow rendering the car dead. Other accessories will still run but the car will not start. I have had the alternator checked and the battery is new. There is no short to ground with the negative cable removed. I have also checked the continuity from the fuse to the ignition switch. The car starts fine and seems to idle with no problem. When it blows, it has only been driven for 5-10 minutes. I also cleaned the ground connection from the battery. Voltage is 14Vdc.	Possibly an internal short in the coil. Try one known to be good.
Should the O2 sensor be replaced when the sensor light comes on?	Probably not, but you should test it to make sure it is alive and well. This assumes that the light you see is simply an emissions service reminder light and not a failure light. A reminder light is triggered by a mileage event (20-40,000 miles usually) or something like 2000 key start cycles. EGR dash lights usually fall into the reminder category. Consult your owners manual, auto repair manual, dealer, or repair shop for help on what your light means.
How do I know if my O2 sensor may be bad?	If your car has developed poor fuel economy and the usual tune up steps do not improve it, this can point to an O2 Sensor failure. Vacuum leaks and ignition problems are common fuel economy destroyers. The on board computer may also set one of several failure "codes". If the computer has issued a code which incriminates the O2 sensor, the sensor and it's wiring should be tested. Usually when the sensor is bad, the engine will show some loss of power, and will not seem to respond quickly.

Table 22 - Fault Location Table (continued)

Fault	Solution/Suggestion
What will damage my O2 sensor?	Home or professional auto repairs that have used silicone gasket sealer that is not specifically labelled "Oxygen sensor safe", "Sensor safe", or something similar, if used in an area that is connected to the crankcase. This includes valve covers, oil pan, or nearly any other gasket or seal that controls engine oil. Leaded fuel will ruin the O2 sensor in a short time. If a car is running rich over a long period, the sensor may become plugged up or even destroyed. Just shorting out the sensor output wire will not usually hurt the sensor. This simply grounds the output voltage to zero. Once the wiring is repaired, the circuit operates normally. Undercoating, antifreeze or oil on the outside surface of the sensor can damage it.
Will testing the O2 sensor hurt it?	Almost always, the answer is no. You must be careful to not apply voltage to the sensor, but measuring it's output voltage is not harmful. A cheap voltmeter will not be accurate, but will cause no damage. This is not true if you try to measure the resistance of the sensor. Resistance measurements send voltage into a circuit and records the returning voltage.
How can I test my O2 sensor?	They can be tested both in the car and out. If you have a high impedance volt meter, the procedure is fairly simple. It will help you to have some background on the way the sensor does its job.
What percentage of emissions problems are caused by bad oxygen sensors?	A study conducted for the California Air Resources Board several years ago stated that 70% of the fuel-injected vehicles that failed the state's emissions test had faulty O2 sensors.
My engine check light comes on intermittently when cruising at some constant speed (60 - 120kmh). It stays on until I shift to neutral. There is no performance loss or unstable reaction. A check of the diagnostic error code revealed a problem with the Oxygen Sensor. Is there a possible cure?	When you use the cruise control the ECU figures you are moving at a constant rate (which you are), so the ECM sends commands to lean out the air/fuel ratio to get better mileage. A faulty O2 sensor will cause the engine to run too lean, so after a while the O2 sensor finally wakes up and says the engine is running too lean. A quick fix is to floor the throttle and then quickly let off, forcing a slightly richer condition for a few ks before leaning out again. The simple solution, of course, is to replace the O2 sensor, and the problem should go away.
How do I do a quick test on the Knock Sensor?	A quick test of the spark timing system is to hit a hammer against the engine near the knock sensor. It should slow the idle down as the timing retards.
My 1968 GM has a problem with voltage surges. At heavy load (headlights, in gear) and low idle, the headlights, dashlights, and all accessories get extremely bright. I read as high as 20 VDC at the battery. The alternator and voltage regulator have been replaced. The surge is erratic and can be brought down to normal (14 VDC) by tapping the regulator.	The most likely problem is a bad ground, and since you can fix it by tapping the regulator the bad ground is probably there, especially if you have painted the fenderwell where the regulator mounts. If the regulator is properly grounded, then look at the regulator itself.

Table 22 - Fault Location Table (continued)

Fault	Solution/Suggestion
My 91 Volvo 240 has a knock-sensing ignition that retards the spark and then richens the mixture if detonation is sensed. Can I advance the static timing several degrees and let the ignition do its thing on regular fuel, and for trailer towing put in premium unleaded for more power? It would seem that the mileage will increase during ordinary gentle driving.	Most ignition systems that have a knock sensor advance the timing according to a very complex algorithm. Making changes outside of the factory specifications could have adverse affects and is highly inadvisable. Usually under load, the timing is advanced to its maximum limits as long as no knock is read from the sensor. Altering your base timing might impede the performance of this operation. Also, using premium unleaded fuel to get more power is a myth. Regular unleaded fuel actually has more energy potential. Premium has a higher octane rating for increased knock suppression in a high compression engine. Using it in a vehicle designed for lower octane fuel invites cold weather starting problems among other things. Highly paid engineers developed the systems on your car to function properly as they are. If you need more power, get a Volvo with a bigger power plant.
In the last couple of weeks, my engine has started to miss when up to speed. If I am accelerating, it rarely happens. It doesn't always happen when I am up to speed, either. The plugs and wires have 45k on them. I think that the plugs were Bosch platinums. The other ignition stuff is stock and has 145k. What could be wrong?	It sounds like you have a lean fuel condition at cruise speed. If that model is carbureted then it probably needs an overhaul. If you have fuel injection, then anything that restricts fuel pressure or flow could be the culprit, ie. dirty injectors, fuel filter, bad regulator, or fuel pump. Your secondary ignition components are also past due replacement. The distributor cap, rotor, plug wires, and spark plugs could be the problem. Of course there are other possibilities, but from the limited information you have given, those are the most likely reasons for the miss.
I'm having a problem with my fuel gauge which reads empty with the key off. When I turn the key on, it goes quickly to past full. I know the tank is only about 1/2 full. Where should I start looking for the problem? I'm not sure if its in the gauge or the sending unit.	If you disconnect the wire from the tank sending unit and the fuel gauge drops back to empty then the problem is in the sending unit. If it stays at full then the wire to the gauge is shorted to ground somewhere.
My 93 Ford sputters and back fires through the intake if the engine is reved in the morning, but once it's on for about 1-2 minutes it runs fine. A few weeks ago I had to clean and dry water out from around the recessed spark plug holes (this water probably got in from cleaning the engine). Any suggestions on what to look for to stop the morning sputter?	Either a vacuum leak or restricted fuel delivery would be the most likely cause. Induction (intake) back firing is usually caused by a lean fuel mixture. When the engine is first started and still cold it needs a very rich mixture. Any vacuum leak or fuel delivery problem can cause it to be too lean and backfire. The problem may not be severe enough to cause backfiring once the engine warms up. It can run well enough on a lean mixture once it is warm.

Table 22 - Fault Location Table (continued)

Fault	Solution/Suggestion
When my engine is started from cold, the alternator will work fine. No red charging lamp throughout the ride. After running the engine for a while (warm up), the red charging lamp stays on until the engine is switched off. Any idea what is wrong with the alternator?	It could be the slip rings and/or the brushes. A slipping belt might cause it to act that way as well.
My car is powered by a 350 V8 that is just hitting 60K miles. Recently, it started getting a strange miss. The problem only occurs when I slowly accelerate above 80k/h (45 mph) or so. The engine misses so bad it jerks the car and occasionally backfires. If I accelerate harder, the miss is much less evident, but still there. I changed the air filter, fuel filter, and fuel, but the problem is still there. The 'check engine' light does NOT come on when this happens, and I checked for any engine computer codes and nothing is being stored - just the code 12. I haven't checked the plugs yet; they are Splitfires that have close to 50k miles on them.	You will more than likely need an ignition repair of some sort - either a wire is cracked or burned through, the wire ends are corroded, or there may even be a cracked spark plug in there somewhere. A good visual inspection would turn up any problems (don't forget to look at the coil wire). Splitfire plugs could also be a problem. A long shot would be a weak coil or primary ignition component - module or pick-up; both problems would definitely be obvious on the scope, provided the engine is loaded properly when testing.
What are the common problem areas resulting in oscillating RPM (neutral and in gear)?	- gunk built up in the throttle body - clean it out. - a bad Oxygen sensor. - a dirty or bad idle speed control motor/solenoid.
My 1977 Mercedes 280 SE will start when I turn the key and will then stop as soon as I release the key, that is, the engine runs as long as the starter is energised. There is power at the ignition coil.	1. The ignition coil has two porcelain resistors nearby- one works while cranking, one while running. Test each for resistance or continuity. 2. Low fuel pressure from a weak pump: the cold-start injector is electric and will spray fuel at whatever pressure is available while the starter is engaged. When you release the key, the (mechanical) injectors need at least 70 psi or so to open.

Table 22 - Fault Location Table (continued)

Fault	Solution/Suggestion
I have an '88 TBI. The other day it wouldn't start. The engine cranked fine, but didn't fire. Looking in the top I noticed no fuel was being sprayed into the fuel body. The fuel filter was OK, and by removing the fuel line and turning the key I could see it spray fuel (Electric fuel pump OK). I removed the fuel injector and again turning the key caused fuel to spray. I replaced the injector which cost $70.00 and it changed nothing. The only thing left is the injector wiring. Any ideas?	Don't we all wish it was that simple. The injector is triggered by the ECM when it receives the proper signals from the crank sensor via the ignition module, so you could have any one of 1000 problems. You could have already had the problem fixed for what you wasted on an injector, which is the least likely problem and could have been eliminated in 2 seconds with simple tests. Do you have spark at the plugs? If you have no spark or injector pulse you probably have a bad crank sensor.
Serious Ford Distributorless Ignition System problem.Once it reaches what seems to be operating temperature, the car will crank and crank and not fire up at all. Replaced the main DIS module at the advice of one shop that did nothing. Car starts fine when it is cold or has sat for a long time, usually in excess of 5 hours. It will also die on me while actually driving the car. Speed does not matter. This has been going on for a while. Can I do any tests for myself? It is very intermittent and I will have to say I think it has to be related to heat because it will do it more so in the summer months, but will still do it in winter months.	First make sure you have NO SPARK when it won't start (otherwise you could have any number of problems). The DIS system in the 3.8 uses 2 main sensors. PIP (Profile Ignition Pick-up-crank sensor) and CID (Cylinder ID-cam sensor). The system can deal with a failure of the cam sensor by randomly selecting a cylinder as #1 at each crank (if the CID has failed you may have to cycle the key 6 or so times to get the car to start). A failed CID will also NOT cause the engine to stall because it has been started the EEC will keep track of which cylinder to fire from the PIP signal. It will also set a code if the signal is lost. The ignition module generates an IDM (Ignition Diagnostics Monitor) signal from the feedback of the primary side of the coils and sends it to the EEC. From this signal the EEC KNOWS if it told a coil to fire and it didn't, so this will set an IDM code in the EEC. So far it looks like the module, coils, and CID sensor are OK. If your car has a Tach does it show no RPM when the engine is cranking but won't start? If so highly suspect the crank sensor. Another thing to check, next time it won't start locate the shorting plug (SPOUT connector) at the right front of the engine compartment. It has two Yellow/Lt Green wires going into it. Pull this plug and try starting it. If it starts you may have a problem in the EEC itself. By pulling this plug you are forcing the ignition system to run on "module" timing, without any intervention from the EEC processor. Also make sure whoever replaced the ignition module used heat sink grease on the back (or it will overheat) and secured it well (the module screws are the main ground for this system).